EXTRAORDINARY BELIEFS

Since the early nineteenth century, mesmerists, mediums and psychics have exhibited extraordinary phenomena. These have been demonstrated, reported and disputed by every modern generation. We continue to wonder why people believe in such things, while others wonder why they are dismissed so easily.

Extraordinary Beliefs takes a historical approach to an ongoing psychological problem: why do people believe in extraordinary phenomena? It considers the phenomena that have been associated with mesmerism, spiritualism, psychical research and parapsychology. By drawing upon conjuring theory, frame analysis and discourse analysis, it examines how such phenomena have been made convincing in demonstration and report, and then disputed endlessly. It argues that we cannot understand extraordinary beliefs unless we properly consider the events in which people believe, and what people believe about them. And it shows how, in constructing and maintaining particular beliefs about particular phenomena, we have been in the business of constructing ourselves.

DR PETER LAMONT is a senior lecturer at the School of Philosophy, Psychology and Language Sciences, University of Edinburgh. He is Programme Director of the MSc in History and Theory of Psychology, and Honorary Secretary of the British Psychological Society (History and Philosophy of Psychology Section). He is also a longstanding member of the Koestler Parapsychology Unit, a former professional magician, an Associate of the Inner Magic Circle and Past President of the Edinburgh Magic Circle. He has published extensively on the history and psychology of magic and the paranormal.

For Mrs McTavish,
an extraordinary woman

Extraordinary Beliefs

A Historical Approach to a Psychological Problem

Peter Lamont

CAMBRIDGE
UNIVERSITY PRESS

CAMBRIDGE
UNIVERSITY PRESS

University Printing House, Cambridge CB2 8BS, United Kingdom

Published in the United States of America by Cambridge University Press, New York

Cambridge University Press is part of the University of Cambridge.

It furthers the University's mission by disseminating knowledge in the pursuit of education, learning and research at the highest international levels of excellence.

www.cambridge.org
Information on this title: www.cambridge.org/9781107688025

© Peter Lamont 2013

This publication is in copyright. Subject to statutory exception and to the provisions of relevant collective licensing agreements, no reproduction of any part may take place without the written permission of Cambridge University Press.

First published 2013
Reprinted 2013

Printed by CPI Group (UK) Ltd, Croydon CR0 4YY

A catalogue record for this publication is available from the British Library

Library of Congress Cataloguing in Publication data
Lamont, Peter.
Extraordinary beliefs : a historical approach to a psychological problem / Peter Lamont.
pages cm
Includes bibliographical references and index.
ISBN 978-1-107-01933-1 (hardback) – ISBN 978-1-107-68802-5 (paperback)
1. Parapsychology. I. Title.
BF1031.L255 2013
130 – dc23   2012035057

ISBN 978-1-107-01933-1 Hardback
ISBN 978-1-107-68802-5 Paperback

Cambridge University Press has no responsibility for the persistence or accuracy of URLs for external or third-party internet websites referred to in this publication, and does not guarantee that any content on such websites is, or will remain, accurate or appropriate.

Contents

A brief reflexive preface	page vii
Acknowledgements	ix

1	Introduction	1
	Observations on an extraordinary feat	1
	Some extraordinary beliefs past and present	8
	Understanding paranormal beliefs	14
	Why history of Psychology?	19
2	The making of the extraordinary	34
	The performance of magic: how it is done	35
	The reception of magic: how it is seen	43
	Framing an extraordinary feat (in performance and reception)	49
	Beliefs and discourse	54
3	The making of mesmeric phenomena	63
	Framing mesmeric phenomena (in performance)	68
	Framing mesmeric demonstrations (in reports): reporting the facts	78
	The construction of a new boundary between ordinary and extraordinary	92
	Framing a failed demonstration of mesmeric clairvoyance	96
	Framing a successful demonstration	100

Framing an exposure of mesmerism 104
Constructing a psychology of error 110
Mesmerism and the constructive powers of psychological knowledge 114
Discussion 117

4 The making of spiritualist phenomena 126
Framing séance phenomena (in performance) 133
Framing séance phenomena (the reception): reporting the facts 139
Framing séance phenomena as not real 149
The framing of failures, duplications and exposures 157
Discussion 162

5 The making of psychic phenomena 166
The birth of psychic phenomena 166
The problems of framing mind-reading: the case of Washington Irving Bishop 172
Scientific psychology and the psychology of error 181
Discussion 195

6 The making of paranormal phenomena 198
The making of parapsychology 201
The making of mind-reading, c. 1900–1970 213
The making of paranormal belief 230
The making of the modern sceptic 234
Discussion 239

7 The making of extraordinary beliefs 242
The particularity of extraordinary beliefs 243
Extraordinary beliefs and expertise 246
On other beliefs about extraordinary phenomena 248
Understanding extraordinary beliefs 253

Notes 260
Bibliography 291
Index 319

A brief reflexive preface

For many years, I have studied the history and psychology of magic and the paranormal. During this time, I have been asked certain questions on a regular basis, and two in particular. The first is: have you ever encountered anything that you cannot explain? The short answer to that question is 'no', but then, for reasons that will soon become apparent, anyone can provide an explanation for seemingly inexplicable events. Whether the explanation is an adequate one, however, is always a matter of debate. When I answer that question with 'no', I am not settling the matter, but expressing a view: I do not believe in the paranormal.

Which brings me to the second question I have been asked on a regular basis: why do people believe in the paranormal? The short answer is that they *have* encountered things that they cannot otherwise explain. But for those who believe that such things are not real, that is not an adequate explanation. We sceptics, convinced that they are wrong, want to know why they come to the wrong conclusion. We say it is because they don't know better, or because they desire to believe in such things. For many years, I said this myself, until I realized that this, too, was simply inadequate. I have met too many believers to think that their beliefs are simply the product of ignorance and wishful thinking. And I know too many sceptics to think that our beliefs are impervious to such human frailties. At the same time, I do not believe in the paranormal. This book is an attempt to provide an alternative approach to the problem.

One of the common arguments made by those who study paranormal belief is to say that the subject is worthy of study because we can bracket the first question, and focus upon the second. In short, even if the phenomena do not exist, countless folk believe in such things, and so we should try to explain this in its own right. However, despite the enormous amount of studies on this question, I think it is fair to say that, to date, we do not have a particularly clear answer. I think there are reasons for this, and I think that in order to understand such beliefs we need to bracket the second question too. We need to step back a little further, and consider the question itself: what are these beliefs that we wish to explain, and why have we tried to explain them for so long? To do so requires a historical perspective, and that is the aim of this book: to provide a historical approach to a psychological problem, by examining the phenomena in which people have believed, the beliefs that have been expressed about these events, and the attempts to understand such beliefs. By doing so, we can see that there are other reasons why extraordinary beliefs have been around for so long.

Acknowledgements

This book is, first and foremost, a historical approach to a psychological topic, and part of a wider argument about the need for historical understanding within Psychology. I therefore want to begin by thanking those with whom I have been fortunate enough to discuss this remarkably important, and remarkably tricky, business. In particular, Alan Collins, who has been an endless help; Graham Richards and Roger Smith, who had already done the hard bits; and my BPS (HPP) colleagues, Geoff Bunn and Peter Hegarty. For their thoughts on earlier drafts, my further thanks to Alan, Graham and Roger, and also to Barry Barnes. Needless to say, the fact that they provided helpful comments should not be mistaken for compliance. They are far too wise to be held responsible for any of the flaws in this book.

In the world of parapsychology, I have benefited from those on both sides of the great divide. More than anyone, the late Bob Morris, whose broad definition of parapsychology managed to include the likes of me. Because of this, I have had many enlightening discussions with folk in parapsychology over the years, with my KPU colleagues and further afield, who have made me think in ways I might not otherwise have done. In particular, however, I want to thank Eberhard Bauer, the late John Beloff, Alan Gauld, George

Hansen, the late Marcello Truzzi, Caroline Watt, Richard Wiseman and Rob Wooffitt.

In the world of magic, I have been helped in word and deed, in long conversations about history and theory, and in the provision of esoteric sources. My particular thanks, for various reasons, to David Britland, Derren Brown, Eddie Dawes, Thomas Fraps, Paul Harris, Guy Hollingworth, Ricky Jay, Bill Kalush, Gary Kurtz, Peter Lane, Brian Lead, Max Maven, Stephen Minch, Jim Steinmeyer, Juan Tamariz, Barry Wiley and the late Tommy Wonder. The simple and indisputable fact (and it is the only indisputable fact in the book) that these people know significantly more about magic than any academic who has written on the subject is a reminder that academic knowledge should not be taken too seriously.

At a local level, I have been on the fringe, first as a magician in a parapsychology unit, then as a historian in a Psychology department. But Edinburgh is a good place to be on the fringe, thanks to Andy McKinlay and Sue Widdicombe, who have helped me fit in because I make them look mainstream; and Sergio Della Sala, because I make him look well dressed. And there are many others I could mention, but to be honest, nobody reads these things. Unless, of course, you are waiting to be mentioned, in which case, you are about to be disappointed. Sorry about that, but you know in your heart how much I appreciate all you have done, and to name you now would be to indulge in the sort of crude flattery that lesser folk (like that lot above) need in order to make them feel important.

However, several institutions certainly need to be thanked, and that means all the folk who work in them, whose individual names I do not know. For providing what we professionals refer to as 'the evidence': the British Library, Edinburgh University Library, the Harry Price Library, The Magic Circle, the National Library of Medicine (USA), the National Library of Scotland and the Society for Psychical Research. And, for providing, at important periods, what we professionals refer to as 'money': the Arts and Humanities Research

Council, who provided a Fellowship in the Creative and Performing Arts, without which I would not have made it to this point; the Institut für Grenzgebiete der Psychologie und Psychohygiene, without whom I would not have made it to that point; and, once again, the Society for Psychical Research, which provided a much-needed bridge between the two.

Finally, thanks to Hetty, Carrie, Belle, Ekta and the other folk at Cambridge University Press, who up to this point have been wonderful. Of course, by the time you read this, anything could have happened...

...oh, did I mention Claudia?

ONE

Introduction

Observations on an extraordinary feat

An extraordinary thing happened... in front of a crowd of strangers, a man asked a woman to think of a word. He asked her to concentrate on the word, and then he looked into her eyes. After a moment or two, he began to speak: it was a word of about six or seven letters, a name, no, an object, and there was a T in the middle, no, there were two. There were two Ts in the middle. She nodded. Don't nod, don't give me any feedback, just concentrate. It's a small thing, not so small, but small in a sense. It's alive, it's an animal, it's a pet and it's very cute. You're thinking of a kitten! She stared at the man. The strangers, who had been staring at him, turned to stare at her. They could tell, simply from the expression on her face, that he had read her mind.

Perhaps this was a magic trick, though it is hard to imagine how it could have been done. The woman was asked to think of any word she wanted, and nothing was said or written down. In any case, there was a magician present, and he said that he could not explain how it was done. Some thought it was the result of clever psychological techniques, of reading subtle facial cues. After all, anyone could tell from her facial expression that the man had read her mind, so perhaps he was able to pick up on more subtle information? However, there was also a psychologist present, and she was certain that psychological techniques could not account for the demonstration. If it was neither trickery nor psychology, then surely, as others thought at the time, this was a genuine paranormal demonstration? Of course, you were not there, and are understandably sceptical. Nevertheless, the description is accurate, since I was there myself, and saw this (with my own eyes, as all competent observers should). You have my word.[1]

This is rather typical, in certain respects, of cases of extraordinary (e.g. paranormal) phenomena throughout history. It begins with a reported observation of something for which there seems to be no ordinary (e.g. normal) explanation. Faced with an anomaly, we are forced to consider whether or not it is real. If we are initially sceptical, as everyone claims to be, then we first consider possible ordinary explanations for it. These may be considered in depth, or far too briefly, and some may not be considered at all. Nevertheless, whatever ordinary explanations come to mind, they need to be rejected before an extraordinary conclusion can be reached. That, after all, is what extraordinary (or paranormal) means: beyond the ordinary (or normal). In other words, belief in anything extraordinary depends upon the exclusion of ordinary explanations.

Others, of course, have not believed, and this is always an option. We can always reject the testimony as untrustworthy, as invention or exaggeration of something less impressive. After all, human observation and memory are notoriously unreliable. Or else we can assume that, though what happened was highly improbable, it was nevertheless coincidence. After all, winning the lottery is highly improbable, yet nevertheless happens to somebody every week. Or else we can assume that it was fraud, despite the failure of magicians and psychologists to explain what was going on. After all, magicians and psychologists are only human, limited in knowledge and capable of being deceived. In choosing one of these options, we might admit that we do not have an adequate explanation, but we can nevertheless believe that one exists. In other words, we can always assume that, though the event is unexplained, it is not inexplicable.

We therefore have a choice between one belief and another. We can believe that the event has no ordinary explanation, or we can believe that it does have one. And the problems of testimony, chance and fraud always make the latter an available option. So why would anyone believe in extraordinary phenomena? This is the question that psychologists have long seen as the one of primary interest in terms of extraordinary beliefs. And yet it has been answered on a regular basis, indeed since before psychologists began to ask the question: people believe because they do not consider the ordinary explanations as adequate ones for the event in question. After all, as in the above case, they are often barely explanations, lacking not only in detail but also in any supporting evidence. This is a point that believers have been making for a very long time, that ordinary explanations are sometimes inadequate, which is why an extraordinary one is sometimes necessary. One need not agree, of course, and people have also disagreed for a very long time, but it hopefully makes the point that disbelief is not a self-evident position. Thus, instead of wondering why people believe, it might be more useful to consider how people come to the conclusions that they do.

This is partly a matter of individual differences, as many psychologists have long stressed, since there are obviously individuals who believe, and individuals who do not. But before we consider individual differences, we need to remember that belief is also a product of social context, since at certain times, and in certain places, almost everyone has accepted the reality of certain extraordinary phenomena. Indeed, what is considered ordinary has varied significantly at different times and places. To take a rather obvious example, mobile phones would have been considered extraordinary by anyone a century ago. Few of us now, of course, truly understand how such things work, but we accept that they are ordinary enough because we are used to them, and because we assume that there are others who know how they work, and who could explain it all if necessary. In other words, people believe according to a wider context of plausibility, based upon what they regard as ordinary, and their trust in those they regard as experts (magicians, psychologists, telephone engineers) to be able to explain things.

There is also the matter of the particular event in question, of what is going on *here*? Regardless of any individual or wider social factors, what someone believes depends upon particular events. It is hard to find a single believer past or present who has not declined to believe in some phenomena. Thus, whether or not someone believes depends upon the event in question, and not only for believers but also for disbelievers. After all, any self-respecting sceptic would have to admit that they would accept the reality of certain phenomena, providing the evidence were sufficiently convincing. Indeed, there are countless reports by those who began as sceptics, but became believers, as a result of particular phenomena that they were unable to explain. That, at least, is what they tell us, though the reliability of testimony has been part of the problem. Meanwhile, to put it another way, which is the way it is invariably put by both believers and disbelievers, it depends upon the evidence, and what counts as adequate evidence will always come down to considerations about particular events. Beliefs are always based upon particular events, since to believe in extraordinary phenomena is to believe that certain events have occurred that are extraordinary.

Within particular social contexts, and in relation to particular events, there will also be differences between individuals – some will believe, some will not – and the question of why some people believe is certainly an interesting question, but it is only one of several. If we are to understand belief in extraordinary phenomena, we must consider both belief and disbelief, since the latter is not an absence of belief, but rather the belief that such phenomena are the result of ordinary processes. We must also consider the social context within which such events took place, since what one makes of an extraordinary phenomenon depends upon what one regards as ordinary. And we must consider the details of the events that are believed to be real, since believers do not believe in just anything.

In the case of the demonstration above, for example, there are several details that made it convincing. The word was freely chosen from millions of possible words. It was not, say, a playing card, which might have been forced, and of which there are only 52. And the word was only thought of, it was not written down, so it is hard to think of any way the man could have known what word was chosen. Furthermore, he could not have divined the word by reading subtle facial cues, since the best this can provide is a reaction to a prompt. For example, if the woman had thought of a letter, and the man had then recited the alphabet, the woman might have reacted when she heard her own letter, thus informing him of what she was thinking. In theory, an entire word could be discovered this way, letter by letter, but it would be a long and tedious process. In any case, this is not what happened. Furthermore, a psychologist was present, and she ruled out psychological techniques, and a magician also saw the trick, and said that he could not explain it. If the choice of word had been restricted, or had been written down, or if neither magicians nor psychologists had been present (or else if they had claimed to know how it was done), then the feat would have been less convincing, and fewer people (if any) would have believed it was paranormal.

The details of the event and the authority of relevant experts are invariably central to the exclusion of ordinary explanations, and have been regularly given as reasons why individuals believe in extraordinary phenomena. Indeed, when we examine particular extraordinary events, and what people make of them, we immediately find reasons for belief and disbelief because, given the opportunity, people tell us. One of the constant themes in the history of extraordinary beliefs has been that people explain why they believe what they do. Ordinary beliefs might be held without a second thought, and may be expressed without justification, but extraordinary beliefs demand reasons, and the expression of such beliefs demands that they are given.

It can be said, of course, that these are not the real reasons for belief, that there are underlying (unsaid) reasons, of which those who believe are unaware, such as gullibility or wishful thinking, to which nobody ever admits. This may be so, but we do not need to take the stated reasons at face value for them to be informative. We can reconsider the questions we ask, and the assumptions we make when we attempt to answer them, including the idea that what people say is a reliable route to belief. As we shall see, in doing so, the reasons people give for their beliefs (which, as it happens, include references to gullibility and wishful thinking) can help us understand why extraordinary beliefs have been, and continue to be, so common.

There are several other questions to be considered, however, not only those above but also ones to do with the nature of psychological knowledge, and the ways in which disputing extraordinary phenomena has shaped the way we think and behave. These require a historical approach because they cannot be understood without historical perspective. History allows a wide range of extraordinary phenomena to be considered, which were the objects of both belief and disbelief, and which occurred in different social contexts, at times when what was thought to be ordinary or plausible was quite different from today. History allows us to consider phenomena that were similarly extraordinary in certain respects, yet had different names that carried different meanings, and thus provoked different kinds of belief and disbelief. After all, if we are to understand extraordinary belief, then we need to consider not only the events that have been the objects of belief, but also what has been believed about them. Furthermore, while psychologists have been primarily concerned with why individuals believe in extraordinary phenomena, this itself has a history. By looking back, we can understand not only why people have believed, but also why this became the key question asked by psychologists.

There is, of course, another obvious question, one that almost everyone asks themselves about an extraordinary phenomenon, such as the one described above: was it 'real'? In this case, at least, the answer is simple: it was a trick witnessed by the author, performed by a fellow magician. The details may be imperfect, since memory is imperfect, but had you been there, you would have seen something very close to what was described. The psychologist could not explain it because it did not rely upon psychological techniques, and the magician who said that he could not explain it said so out of politeness. This is a not uncommon ruse used by magicians when asked about a performance of a fellow magician. The result is that this particular feat remains unexplained, but it is not inexplicable (though you, the reader, have to trust me on this, since I am not about to reveal the secret).

There is one more point worth making now, regarding the distinction between belief and disbelief, the crudeness of which shall later be shown to be problematic in a variety of ways. Meanwhile, however, one might ask: what about those who have no particular beliefs about extraordinary phenomena? In many years of discussing such things, I have never met anyone with no view on the matter. No doubt such folk exist, but an absence of belief is an absence of thought, and could only be found in an individual who had genuinely never considered the matter. And if such an individual does exist, we would not know, unless we asked, at which point they would have to consider the matter. Having considered it, there are some who express the view that they have no particular belief about extraordinary phenomena. If we take that expression at face value (i.e. as what they really think), it is clearly a point of view. We might call it an agnostic, even neutral, position, but it is not an absence of belief, since any position must be taken, and taken in relation to other options. To reject both the belief that such phenomena are real, and the belief that they are not, is to reject those beliefs in favour of an alternative (i.e. that they may or may not be real). To be agnostic, or ostensibly neutral, is merely to consider two positions, and then come down somewhere in between. If we treat such expressions of neutrality as representations of a neutral position, then they are based upon a combination of at least some of the pro and con arguments that we shall be examining. On the other hand, avowals of neutrality are not merely representations of internal mental states, but can serve certain social functions. As we shall see, they can be deployed in order to present oneself as a balanced commentator, as one who has no particular axe to grind, even when expressing and warranting less than neutral positions.

For the moment, however, it has been argued that beliefs in extraordinary phenomena depend upon the exclusion of ordinary explanations, and that disbeliefs are simply beliefs that some sort of ordinary explanation is adequate. Thus, we need to consider both beliefs and disbeliefs, that is, beliefs *about* extraordinary phenomena. These are based upon particular events (the objects of belief) and are shaped by the social context in which they occur, which provides a list of plausible explanations (what might be believed about them). This becomes clear when one takes a historical perspective, as even the briefest glances at the past will show.

Some extraordinary beliefs past and present

The term 'extraordinary' has been chosen because we are discussing events that are, and consistently have been, beyond ordinary human experience. Nobody wonders why people believe in gravity (or in the efficacy of mobile phones), since such things are (now) common features of human experience. Yet even spiritualists and psychical researchers, who claim to have witnessed many psychic phenomena, and orthodox Christians, who believe in the reality of biblical miracles, accept that such things are extraordinary; indeed, that is precisely why they matter to spiritualists, psychical researchers and Christians.

There have long been reports of extraordinary phenomena, but the terms that have been used to describe them have changed. The events in question have been similar in certain respects, yet understood in quite different ways. Continuity can be found in the forms of the phenomena that have been described in various ways. For centuries, things have mysteriously appeared (plagues of locusts, fish and loaves, spirits of the dead), transformed from one thing into another (water into wine, witches into cats, straight spoons into bent spoons), and floated in the air (medieval saints, broomsticks, tables in Victorian drawing rooms). There have always been, or so it has seemed, magical or miraculous cures, exhibitions of clairvoyance, and predictions about the future.

Throughout the last two centuries, the period with which we are concerned, both believers and disbelievers have regularly compared earlier magical and miraculous phenomena to the phenomena associated with mesmerism and spiritualism, and later psychic and paranormal phenomena. That these various forms of extraordinary phenomena were similar in certain respects has been recognized by every generation, as they have been compared and contrasted by those who have found them similarly real or similarly false, or have discriminated between the real and the false. In doing so, however, the categories used, and the meanings associated with them, have been disputed and changed significantly.

It is in these recognized similarities, disputed differences and various understandings that beliefs about extraordinary phenomena can be understood in a way that gets beyond some of our current assumptions about the paranormal. The term 'paranormal' refers to events that are anomalous in terms of current scientific knowledge. This places paranormal phenomena, by definition, outside of orthodox science. This may seem a rather obvious assumption, but there are practical implications of this for understanding paranormal beliefs today, which shall be considered shortly. For the moment, however, the point is simply that whether such phenomena are considered normal, or incompatible with current scientific knowledge, depends upon the phenomena in question and the historical context in which they reportedly occur. That this is the case today is not always obvious, since we often miss what we take for granted, hence the need for a historical perspective to remind us that it has always been the case.

In seventeenth-century Britain, for example, it was normal to believe in miracles, witchcraft, ghosts and other extraordinary phenomena. Beliefs in ghosts had survived the Reformation, when the rejection of Purgatory had made them homeless, but their obvious link to the existence of the soul had made them indispensable.[2] Belief in witchcraft and the occult was equally common, and Christian miracles were taken for granted. Even heroes of the scientific revolution, such as Isaac Newton and Robert Boyle, could study alchemy and investigate second sight, could believe in the miracles of the Bible and the truth of the Genesis story of Creation.

It is easy simply to dismiss such beliefs as the product of a more primitive time, a time when early modern folk were incapable of discriminating between the truth and falsity of magic and miracles, but that is not the case. Most took the miracles of the Bible for granted while rejecting other miracles, most obviously those associated with Roman Catholicism, since it was widely understood (by the Protestant majority) that the age of miracles was over. Various extraordinary phenomena were disputed, in terms of their reality and their extraordinariness, as part of a developing discourse of facts within natural philosophy.[3] In short, beliefs were evidence-based, but what counted as evidence, as adequate evidence then and there, was based upon different assumptions than at present. Meanwhile, everyone else, from royalty to the lesser sort, could watch the extraordinary feats of jugglers (the term then used to refer to performers of conjuring tricks) without mistaking them for feats of witchcraft.[4] Of course, there would have been some people who believed that these tricks were real, but that has always been so, and as we shall see, has remained so ever since.

In other words, even the briefest of glimpses at the period prior to that which concerns us here reveals that beliefs were based upon particular phenomena (certain miracles, certain extraordinary claims, certain magical feats, but not others), and shaped by a social context that provided a sense of what counted as ordinary (in relation to, for example, contemporary science, religion or entertainment).

When we turn to the period with which we are concerned, beginning in the early nineteenth century, we see a different context of plausibility, within which different assumptions and discriminations were made in relation to the extraordinary. Beliefs in witchcraft, once common, were now rare, except in certain rural areas. For the educated, there were already hallucination theories to allow one to believe in ghost experiences, if not in ghosts themselves.[5] Almost everyone still took the miracles of the Bible for granted, though scholars were already questioning the validity of some of them.[6] And when one saw a conjuror, the term that had now replaced 'juggler', performing ostensibly magical feats, it was clearer than ever before that his feats were merely trickery.[7] For the majority of modern people, witchcraft, ghosts and other superstitions were now relegated to the past, and beliefs in them associated with primitive thinking. Meanwhile, the miracles of the Bible could be believed without seeing, and the extraordinary feats of conjurors could be seen without believing.

For all the Victorian talk about the rise of science and rational thinking, and later characterizations of the modern world as 'disenchanted', things were never so simple.[8] So far as the modern world was accompanied by a new norm of disbelief, this was only in relation to certain kinds of extraordinary phenomena. As magic and witchcraft were consigned to the primitive past, or to parts of the contemporary world deemed primitive, and as a special case was constructed for the miracles of the Bible, new kinds of extraordinary phenomena began to appear. The phenomena associated with mesmerism and spiritualism were observable by anyone who took the time to look, and what became known as 'psychic' and 'paranormal' phenomena are with us still, as objects of belief and disbelief, having been taken seriously by many educated and scientific folk. And, as people have continued to believe in extraordinary phenomena, even though they are supposed to know better, so historians and psychologists have provided explanations for this.

Historians have tended to understand such beliefs in terms of wider religious, scientific and social concerns. For example, spiritualism has been seen as a response to increasing doubts about Christian faith in the wake of emerging scientific knowledge, and psychical research as a surrogate faith that satisfied spiritual, philosophical and empirical needs.[9] The interests of scientists in such phenomena have been understood in terms of other contemporary scientific discourse and practices, whereby individual scientists regarded such phenomena as compatible with related natural phenomena and, therefore, not so extraordinary after all.[10] More broadly, they have been understood, to varying degrees and in all manner of ways, in terms of the radical social and cultural changes that characterized the emergence of modern industrial Britain, as individuals and groups negotiated status and authority, and as part and parcel of broader cultural shifts in how modern people saw themselves and their world.[11]

Understandably, the primary focus of such studies has been on the relationship of interest in such phenomena to various intellectual, social, cultural and scientific topics, from faith and secularism, to class and gender, to literature, technology and expertise. But so far as they have suggested explanations for belief, they have generally done so in terms of individuals' desire to believe, the social function of belief-related practices, and the compatibility of such beliefs with wider cultural views and scientific knowledge. These are all relevant reasons, of course, but not necessarily the ones of primary importance to those who expressed beliefs about such phenomena. Indeed, when one examines how people expressed their beliefs, one finds that there is an overwhelming stress upon the primacy of the evidence: in short, that less extraordinary explanations were simply inadequate to account for what had been observed. The extraordinary phenomena associated with (indeed, which were the very basis of) mesmerism, spiritualism, psychical research and parapsychology have always been defended and disputed in this way.

For the most part, the matter of evidence has been side-stepped by academic historians who have been more interested in understanding why such phenomena were of interest to people at the time, rather than simply dismissing them as examples of pseudo-scientific thinking, as some earlier historians tended to do.[12] However, if we wish to understand such beliefs, then we need to consider in rather more detail the views of believers and disbelievers, and that means examining the events about which beliefs have been held, as well as what has been believed about them. Historians have not done this in depth because they have been primarily concerned with matters other than belief per se, such as wider theoretical debates about science or modernity. Psychologists, however, have been directly concerned with trying to explain such beliefs. Indeed, the psychology of belief was itself a product of the nineteenth-century disputes about extraordinary phenomena, and its current form emerged from more recent disputes about the paranormal. Its very existence and form has a history and, as we shall see, a historical perspective reveals that the form of enquiry and the object of enquiry have been inextricably linked.

But this is not only a historical enquiry, it is also a psychological one, which seeks not only to explain why we examine beliefs in the way that we do, but also to provide an alternative way of understanding extraordinary beliefs themselves. In order to do so, we need to consider the limits of current psychological methods, and in particular the fact that they do not adequately consider either the objects of belief, or what is believed about them.

Understanding paranormal beliefs

Beliefs are generally understood as propositional attitudes. To take a classic example, belief that it is raining is an attitude (belief) towards a proposition (it is raining). People may believe that it is raining, or they may believe that it is not, but nobody talks about belief in rain. 'Belief in' is reserved for things the existence of which is somewhat dubious. People believe in unicorns, but not in horses, they believe in witches, but not in watches. Of course, 'belief in' the existence of something is 'belief that' the thing exists, but some beliefs are less obvious than others. Thus, one might implicitly believe that watches exist without so much as a conscious thought, but belief that witches exist requires (in our time and place) some consideration. In other words, whatever the nature of certain implicit beliefs, extraordinary beliefs are like what Daniel Dennett calls 'opinions', dependent upon language, and upon some sort of decision about the truth of sentences.[13]

As a propositional attitude, belief in the paranormal is the belief that paranormal phenomena exist, this being the proposition ('paranormal phenomena exist') towards which an attitude is taken. An advantage of translating 'belief in the paranormal' to 'belief that paranormal phenomena exist' is that it reminds us that we are talking about beliefs relating to certain phenomena that are classed as paranormal. But it does not get to the heart of the matter unless we consider the phenomena in question, and what is meant by 'paranormal', not only according to psychologists but also to those whose beliefs we seek to understand. After all, if believers do not believe what we think they believe, then we are failing to understand their beliefs.

In Psychology, the most commonly used measure of paranormal belief is the Paranormal Belief Scale (PBS); most studies of paranormal belief having been based upon a version of this scale.[14] The PBS asks for responses to statements about such things as the existence of witches, the possibility of mind-reading and the ability to predict the future with accuracy. To agree with the statement 'Witches do exist', for example, is taken to indicate a belief in witchcraft. This, of course, is a rather clumsy statement, since clearly witches do exist – I have seen them (with my own eyes), and have discussed post-punk goth bands with them – though whether they have any magical powers is, of course, another matter. Similarly, it is possible to read minds, since we can know what others are thinking (we can often tell when others are lying, or fancy us, or want to borrow something). And many people can predict the future accurately (such as weather presenters, economists, or the makers of railway timetables), though (like astrologers and psychics) they are often wrong.

In other words, one can believe in the existence of these things without believing in the paranormal, and the same might be said for the following which, according to the PBS, also indicate belief in the paranormal: black magic (which is practised by real people), cases of witchcraft (which are reported in the news), life on other planets (in which most scientists now believe), the Abominable Snowman and the Loch Ness Monster (even if one believes that they are, respectively, a form of primate or fish, not so different from currently known creatures). It is also possible to cast spells, as it is to read minds or predict the future, without any paranormal processes being involved.[15] In short, belief in the existence or occurrence of these things is not necessarily belief that they are paranormal.

This is primarily a problem of clarity, but it points to a more fundamental matter. Beliefs in witchcraft, mind-reading, predicting the future, or the existence of crypto-zoological beasts are only meaningful for paranormal belief if they refer to things that are not in line with orthodox scientific knowledge. As noted above, this is what 'paranormal' means in academic circles; it refers to phenomena that are defined as outside (anomalous in terms of, contrary to, not currently understood by) current orthodox science. Belief that paranormal phenomena exist is, by definition, belief in phenomena that are outside current scientific knowledge. However, that is not necessarily what it means for those whose beliefs we seek to understand.

After all, there have always been scientists who have claimed that such phenomena are real, and that they are compatible with scientific knowledge. Newton and Boyle believed in miracles; senior figures in the Royal Society since, and even recent Nobel Prize winners, have claimed that such phenomena are real and that they are compatible with scientific knowledge.[16] In recent times at least, these scientific authorities have been in the minority, and their views have not been considered part of orthodox science, but their scientific credentials have nevertheless been influential in swaying opinion. To take just the most recent example (at the time of writing), an internationally respected psychologist has just published, in a major peer-reviewed psychology journal, experimental evidence for the existence of extrasensory perception (ESP), and this has naturally been reported more widely in the popular press.[17] Anyone who has read or heard about this might reasonably believe that ESP is part of current scientific knowledge.

In addition to 'proper' scientists in 'proper' scientific journals, countless others have appealed to scientific credentials, expertise and knowledge that many scientists might regard as dodgy, but that the public might not realize are not 'proper' after all (though, of course, what is proper or not has long been a matter of debate, and one that shall be discussed later). It has often been reported in the media that there is scientific evidence in favour of such things, and that they are compatible with scientific knowledge, and science has often demonstrated that remarkable things are nevertheless true. In other words, it is far from easy for non-experts (the people whose beliefs are of interest) to know what is compatible with orthodox scientific knowledge. From their point of view, belief in such things is not necessarily belief in things that are contrary to scientific knowledge.[18]

If we are interested in what they believe, rather than simply what they believe in, then we need to get into rather more detail. Indeed, even if it is simply belief in the existence or occurrence of things that is of interest, regardless of what is believed about them, then more detail is needed, because this begs the question: belief in what things? When one compares different belief scales, one immediately sees that what counts as paranormal varies radically among them. In this sense, different measures of belief are quite literally measuring belief in different things.[19] But even if we stay with the PBS for the moment, and consider only belief in ESP and psychokinesis (PK), which all scales attempt to measure, we see that the objects of belief are general rather than specific, referring to 'mind-reading' or the 'movement of objects through psychic powers'. So what is the object of belief for the participant (i.e. of what are they thinking when they respond to such statements)?[20]

In responding to a statement about 'mind-reading', for example, one might think of a demonstration like the one at the start of the chapter. After all, similar demonstrations have been performed live and on television on countless occasions in recent years. If one believes that this is a psychological feat (e.g. that thoughts can be read by reading subtle body language), then presumably one is not, on this basis, a believer in the paranormal. But what if this belief relates to a feat that cannot be done by reading subtle body language (such as the one at the start of this chapter)? Such a feat is far beyond the limits of such a technique and, if real, would have to count as an example of ESP. People have believed that such events are real, but not that they are paranormal, though experts would say that if they were real, then they would be paranormal. So are these people believers in the paranormal or not?

The point is that one cannot begin to answer this question without considering what is meant by the terms used to describe such things, and one cannot assume that they mean the same to those who hold beliefs as they do to those who study them. We are dealing with beliefs about phenomena that are, by definition, on the margins of ordinary knowledge, and ambiguity is not only understandable but also to be expected. Without understanding what the relevant terms mean to those whose beliefs we are studying, we cannot understand what they believe. And unless we know what events are the objects of belief, we do not know what they believe in.

In responding to a statement about the 'movement of objects through psychic powers', for example, one might think of when, during a round of golf, one willed the ball to go into the hole, and it did. Or one might think of a stage conjuror levitating an assistant. Or, if one knows anything of the subject at all, one might think of the famous experiments of William Crookes, the first to describe the movement of objects through 'psychic' powers, and which, to date, have never been fully explained.[21] In other words, one might express belief (or disbelief) in the flimsiest or silliest of examples, or in the most carefully examined evidence, and the scale makes no distinction between the two. One might believe (or disbelieve) on the basis of prolonged rational enquiry or else on the basis of total ignorance of the subject, and these will count as identical beliefs.

If we wish to understand extraordinary beliefs, then we need to consider the objects of belief, and what is believed about them, and this means getting into more detail concerning the phenomena about which beliefs are expressed, the causes to which they are attributed, and what the relevant terms mean to those whose beliefs we seek to understand. The good news is that there is already considerable data with which to work, since extraordinary beliefs have been expressed for a very long time. In the process, both believers and disbelievers have explained what they believe, and on what basis. And, as we shall see, the relationship between extraordinary beliefs and the boundaries of scientific knowledge has been another recurrent theme. In other words, we can get at the very matters that are currently being missed.

Of course, what people say and what they believe is not necessarily the same thing; which is an inherent problem of questionnaires too.[22] To assume that any expression of belief produced in a particular context represents an ongoing internal mental state is a significant assumption, and one that shall be avoided here. An alternative approach to understanding beliefs shall be outlined in the next chapter, one that allows for a historical enquiry into beliefs about various kinds of extraordinary phenomena at different times and places. It will examine how they were made convincing by those who demonstrated them and those who reported them, how believers and disbelievers constructed and maintained their views, and how beliefs came to be understood by psychologists in the ways that they currently are. This, to use Graham Richards' distinction, is a history of psychology (the subject matter) and Psychology (the discipline), of extraordinary beliefs and of how psychologists have understood them, because the two things are inextricably linked. As such, it is part of a wider argument about the need for history in psychological understanding, one that will now be considered.

Why history of Psychology?

The history of Psychology is relevant to a wide range of disciplines, but the primary argument for the need for historical studies within Psychology is based upon the reflexive nature of psychological knowledge; in short, it is both constructed and constructive. Psychological knowledge is not only the study of thought and behaviour but also the product of thought and behaviour: it is produced by particular people (i.e. psychologists), as a result of them thinking and acting in particular ways (i.e. doing Psychology). It is not only constructed but also constructive, in the sense that the knowledge produced can affect its own subject matter. For example, it defines people in particular ways, and changes thoughts, feelings and behaviour via dissemination and application. All of this happens over time, and how it happens depends upon the time and place in which psychological knowledge is produced, disseminated, discussed and deployed. Only history can provide the perspective needed to understand how we produce the particular understandings of how we think and behave, and how this in turn affects the ways in which we think and behave.[23]

Psychological knowledge as constructed

Psychological knowledge is constructed because it has to be. Invisible, intangible stuff such as thoughts and feelings, beliefs and desires, intelligence and personality cannot be observed directly, nor can they be pointed at, or held up and displayed (like a rock or a hamster) if we want to show them to someone else. This is hardly a unique problem in the sciences, but it is perhaps a more obvious one in Psychology, where brains may be scanned, but minds are not seen. Mental stuff may be reducible to the physical, though there is, of course, a debate about that, but as long as we talk about mental processes, whether as functional or as something else, we will not be able to see them. We will, of course, depend upon language, one that reflects the observable, physical world in which we live.

The inner world is commonly understood via metaphors that compare the psychological with the physical.[24] Our thoughts are like vision (we can see what others mean, but we have our own views, according to how we look at things) and our memories are like containers (in which we hold a thought, by keeping it in mind). Our traits and states are understood in physical metaphors because, whether we are bright or dim, outgoing or depressed, or have minds that are open or closed, balanced or disturbed, we struggle to see ourselves without the use of outside help.

Scientific psychology seeks to get beyond such commonsense understandings, but however rigorous the methodology, the problem does not go away. Observation and measurement are never self-evident matters, but when dealing with what cannot be seen, they become that much more problematic. What does one look at? How does one see it, count its components, or measure its size? The basic stuff of psychological enquiry must first be identified as something or other, and the categories we use carry meanings that are part and parcel of our time and place. For example, emotions, attitudes and personality are basic psychological terms now, but not so long ago, people spoke of passions, sentiments or affections (not emotions), attitudes were physical (not psychological) and individuals had character (not personality).[25] The words were different, and so were their meanings, as people understood what it was to be human in quite different ways than we do today.

Perhaps we know better now, but even if we do, we nevertheless see ourselves in a particular way, shaped by the world in which we live, most noticeably today through the computer metaphor of mind. New technology has provided not only new metaphors (such as the information capacity of memory) but also new methods (such as eye-trackers, IQ tests, attitude scales) that reduce psychological stuff to countable things, ripe for statistical analysis. This makes possible a scientific discipline, though its status as a science has been a sensitive matter, and the attempt to see ourselves scientifically has continually determined the direction of the discipline, what it studies, how and why. Thus, scientific Psychology has been defined in many ways at different times, and in different places at the same time.

The origins of scientific psychology are, perhaps, a logical example with which to begin. It offers one definition, since stories about origins are always forms of definition: to say that scientific psychology began with X is to define X as scientific psychology. But history shows that it is only one of many different definitions, and each in turn has produced radically different kinds of psychological knowledge.

According to the standard version of history, the origins of scientific Psychology are to be found in the establishment of Wilhelm Wundt's research laboratory in Leipzig, 1879. The prior thoughts of philosophers such as Descartes, Lock, Hume and Kant are invariably mentioned, but not as scientific work, while the prior work of physiologists such as Bell, Muller, Helmholtz and Weber is generally cited as scientific, but not as Psychology proper. Thus, Psychology's founding father is typically seen as Wilhelm Wundt, though other candidates are available, of course, most obviously Gustav Fechner, founder of psychophysics. Nevertheless, it was Wundt who established the first research laboratory, founded a journal in which research could be published, and taught students how to conduct experimental research, who then went on to establish Psychology as an academic discipline. As candidates for parenthood go, Wundt remains the most popular choice (despite his reservations about the independence of Psychology as a discipline, and his scepticism about the role of experiments in the study of higher mental functions, such as thought and language).

However, as Danziger has pointed out in *Constructing the Subject* (1990), Wundt's psychology was not the only psychological research being done at this time, and the form it took reflected the social context in which it took place. It was a study of the content of consciousness, primarily sensations, based on the method of experimental introspection. This took place in a university laboratory, and was conducted by colleagues who played the respective roles of experimenter and subject. These roles were interchangeable, since the data provided by the source (the subject) were taken to be representative of the human mind. Meanwhile, Francis Galton was conducting a quite different form of psychological research in his anthropometric laboratory in London. This was not an academic context but rather a commercial one, in which he collected data from members of the public who paid money in order to learn more about themselves. The relationship between experimenter and subject was one of service-provider and consumer, and the data provided by these sources, far from being representative of the human mind, were taken to represent individual abilities, for the express purpose of comparison. At the same time, Jean-Martin Charcot was studying hysteria in France, in a hospital (i.e. in a context that was neither academic nor commercial, but medical), and his knowledge was the product of an interaction between doctor and patient. The data provided by his patients (who were neither colleagues nor customers) represented neither the normal human mind nor a particular individual, but rather a pathological condition. Thus, at the same time but in different contexts, and as a result of different kinds of interaction between different kinds of people, fundamentally different kinds of psychological knowledge were being produced.

When we consider changes over time, the sheer variety of scientific psychologies becomes even more apparent. For example, as the discipline of Psychology emerged shortly afterwards in the United States, it came to focus on the function (rather than the content) of consciousness, including the higher functions (that Wundt had not thought amenable to experimental investigation), and employed a wider range of methods (that he would not have used). Throughout all of this, psychologists argued that what they did was scientific, until the next generation of psychologists, led by J. B. Watson, told them that it was not. Behaviorism was, of course, a rejection of the study of unobservable mental stuff in the interests of (what was now deemed) proper scientific enquiry, but its dominance was primarily an American affair. Meanwhile, a radically different kind of scientific Psychology dominated in Germany, one that continued to focus on experience and was, in stark contrast with behaviourism, nativist and anti-reductionist.[26]

There has since been the so-called cognitive revolution, providing one uses the term rather loosely, and we may be in the midst of a 'biological revolution', as brains are scanned because we can. And as we drift from mind to brain, in how we talk and what we do, other topics, questions and methods gradually attract less attention. The wider social context continues to guide the direction of the discipline, as the demands of science, government and business shape the kind of psychological knowledge that is deemed useful (e.g. worthy of funding), and contemporary attitudes about the way we are (e.g. in terms of gender, race or sexuality), and the way we should be (e.g. in terms of mental illness or criminality) lead to questions being asked that were not asked before (and others no longer being asked), because what is normal or taken for granted is different from before. They are based upon psychological categories that we now regard as basic, using methods that were not available in the past (but not those now considered unethical), according to paradigms and research programmes that we now consider most appropriate.

Psychological knowledge continues to be the product of psychologists thinking, acting and interacting with others, and in particular ways that cannot be isolated from the wider social context that shapes the way people think and act, because psychologists are people too. The categories we use determine the object of enquiry (what we are asking questions about), and the approaches we take determine the line of enquiry (the questions we wish to ask). The enquiry is limited by ethics (what we can ask, how we can answer it), and by what is simply taken for granted (the questions we do not bother to ask), while the methods we choose determine the form of the results (the kinds of answers that we get). In short, the context in which Psychology is done shapes, in countless different ways, what it studies, how and why. Psychological knowledge is necessarily constructed, but in ways that are not necessarily obvious to those who produce it, let alone those who consume it. What history provides is the perspective needed to see not only how this has happened, but also with what *psychological* consequences.

Psychological knowledge is constructive

The most obvious psychological consequences come from the fact that psychological knowledge is not only constructed, but also constructive of its own subject matter; in short, it can change how people think, feel and behave. It is, after all, the explicit purpose of much applied psychology, a purpose defined by people according to a particular social context, to change people through changing their knowledge and understanding of themselves. This has led to changes in the thoughts, feelings and behaviour of children at school, employees at work, soldiers at war, and those regarded as deviant in particular ways, in relation to particular norms. How psychological knowledge has been 'applied' has itself changed significantly over time, transforming psychologists' own understandings and practices (which have, in turn, changed the manner in which their patients or clients have been changed as a result of such practices). In fairly direct ways, then, changes in psychological knowledge, shaped by particular historical contexts, have produced changes in psychological reality.

The dissemination of psychological knowledge, its language and its theories, has had a wider impact upon how we see ourselves (as left-brained or right-brained, extravert or introvert, as in denial, seeking closure, or suffering from depression) and how we see others (as more or less intelligent, normal or abnormal, mad or bad, in need of treatment or locking up). How we think, feel and act towards people depends upon whether we think they are responsible or victims (such as children who fidget, employees who miss work, people who break rules that we do not), or whether they can or deserve to be helped (special education, paid leave, punishment or rehabilitation). Our thoughts, feelings and behaviour, in being ourselves and in relation to others, are shaped in all manner of ways by psychological language and theories.

However, psychological knowledge also plays a more fundamental role in the construction of psychological matters. Psychology, after all, defines its subject matter. Psychologists decide what is of interest by identifying relevant psychological categories and ways of studying them and, in doing so, shape how we understand ourselves at the most basic level. Thus, for example, when Watson defined Psychology as the study of behaviour, he provided a radically different way of understanding what we are from that provided via introspective methods. This was not merely an alternative method, it was a redefinition of the subject matter. It was later argued, of course, that this understanding was too narrow and that we are, in fact, more than organisms who respond to stimuli, and the success of the critics led to a significant change in how psychological research was carried out. The new forms of psychological knowledge that followed, directed towards a quite different subject matter, defined us in a radically different way (i.e. primarily as cognitive beings, whose minds are like computers).

This is not merely a matter of studying different aspects of ourselves. In deciding what counts as psychological knowledge, psychologists not only define their subject matter but also, in doing so, define what we are as psychological beings. Psychological language, the categories, theories and metaphors that psychologists employ, define what we consist of and place the various components in a particular relationship. To talk of emotions rather than passions (or personality rather than character) is to define our feelings (or our selves) in one way rather than another. And though we may wish to distinguish between descriptions and reality, we cannot do so without resorting to descriptions. Since language is necessary for understanding, or indeed, any meaningful experience, it is, in practice, impossible to distinguish between psychological reality and particular descriptions of it. This is not to say that there is no psychological stuff beyond language, but rather that, whatever it might be, we cannot say anything about it (or meaningfully experience it) without employing particular psychological language.[27] In short, the way we define ourselves is, by definition, what we are.

One of the upshots of this has been that, to use Ian Hacking's term, new 'kinds of people' have been created, as a result of new classifications that have defined people as of a particular kind.[28] The creation of new psychological categories (such as multiple personality disorder or post-traumatic stress disorder) has created new ways of being for those classified as such.[29] Unlike kinds of rock or hamster, the classified human interacts with the classification, either directly or via the practices of others, not only by being treated according to the classification, but also by adopting or actively seeking it (e.g. to gain access to special treatment), or perhaps by resisting it (e.g. by rejecting its classification as a mental disorder).

Psychological knowledge has the capacity to change how we think, feel and behave, through application, dissemination and definition of what we are. By giving particular meanings to our experience, it defines our experience. How it does so depends upon the particular form of psychological knowledge in question, and its relationship to wider understandings at any given time and place. This is not obvious to psychological scientists there and then (or here and now), because they are part of that context too, and share what others at the time take for granted, deem appropriate, valid or useful. To understand how this has been the case thus requires historical perspective.

This might be seen as the main argument for the role of history within Psychology, that it is necessary for adequate psychological understanding because of the nature of psychological knowledge. That psychological knowledge is constructed and constructive does not necessarily mean that it is invalid, or that there is no improvement in scientific knowledge over time, or that there are no psychological phenomena independent of such knowledge. Indeed, it might benefit scientific psychology since, as Danziger has pointed out, only a historical psychology can show how psychological enquiry has been directed by taken-for-granted assumptions about the objects and methods of enquiry.[30] The details of the argument naturally depend upon the topic in question, and in this case we are concerned with beliefs about phenomena that have long been seen (by most) as contrary to scientific knowledge. This requires us to consider bodies of knowledge within which such phenomena could be understood, but which came to be rejected by mainstream psychology. The relevance of knowledge that has been dismissed may not be immediately apparent to psychologists, but there are nevertheless lessons to be drawn from a historical examination of rejected areas of psychological knowledge.

A history of unorthodox Psychology

It is essential to the existence of the discipline of Psychology that it is recognised as the most reliable source of psychological knowledge. It needs to be seen as superior to the claims of others who profess expertise on psychological matters, and to the understanding of the wider public, who also tend to have views about such things. Thus, it is invariably argued (e.g. in introductory Psychology textbooks and lectures) that Psychology is a science and, therefore, more reliable than unscientific theories and commonsense. But if the philosophy of science has shown us anything, it has been that 'science' is a category with no self-evident boundaries, and as the brief glance at the history of Psychology above illustrates, what counts as scientific psychology has varied significantly at different times and in different places. In short, what counts as scientific psychology, and what does not, needs to be constructed as such.

How the boundaries of scientific knowledge and expertise have been negotiated has been a significant theme in the history of Psychology.[31] This should not be surprising since it is a matter of fundamental importance to understanding not only the history but also the present form of the discipline. Psychology is what it is precisely as a result of such boundaries being drawn. And while it may be tempting to think that this is simply because we have identified what is right and what is wrong, history shows that this is an inadequate explanation. How this relates to the psychology of belief shall be an ongoing theme in this book but, for the moment, it is worth briefly considering the case of phrenology, since it is a useful example of psychological knowledge being constructed and constructive, and of the kinds of boundary-work that can take place.

When the eminent French physiologist, François Magendie, first coined the term 'pseudo-science' in 1843, he was referring to phrenology.[32] The original pseudo-science has become something of an exemplar for those who see its indifference to the evidence as directly contrary to the essence of science, falsifiability. But phrenology had critics before Magendie (and long before Karl Popper), and when one considers what was said at the time, one quickly sees that this was not simply a battle between science and pseudo-science or, for that matter, between true and false. For example, critics such as the equally eminent physiologist, Pierre Flourens, were adamant that phrenology was false because, in their view, the mind was indivisible and independent of the brain; indeed, he carried out experiments to demonstrate the indivisibility of mind, and dedicated the work to Descartes.[33] Yet most current psychologists and neuroscientists would side with phrenologists on this matter. This is also the case for what was the most common criticism of phrenology at the time, that it suggested materialism, a criticism precious few scientists would make today. Indeed, phrenology can easily be seen not only as the root of the idea of localization of function in the brain, but also as a pioneering secular psychology, and as the original psychology of individual differences.[34]

But so far as phrenology was wrong, its wrongness was not obvious at the time. When the *Edinburgh Review* published a scathing review (by the anatomist, John Gordon) of Johann Spurzheim's seminal book on phrenology, *The Physiognomical System of Drs Gall and Spurzheim*, Spurzheim travelled to Edinburgh in order to lecture for anatomists at the University of Edinburgh, and seems to have convinced the majority.[35] Specific criticisms were not obviously correct at the time, such as criticisms of the assumption that the brain and skull were parallel, which was the basis upon which minds could be read by feeling skulls. Critics pointed to the frontal sinuses as significant gaps between the brain and the skull; they claimed that these were common, usually large, and covered up to a third of the phrenological organs. Proponents, on the other hand, claimed that the frontal sinuses were rarer, usually small, and covered (possibly) two organs. When a panel of experts was formed, in order to examine skulls and make a decision, they disagreed on the matter.[36] In other words, even observations at the time failed to determine who was right and wrong. There were also accusations of bias and stubbornness towards proponents of phrenology, but then there were similar accusations by phrenologists towards their critics, as both sides, in the process, continually appealed to the facts.[37]

Critics not only expressed views but also acted in order to draw the boundaries of science in ways that kept phrenology on the outside. When a phrenological section was sought in the British Association for the Advancement of Science, it was refused. When phrenologists submitted papers to be given to the Royal Society, they were rejected. And when George Combe, the Edinburgh lawyer who became phrenology's greatest advocate, requested to lecture at the University of Edinburgh, he was declined permission.[38] Ironically, it was a bequest from Combe that subsequently paid for the first psychology lecturer at Edinburgh, and his portrait now peers over psychology students, who continue to be oblivious to his views.

All of this reflected religious, philosophical and political concerns, the interests of groups (dualists, anatomists, conservatives) and individuals (personal authority, career opportunities).[39] In a variety of ways, phrenology shows that, how and why psychological knowledge has been constructed, if only because its rightness and its scientific status were not self-evident, and so had to be constructed through discursive and institutional boundary-work. Both sides of the dispute, in their words and deeds, reflected wider social, group and individual interests.

In the process, they shaped the thoughts, feelings and behaviour of others, as part of, and indeed because of, the constructive potential of phrenology. For its proponents, phrenology had the potential to reform society, through the education of the poor, the rehabilitation of criminals, more humane treatment of the mentally ill, indeed through the improvement of every individual. In private consultations, lectures and booklets, phrenologists provided advice on self-improvement in every area of life. The applicability of phrenological knowledge eased its dissemination, of course, but so did its sheer accessibility, and its relevance to any conversation about human nature. For those who adhered to the original doctrine, it defined individuals as innate but mutable, the product of the shape of a material brain. One did not have to be a materialist to be attracted to phrenology, but the potential challenge to religious, political and philosophical authority drove many to express negative thoughts and feelings, and to behave in rather critical ways.

All of this is a matter of history but it also gets at psychological matters. Indeed, one need only look at the categories chosen by phrenologists to describe basic brain functions to see the influence of cultural assumptions upon empirical psychological enquiry.[40] Of course, we might say, phrenology was wrong, but that it was wrong, or pseudo-scientific, was not self-evident at the time; even if we judge it by current standards, it was not entirely wrong, while its critics often made assumptions now considered unscientific. To dismiss it as wrong and pseudo-scientific is to miss the fact that what counts as 'right' or 'scientific' has to be constructed as such via words and deeds, and that this does not simply reflect the discovery of psychological reality. However reliable psychological knowledge may be, it is made according to certain assumptions, and in line with certain wider concerns, and the history of psychology shows that these assumptions and concerns have varied significantly. In the process, particular forms of psychological knowledge have emerged, which in turn have had an impact upon human thought and behaviour. The details, of course, depend upon the particular topic in question, and here we are concerned with extraordinary beliefs.

It has been argued that, if we are to understand them, there is a need to be clearer about what is believed, and that this requires deeper consideration of the objects of belief and what is believed about them. Since extraordinary beliefs depend upon the exclusion of ordinary explanations in relation to particular events, and disbeliefs are beliefs that ordinary explanations are adequate, we need to consider the events in question and the ordinary explanations that are available at any given time. These events, and the relevant available explanations, have changed over time, but there have nevertheless been continuities in how they have been described, disputed and defended by those who have expressed beliefs about them. Indeed, it was from this ongoing dispute that the psychology of belief emerged, which eventually led to the current approach to understanding paranormal belief. What history provides is the necessary perspective to understand the reflexive relationship between the psychology of belief and its subject matter. In short, it shows how the psychology of belief has been shaped by, and in turn shaped, the very beliefs it has sought to explain.

Indeed, phrenology is itself a minor example of this since, were it anywhere near as influential as it was, psychologists concerned with superstitious beliefs would include an item about it on their questionnaires. And this is not a hypothetical point, but rather a historical one, since belief in phrenology used to be included as an item on such questionnaires.[41] Phrenology is one example of how what counts as superstitious belief depends upon what psychologists believe to be relevant objects of belief at a particular time. But phrenology is not our primary concern, and the wider significance of this point to current psychological enquiry shall be discussed more fully later.

We are concerned with beliefs about extraordinary phenomena, because these provoked disputes in ways that phrenology did not. Unlike phrenology, these phenomena were demonstrably extraordinary, and this made them that much more convincing. When phrenology came to combined with mesmerism, for example, demonstrations of phreno-mesmerism convinced more in the truth of phrenology than any lecture on phrenology had.[42] Whether people believed depended upon the objects of belief, and rather than being pieces of abstract knowledge, these were demonstrations that could be observed by anyone. It was observations of particular events that converted so many to a position of belief, and it is a reminder that the reception of extraordinary phenomena cannot be isolated from their production. If we are to understand extraordinary beliefs, then we need an approach that includes an examination of what made such events so convincing. After all, as was noted above, believers do not believe in simply anything. The next chapter, therefore, outlines a basic theoretical framework that allows belief in extraordinary phenomena to be understood in terms of what made them convincing, as well as what was made of them. By drawing upon conjuring theory, frame analysis and discourse analysis, we can see how such phenomena were made convincing by those who demonstrated them and those who reported them, and how different positions of belief were formed and maintained.

TWO

The making of the extraordinary

Derren Brown looked into the eyes of the famous chef, Michel Roux. It was 2004, and Brown was already the best-known mind-reader in Britain. He asked Roux to think of a memory from his distant past, then told the chef to look directly at him. A few moments later, he announced the name of Roux's childhood dog.[1] Brown had already performed a similar feat on a popular daytime television programme, as part of a seemingly genuine demonstration of his ability to read unconscious eye movement. Looking into the eyes of the television presenter, Phillip Schofield, Brown managed to discover that Schofield was thinking of the death of his childhood pet hamster.[2] These were presented as psychological feats and, as in any magic trick, there was an element of psychology involved. However, they were illusions, which relied upon techniques of which the viewers (and, presumably, the former pet owners) were unaware.

Brown is only one of countless performers who have demonstrated such extraordinary feats, which seem to be the result of extraordinary psychological abilities, but which are not what they appear to be. Such mind-reading abilities are far beyond what anyone can do, according to our current understanding of the mind. Thus, if they are real, they should be called paranormal. However, they have been presented not as paranormal, but rather as psychological, and many people have believed that, as such, they are real.[3] These people, then, have believed in the paranormal, though if asked, they probably would have denied it. On the other hand, had these feats been presented explicitly as magic tricks, few people would have believed that they were genuine (indeed, fewer people would have been interested in the first place). Those who have demonstrated extraordinary phenomena have presented them in particular ways, and these have directly influenced what people have made of them. In order to understand their reception, then, we need to understand their production. Hence, we shall begin, as so many of these performers did, with the performance of conjuring tricks.

The performance of magic: how it is done

How does one produce an extraordinary phenomenon? Some have sought the help of the spirits, others have appealed to their own extraordinary abilities, yet history shows, and as we shall see, these have not always proven reliable. The methods of conjurors, on the other hand, are designed for use at every performance. If one wishes to demonstrate an extraordinary feat, conjuring techniques are the most reliable means; indeed, many mediums and psychics have themselves resorted to trickery when the spirits, or their powers, have failed to materialize. The ways in which conjuring feats are made convincing are, of course, a matter of performance, but they also reveal a great deal about how such feats are viewed by an audience. Thus, to understand what people make of extraordinary phenomena (whether real or not), we can begin with how they are made to seem real (even when they are not).

Effects, methods and misdirection: what you see, and what you don't

Conjuring is typically understood by magicians in terms of effects and methods. The effect is the fundamental point of magic, the effect being that something happens that cannot happen. Things appear or disappear, or transform into other things. They vanish from one place to appear in another, or are destroyed then restored to their original condition. Objects pass through solid matter, or float in the air, or move by themselves. Minds are read, the future is predicted, and increasingly there are more psychological feats to do with influencing behaviour, or reading subtle body language.[4] All of these extraordinary feats have been performed by magicians, and most have also been demonstrated by mesmerists, mediums and mind-readers who have claimed that, in these instances, they were not the result of trickery.

Those who cannot do it for real, however, have had to rely upon trickery, hence the need for methods: the unseen secrets behind the effects. The methods used by conjurors are innumerable and astonishingly diverse, from smoke and mirrors, sleeves and trapdoors, to more esoteric stuff that we really cannot go into. Nevertheless, there are common strategies and devices used in countless specific ways: things are often concealed from view, or simulated (as if they are there, when they are not), objects are duplicated, disguised as something else, substituted for something else, sneaked from one place to another.[5] These general methodological strategies and devices are employed in countless particular ways, individually or together, and might be used in the production of any effect. Thus, a ball of paper might be concealed prior to its appearance, or following its disappearance, or during a 'torn and restored paper' effect (that relies upon a duplicate piece of paper), or as part of a mind-reading (or prediction) effect in which the thought (or prediction) has been written down. It might be concealed in the palm, up the sleeve, or in various less obvious hidden locations, and in such a way that there appears to be nothing hidden there at all.

Though there may be a limited number of general strategies, it is hard to convey the sheer range and diversity of the specific methods used in conjuring. And however long the list, it continues to grow, as magicians continually invent new methods, and often, in the process, manage to fool each other. However, the focus upon 'secrets' in magic can create the illusion that magic is simple: that there is a trick, that it has a secret, that when you know the secret, you can do the trick. Indeed, this is not entirely untrue, since many tricks have been invented that are 'self-working' (no sleight of hand necessary, nor talent, nor experience). It is true that such tricks can be performed by anyone in possession of the secret, just as some things can be painted by anyone in possession of a brush (a fence, perhaps, or the children's bedroom). However, in the production of anything extraordinary, mere ownership is inadequate.

So, contrary to the impression given by public exposers of magic's 'secrets', the real secrets of magic have little to do with a fake prop, a gimmicked box, a switch, a steal, a palm or a shift. The true secret of magic is not the method itself, but how the performer produces the effect without revealing the method. And this is not simply a matter of preventing the audience from seeing how it is done; it is about avoiding even suspicion about the method being used. There is little mystery, and therefore little point, in performing an effect in which something vanishes, and the audience thinks that it went up the sleeve, but did not actually see it go.[6] How the effect is demonstrated, clearly and convincingly, while avoiding even suspicion about the method, is a complex process of interaction between performer and audience. It can be briefly considered, however, under the umbrella term 'misdirection'.

Misdirection is a term used by magicians to cover an enormous range of techniques, all of which can be seen as ways to direct the audience towards the effect and away from the method.[7] There are the techniques of physical misdirection, which direct the attention of the audience. For example, like the actor, the magician can use his eyes, his words and his body language to direct attention to one place rather than another. He can also exploit what is inherently interesting, such as novelty (e.g. an appearing dove...) or movement

(... that flies upwards) to create areas within the visual field that are naturally interesting to look at (and, in the process, create other areas where nobody is looking). He can direct not only where the audience looks, but also when they pay attention. For example, he can exploit attention levels by the use of pace and rhythm, or by doing surreptitious things when the audience is relaxed (as they laugh, perhaps, or as they applaud what they think is the end of the trick).

In addition to directing the attention of the audience, the magician can also direct their suspicions. Suspicions are immediately raised by actions that seem unnecessary to the plot, or are inconsistent with previous ones. These may be minimized, but in the absence of genuine magical powers, certain actions are necessary to execute the method. And, unless they seem necessary to the effect, these can provoke suspicion. For example, if he puts his hand into his pocket (in order to ditch an object hidden in his hand), this will obviously provoke suspicion. However, if he removes a different object as he does so (a magic wand perhaps?), this provides a reason for going to the pocket that is part of the effect and makes the action less suspicious. Suspicions can never be eliminated, of course, since the audience knows they are being deceived, but they can, like attention, be diverted. This can be done by misleading the audience about the effect. For example, if they think that a coin is going to vanish from the hand, they will be less suspicious about an extra coin being sneaked into the hand. The audience can also be misled about the method. For example, if the magician holds his hand in an awkward manner (as if it conceals a coin), the suspicions of the audience can be diverted towards that hand and away from the real method. Later, of course, the hand can be shown empty, thus removing the pseudo-explanation, but by now the dirty deed has been done.

These are merely a handful of ways in which the conjuror directs where the audience is looking, and what they are thinking about what they are seeing. The fact that magicians can use such strategies in order to successfully fool each other should make the point that there are endless possible applications, but it is enough to allow us to consider the relationship between performance and belief. It follows that such strategies could be used in order to convince others that such feats are real. Indeed, magicians have tended to make a basic distinction between the magician and the pseudo-psychic, who may employ similar methods and strategies but who make radically different claims; the magician is presented as the 'honest deceiver', the pseudo-psychic as one who lies about his use of deception. But this simple dichotomy misses an important part of the way in which magic is often performed, and which in turn is fundamental to how magic is seen.

The distinction between the claims of the pseudo-psychic and the magician, between what is supposed to be real and what is not, is not as clear as it may appear. After all, there are countless ways in which the magician can make the effect convincing, but of what is it meant to be a convincing demonstration? What, as far as the audience is concerned, is actually going on? As mentioned above, psychological misdirection can involve the misrepresentation of the method: by implying that the trick is done in one way, the audience can be diverted from suspecting another way. And sometimes, as in the example above, the pseudo-method is shown to be invalid before the end of the trick, having served its purpose, and leaving the audience with no explanation. But pseudo-explanations are also used by magicians as general presentational tools, and as such play a significant role in how the audience views the effect.

The role of pseudo-explanations in magic

A common way to divert the audience away from the method that is being used is to provide them with a pseudo-explanation. According to Robert-Houdin, who is often regarded as the father of modern magic, the conjuror should 'induce the audience to attribute the effect produced to any cause rather than the real one'.[8] In one of his most famous illusions, for example, he suspended his son in the air, and told his audience that this was due to the mysterious powers of ether.[9] This, it should be said, was in the 1840s, when ether was widely regarded as a substance with rather mysterious properties. In other words, it was not quite so implausible then, but whatever his audience thought about ether, it diverted them from thinking, at least temporarily, about wires and other hidden supports.

Conjurors almost always employ some form of pseudo-explanation, even if it is only implicit in the performance. The snapping of fingers, a gesture of the hand, the saying aloud of the magic words, these are (in the context of the performance) the implied causes of the effects that follow. But pseudo-explanations are often narratives used to frame the performance of the effect, and these may serve as plausible explanations even after the performance is over. It has been claimed, for example, that Robert-Houdin's audiences really believed the ether explanation.[10] Whether or not this is true, and regardless of whether this was the intention of Robert-Houdin, the pseudo-explanation is central to how the audience views the feat, certainly while they are watching it and, possibly, afterwards too. In order to provide a relevant example that will not incur the wrath of fellow magicians, let us consider a trick using a method that is not (to the best of my knowledge) actually used by anyone.

Imagine a card trick in which you choose a card, place it in your pocket and the magician tells you the name of your card. That is the effect, and it is hardly novel: the magician somehow knows which card you chose. There are countless possible methods, but let us assume that he uses a special deck in which all the cards are the ten of clubs. The advantage of this method is that it allows an entirely free choice of any of the 52 cards, but the obvious disadvantage is that he cannot show you the faces of the cards. This, of course, makes it rather unconvincing. So, in order to make it more convincing, let us assume that he begins with a normal deck (minus the ten of clubs), and allows you to examine these cards and shuffle them (nobody will notice a missing ten of clubs). Then, before you realize the trick has really begun, he secretly switches that deck for the one in which all the cards are the ten of clubs. You then choose any card, put it in your pocket, and he announces, after a bit of theatrical patter, that it is the ten of clubs. As you retrieve the card from your pocket to confirm this (i.e. while your attention is elsewhere), he secretly switches the decks again, and leaves the original deck on the table, in case you want to examine it.

From the point of view of the audience, what has just happened? A deck of cards has been examined and shuffled (apparently ruling out a trick deck). A completely free choice of a card has been made (apparently ruling out any kind of 'force') and the card has been placed in a pocket out of sight. At the end of the trick, the other 51 cards in the deck are sitting on the table, offering no clues as to how it could have been done, even to the sceptical investigator. This is the basic job of the magician, to perform an extraordinary feat for which the audience has no explanation. But again, from the point of view of the audience, what has just happened?

Magicians rarely present such tricks without some form of pseudo-explanation. This is partly because, for reasons discussed, they serve as misdirection, but also because raw effects (e.g. I chose a card, then he told me what it was) lack clarity and drama. In this case, there are several choices. The performer can claim to divine the card that is hidden in your pocket (clairvoyance), or read your mind (telepathy), or he might prepare a prediction ('You will choose the ten of clubs') and place it on the table before the trick begins (precognition). Or else, as increasingly is the case these days, he might present the feat as a psychological one. He could ask you to answer some questions ('Is it red?', 'Is it an even number?') by either lying or telling the truth, and then pretend to know when you are lying by reading your facial expressions. Alternatively, he could claim that this is a feat of super-memory, and rapidly glance at the cards in his hands, then announce that the one that is missing is the ten of clubs. These pseudo-explanations not only divert attention and suspicion away from the method being used, but also provide a narrative for the performance. It is no longer merely a card trick, but a demonstration of extraordinary human abilities, something more meaningful for the audience. But surely this is merely theatre; it is still just a trick, isn't it?

This is where the pseudo-explanation provided by the magician is central to the question of belief: in short, what if the audience takes him seriously? What if they think this is real ESP, or a demonstration of genuine psychological abilities. Indeed, it is the experience of most professional magicians that if one performs a trick such as this, at least some will believe that it is not a trick. And why would they not, in the absence of an alternative explanation? It may look like a magic trick, because of the props (cards are things that magicians do tricks with), or the manner of the performer (he was entertaining us), or the context in which it took place (it was a show, we bought tickets, it was in a theatre). Nevertheless, some will believe, and then again, what if they had been tarot or ESP cards, if his manner had been different and the context more serious?

All of this is a matter of belief, of course, but belief in what? Many who do not believe in ESP find esoteric psychological techniques far more plausible. After all, we can often tell what people are thinking from their facial expressions, and we can spot a lie as well as most, but perhaps not as well as those who have studied the science of non-verbal communication. And are there not memory experts who can rapidly memorize a deck of cards? Thus, we might believe that it is not a psychic feat, but a genuine psychological feat, particularly if the performer has pointed out how the gullible are fooled into mistaking such things for paranormal demonstrations. And we would be wrong, and no less gullible, yet pride ourselves for not being so.

A conjuring effect, in the hands of a professional, is specifically designed to leave the audience with no explanation for how it might have been done. In the process, however, the conjuror regularly offers an explanation, whether seriously or tongue-in-cheek, and in the absence of an alternative, this *may* remain the most plausible explanation for some observers. Indeed, many magicians, aware of this issue, are quite explicit about their use of trickery. However, those who make references to psychic or pseudo-psychological processes differ from the pseudo-psychic only in degree (i.e. the degree to which they intend to induce the false belief that what they are doing is genuine). And regardless of what the magician may say, their manner, or the context in which they perform, there are invariably some observers who nevertheless view such feats as genuine.[11] Despite the general assumption that magicians simply do tricks (that are not 'real'), the performance of magic often involves a claim (however seriously it may be intended) that the effect is due to some kind of process that might be regarded as 'real'. This pseudo-explanation directs the audience view about what is actually going on, though whether it is accepted as real is, at the end of the day, up to the audience. What people make of conjuring tricks is, therefore, an ideal subject in which to explore the fuzzy distinctions between belief and disbelief.

The reception of magic: how it is seen

To understand how magic is seen, we need to begin with what magic is: the essence of magic is the effect. It may be accompanied by an entertaining narrative, a mythical tale or a series of jokes, elaborate costumes and sets might be used, roles might be played, music might be played. But what makes it magic rather than story-telling, comedy or theatre is that there is an effect of something magical happening. Singers may dance, tell stories, wear costumes, but singing is the song, and magic is the effect. So what, precisely, is the magic effect?

Effects can be seen as extraordinary events, ones that cannot happen, yet nevertheless happen. In terms of performance, examples have been given, objects disappear, transform, and so on. In terms of reception, however, the effect does not happen on stage, but in the minds of the audience. It is a mental state, created by a dilemma, based upon a contradiction – X cannot happen, X happened. The more convinced the audience that the effect cannot happen, yet happens nonetheless, the more powerful the effect. Thus, good conjuring theory and practice seek to exclude every possible method for how an effect might be done, in order to create an effect that has, from the audience view, simply no explanation.[12] And while not all magicians engage in such theoretical considerations, the basic point is understood more widely. There is, for example, a recent popular trick, 'NFW!', named after the desired response of the audience. It is, then, generally understood by magicians that the strength of the effect is directly proportional to the conviction of the audience that what is being observed simply cannot happen.

If we define magic in terms of the effect, and the effect as an event that cannot happen, yet nevertheless does, then it makes no sense to speak of a willing suspension of disbelief. Following Coleridge, who had poetry in mind, several scholars (and even some magicians) have spoken about magic as if it involves a willing suspension of disbelief.[13] Clearly, one willingly suspends one's disbelief in order to appreciate literature, film and theatre, but not to appreciate magic. Take a simple example: if you go to the theatre to see Peter Pan, and when he flies above the stage, you ignore the wires, then that is a willing suspension of disbelief. But if you go to see David Copperfield, and see him fly above the stage, you do not ignore the wires. You look for the wires. You do not see them. That is magic.

If you look for the wires and see them, then it is ineffective magic. If you do not look for them because the possibility of wires did not cross your mind, then you do not need magic because you must live in a world of endless wonders. If, on the other hand, the possibility of wires does indeed occur to you, but you decide not to look for them, then that is a willing suspension of disbelief. But it is not magic.

We are not concerned here with the magic of theatre, or the magic of literature, prose or poetry, but with conjuring effects, the apparently impossible events that rely upon the esoteric methods of the magician. Magic is neither theatre nor fiction in the sense that, whatever theatrical or fictional elements might be involved, the essence of magic is that something impossible appears to happen in real time and space. To truly experience an impossible event, you must observe an event that you truly believe to be impossible. A willing suspension of disbelief can only diminish that experience.

Another example: perhaps an object vanishes or transforms into something else. This requires the audience to observe that it was there, but is no longer there, or that it was one thing but now is something else. It does not involve any suspension of disbelief. On the contrary, it requires genuine belief that what you are seeing prior to the magical effect is really happening (that the object really is there, that it really is what it appears to be), or else the effect (that it is no longer there, that it is something else) cannot work. This belief is not willingly suspended disbelief; it is belief based upon observable evidence. The more convincing this evidence (e.g. the more convinced the audience that the object is really there), the stronger the magical effect (e.g. when they see that it is not there). The strength of the effect is directly proportional to the belief (not willingly suspended disbelief, but genuine real-time conviction) that it was truly where it was supposed to be. This is the primary aim of magic as a performing art: the creation of a dilemma between the conviction that something cannot happen and the observation that it happens. It requires disbelief (it cannot happen) based on real-time conviction (in these conditions, it is impossible) in order for the effect (it happens) to produce the experience. In short, if you suspend disbelief, willingly or otherwise, the magic disappears.[14]

In terms of a stereotypical magic trick, the willing suspension of disbelief is antagonistic to the effect. It is true that magicians invariably use narratives in order to frame an effect, and stories are natural targets for a willing suspension of disbelief. But the story is not the effect, it is part of the presentation; without the effect it is merely a story. The story may include a pseudo-explanation, for example about ESP or psychological processes, and some people may find this to be a plausible explanation for what is actually going on. But even if they do, that is not a willing suspension of disbelief either; it is an attribution for what they have seen, and this we shall consider in a moment.

The stereotypical magic trick, however, is an effect for which the audience has no explanation. They may conclude that it is a trick, but to call it a trick is to provide a name, not an explanation. They must believe that it really happens (X is really there, X is really gone), and that this is impossible, to be left with a mystery for which 'magic trick' is merely a label. This is the goal, and it is not always reached, but that is usually a matter of competence. If it falls short, then it is because the audience has some sense of how it might have been done. But when it succeeds, the audience witnesses an event that they simply cannot explain, that they *really* believe could not have happened. NFW.

This is the primary aim of the magician, but what the audience believes is another matter. Rather than suspending their disbelief, they are being asked to believe that the effect really happens, and that it does not, not really. Faced with this smudged line between reality and illusion, what are they to believe?

Believing in magic

If the primary aim of the magician is to provoke an effect in the mind of the audience, it is often a short-lived experience. This is not necessarily a problem, and some conjuring theorists argue that this momentary experience of astonishment is what matters.[15] Others have been more concerned with the reconstruction process: the subsequent attempt by the audience to understand what has just happened.[16] But whatever one does to direct the process, one cannot prevent an audience from thinking about what they have seen. And, faced with the dilemma of an effect that cannot happen, yet nevertheless happened, there is an obvious choice to make. The first option is to conclude that such things cannot happen, therefore it did not really happen; it was an illusion, based upon a method involving sleight of hand, special props or some other form of trickery. The greater the inability to imagine the method, the stronger the effect, but it remains an illusion. This might be seen as a stereotypical response to a magic trick.

The alternative, however, is to conclude that it was real, which then begs the question of precisely what was real? This is where the pseudo-explanation may be accepted as the real explanation for the effect. Traditionally, this is the world of the pseudo-psychic, who claims to be psychic but relies upon tricks. However, there are many examples of pseudo-explanations that have nothing to do with the paranormal. As mentioned already, the effect may be a demonstration of remarkable psychological abilities, such as super-memory or lie detection, but one that actually relies upon trickery. Or the effect may be a demonstration of gambling techniques, but one that is actually a pseudo-demonstration, in which the magician relies upon a stacked (prearranged) deck and some basic sleight of hand, in order to give the illusion of astonishing skill. Indeed, it may even be a conventional magic effect that is presented as the product of one kind of method, but actually uses another. All of these presentations have been used by magicians (including the author), and are remarkably effective, because the pseudo-explanation is a plausible one. In other words, there are a variety of ways in which the magician can provide a false explanation that the audience can take to be the genuine explanation.

Now clearly this is not the same as seriously claiming psychic abilities, but these are nevertheless false explanations that some people believe to be true, and they are used to demonstrate extraordinary abilities that the performer does not have (and, in many cases, nobody has). This is not a moral argument, nor is it intended as a criticism – many of the best performers have played with the boundaries between illusion and reality – but it hopefully shows that simple dichotomies miss the complexity of what is going on. It may be difficult to talk about such matters without distinguishing between belief and disbelief, or reality and illusion, but it makes no sense to do so until we are clear about what is being believed, and what, precisely, is meant by 'real'. For example, if the magician claims to be using skills that are beyond his abilities (or, indeed, those of anyone else), and if the audience believes this to be real, then one has to wonder in what sense this is different from belief in the paranormal?

The boundary between 'trick' and 'real' is therefore fuzzier than might initially seem to be the case, and this matters because the extraordinary phenomena to be discussed are, and always have been, on the boundary of what is considered possible. But what is considered possible has varied significantly at different times, in different places, and among different people in the same time and place. If the smudging of the boundary between reality and illusion (in the performance of magic) can lead to a fuzzy reception, the disputed boundaries between what is possible and what is not (in the real world) only complicate matters further.

What, for an audience in the 1840s, were the limits of ether's mysterious properties (if it could eliminate pain, then what else could it do)? How plausible was communication with the other world to Victorians, almost all of whom believed in an afterlife, and were at the time witnessing new ways of communicating with others they could not see, in other parts of the world? Where precisely, in a society now obsessed with psychological matters, are the limits of our mental abilities? How rapidly can someone detect a missing card, how accurately can someone detect lies? We can all read the minds of others to some extent, but to what extent?

This is why we need to consider the event in question, and the context in which it took place, but it is also why we need to consider its production as well as its reception. No believer believes in everything, because not all such events are equally convincing, just as not all explanations are equally plausible. It is invariably part of the demonstration of a magic trick, as it is in the case of any extraordinary feat, to exclude various explanations and, in the process, to suggest a particular one. Some are obviously more convincing than others, and there are reasons for this, and these are not simply 'convincing' but are convincing examples of particular things. Whether people believe, then, depends in part upon how convincingly the demonstration excludes alternative explanations, and upon how plausible they find the one being offered... He said that he would suspend his son in the air using the power of ether, then he suspended his son in the air... she asked the spirits to move the table, then the table moved... he said that he could tell when I was lying by reading my body language, then he spotted when I was lying... in the absence of alternative explanations, such presentations will shape not only whether people believe, but also what they believe. If we are to understand all of this, then we need a theoretical approach that can accommodate both the performance and reception of extraordinary feats.

Framing an extraordinary feat (in performance and reception)

Whether it relies upon trickery or not, an extraordinary feat is always presented as if it relies upon something. As we have seen, the simple dichotomy between 'trick' and 'real' is not so simple after all. Since the way in which an extraordinary feat is presented will shape how it is seen, we need to consider the presentation as part of the process through which observers choose whether and what to believe. A useful theoretical approach that encompasses both performance and reception of such feats is frame analysis, and since we will later be speaking of framing, a brief outline of this may be useful.

Frame analysis is concerned with the definition and organization of experience, and describes how actions are recognized as, for example, 'serious' or 'play'.[17] According to Erving Goffman, a frame can be seen as an answer to the question 'what is going on here?'. At any given moment, we might consider what is going on, and the answer we produce defines our experience. In answering this question, according to Goffman, we perceive events in relation to 'primary frameworks' that give meaning to our experience. For example, one might see two children rolling about on the floor, with arms and legs flailing, and ask oneself 'what is going on here?' One might answer this question (frame the event) as 'they are fighting'. Such frameworks are called 'primary' because they are not dependent on prior interpretation, but they can be transformed in a variety of ways. For example, we might look again at these two children fighting, and decide that they are not actually fighting, but merely playing at fighting. Perhaps there is something in their actions, a pulled punch or a relaxed grin, that suggests to us that they are only playing. Thus, the primary framework 'they are fighting' is transformed into 'they are playing (at fighting)'. Such transformations Goffman calls 'keyings', and can take various forms, such as practising or demonstrating. For example, one might practise playing the piano or demonstrate playing the piano, both of which are keyings of the primary framework 'playing the piano', but each having a different meaning.

In addition to keyings, primary frameworks can be transformed through fabrication. Goffman defines fabrication as 'the intentional effort of one or more individuals to manage activity so that a party of one or more others will be induced to have a false belief about what is going on'.[18] Fabrications of primary frameworks include hoaxes, lies and practical jokes. For example, two children might pretend to fight, or someone might mime playing the piano to music, in order to convince an observer that these events are real. Framing, then, refers to the ways in which actions may be demonstrated to others (as real or not, as one thing or another), but it can also be seen in terms of belief – as the answer to the question: what is going on here? To answer that question with 'they are fighting' (or 'she is playing the piano') is to express the belief that they are fighting (or that she is playing the piano). In other words, any primary framework may be transformed by the performer (e.g. as a demonstration, or as a fabrication), and framed by the audience in terms of what they think is going on.

Frame analysis has a clear relevance to the performance of magic and psychic fraud, since a magic trick might easily be framed as a genuine psychic event, and both magic and psychic fraud are particularly complex forms of fabrication.[19] Indeed, magic and psychic fraud have often been regarded as similar forms of activity.[20] However, a frame analysis of magic and psychic fraud actually clarifies the fundamental differences between the two forms of fabrication rather than the superficial similarities. Magic clearly involves fabrication since there is an intentional effort to induce a false belief about what is going on, but this is typically only the case within the frame of the trick itself. If asked what is going on, for example, an observer might state that a coin is in the magician's hand (when it is really up his sleeve), or that a box is empty (when it secretly contains a rabbit). Nevertheless, outside the frame of the trick, there is no fabrication, since at that level the observer knows what is going on (that this is a magic trick). Thus, in terms of frame analysis, a typical magic trick can be seen as a demonstration (keying) of an illusion (fabrication) of real magic (the primary framework).

This is quite different in the case of psychic fraud, where the intention is to induce a false belief not only about the details of the event but also about its cause. The pseudo-psychic claims to be demonstrating genuine magical, paranormal or supernatural phenomena, and seeks to induce a false belief in others that this really is the case. Thus, in terms of frame analysis, and in stark contrast to a typical magic trick, a pseudo-psychic feat can be seen as a fabrication of a demonstration (keying) of real magic (the primary framework).[21]

As noted above, the distinction between magic and psychic fraud is fuzzier than is often thought, and one thing that frame analysis offers is a more adequate distinction. By distinguishing between demonstrations and fabrications, we can see that most magic tricks are demonstrations of fabrications (displays of trickery) but some are fabrications of demonstrations (fake displays of psychological or physical skill). For example, a magician who claims to read minds by reading subtle body language relies upon trickery to fabricate such skill. The difference between this and psychic fraud is in terms of the primary framework being fabricated: in the former case, the primary framework is psychological skill; in the case of psychic fraud, it is psychic ability. And, as discussed above, the distinction between such psychological skill (which is, in fact, beyond scientific knowledge) and paranormal abilities (which are, by definition, beyond scientific knowledge) is not always clear to the public.

To see why this matters in terms of belief, let us take a recent example, the case of Derren Brown, the magician who rose to fame by presenting his performances as psychological feats. In subsequent years, he has become increasingly open about his use of trickery, but he began by explicitly claiming that what he did was 'mind control', not 'magic tricks'.[22] In terms of the framing of the performance, and unlike typical magic tricks (which are demonstrations of fabrications) these were fabrications of demonstrations (of psychological skill). When we consider the primary framework (psychological skill) in terms of scientific knowledge, we see that Brown's feats far surpass what is known about the limits of such psychological processes. Of course, one can influence others' choices, or tell what others are thinking, to some extent, but one cannot do it in the way that Brown has often suggested. In that sense, he has demonstrated para-psychological abilities, even though he has not claimed to have paranormal powers.

When we turn from performance to reception, we can see that the way in which he framed his feats has influenced how they were framed by the audience. There is little doubt that many (perhaps most) viewers framed his feats as the result of extraordinary psychological skills. No doubt some attributed them to paranormal powers, but Brown himself has actively sought to deny the existence of such powers. In doing so, he has often been praised by critics of the paranormal. Nevertheless, those who framed his feats as real (psychology) rather than not real (trickery), were expressing belief in what, according to science, are paranormal abilities. And yet, if asked whether they believed that these feats were paranormal, they would have said that they were not.

As we shall see, there is nothing new about this, but it is a recent example of how the ways that extraordinary phenomena are framed in performance is relevant to how they are framed by the public, and that the ways in which they are framed cannot be understood adequately without consideration of what is meant by the relevant terms, according to both science and those whose beliefs we seek to understand. Frame analysis, then, helps clarify much of the fuzziness surrounding the production of extraordinary phenomena, but it also provides a way of discussing belief that avoids some of the problems discussed so far. By asking 'what is going on here?' rather than 'do you believe in [a paranormal category]?', we direct our enquiry towards particular events (the objects of belief), and what is believed about them (the forms of belief).

There is, however, another advantage of talking about framing. To state that an event is paranormal is to define what is going on. It is to frame the event as paranormal, but it is not a belief in the paranormal. It may, of course, be taken as an indicator of belief, but the advantage of talking about framing is that one can speak of how people frame things without assuming that this is a reliable indicator of an ongoing internal mental state. In short, it allows the discussion to be grounded in discourse, rather than cognition, and the former, unlike the latter, is directly accessible to the analyst. The shift of focus from cognition to discourse is already a significant area of psychological enquiry, and its relevance to this particular enquiry shall now be considered.

Beliefs and discourse

Psychologists have invariably relied upon expressions of belief in order to access actual beliefs. To talk of belief in the paranormal is to refer to a mental state, an attitude towards a proposition about an abstract category ('paranormal'), and to access belief one assumes that expressions of belief are reliable indicators of such mental states. This, of course, is a basic assumption of studies based upon questionnaires, but some psychologists have identified a number of problems with such an assumption. One of these is the problem that was discussed in the previous chapter, that the categories used in questionnaires may not adequately reflect what respondents actually have in mind. There is also the problem of variability, that people often express different beliefs in different contexts. But the main problem that concerns us here is that of representation, that is what people say is not necessarily what they think.[23]

To take a rather recent but relevant example, it is remarkably common for people to include an avowal of prior scepticism (e.g. 'I was a sceptic...') as part of a description of an event they define as paranormal (e.g. '...until a medium told me things she could not possibly have known').[24] If we take such expressions of belief as an indicator of actual beliefs, then such a statement can be seen to represent a conversion from disbelief to belief. This may be the case, but if it is, then it goes against much of what psychologists have claimed. After all, paranormal belief has been associated with low intelligence, lack of scientific knowledge, low social status, and certain types of personality (not to mention, more generally, with gullibility and wishful thinking).[25] How, then, do we explain all these people who began as sceptics and became believers: did their IQ, scientific knowledge or social status decrease, did their personality change, did they become more credulous? How does this fit with the regular claim that believers are more likely than disbelievers to misinterpret normal events as paranormal, and even that belief *causes* such misinterpretations?[26]

One might argue, of course, that such people were not truly disbelievers, but rather closet believers, whose beliefs lay dormant until the opportunity arose to misinterpret a normal experience. This would address the problem in terms of such theories, but not in terms of the methods upon which the research rests, since a questionnaire cannot distinguish between a genuine sceptic and a believer-in-waiting. On the other hand, one might simply dismiss such avowals of prior belief as unreliable, but then that begs the question: how does one distinguish between avowals of belief that are reliable and those that are not?

Problems such as these reflect a more general dissatisfaction with questionnaires that has led many psychologists to change their focus of enquiry from cognition (as represented in expression) to the form and function of discourse itself.[27] In this particular case, by examining avowals of prior scepticism in terms of rhetorical function, we can see how they portray the speaker at the time of the event as a disinterested observer (as opposed to one of those gullible believers), and present the facts about the event in question as convincing (sufficiently so to overcome his initial scepticism).[28] In the process, his current belief is not only described but also justified. As we shall see, real world expressions of belief about extraordinary phenomena invariably include forms of justification. By examining the form and function of discourse, we can see directly how reports of extraordinary phenomena have been made convincing.

Those who have pioneered the analysis of discourse have identified several common themes in the form and function of descriptions of both extraordinary and ordinary events. For example, Rob Wooffitt has shown how accounts of paranormal phenomena are designed in ways that present the speaker as normal and competent, and the facts as real.[29] Indeed, one of the key areas of discursive psychology has been that of fact construction, the ways in which descriptions are made factual (since facts do not actually speak for themselves). As in the case of avowals of prior scepticism, speakers often present themselves as having no stake or interest in what is being described. Certain categories of people are also used in descriptions to warrant the facts, since particular categories (such as doctors) are seen as being entitled to particular knowledge. Hence, the 1940s advert 'More doctors smoke Camels than any other cigarette' was used rather than 'More plumbers smoke Camels than any other cigarette', even if the latter might have been an equally accurate description of the facts. Several rhetorical devices have been identified that are commonly used in order to present the facts as 'out there', independent of the speaker. For example, by attributing agency to the facts ('the facts show', 'the data suggest'), they are presented as being independent of the person who is showing the facts, or suggesting what the data mean.[30] This sort of language, of course, is typical of scientific discourse, in which scientists are presented as disinterested possessors of expert knowledge, and objective describers of the facts. In short, this is part and parcel of how scientific knowledge is presented, and has been part of the process through which the boundaries of science and non-science have been drawn.

This matters for extraordinary beliefs because the relevant phenomena have invariably been disputed in terms of scientific knowledge, as those who have framed such events as real or not, or as one thing or another, have invariably warranted their positions by appealing to scientific expertise, and to what counts as proper science. Even when not referring to science, they have referred to matters of stake and interest, competence and the objectivity of the facts. They have framed such events as one thing or another by appealing to a lack of personal interest, to competence in observation, and to the reality of the facts regardless of how extraordinary they may seem. In doing so, as we shall see, they have reported extraordinary phenomena in ways that are designed to make them factual. Just as demonstrations are made convincing in performance, reports of them are made convincing in discourse, and these are an essential part of understanding beliefs about extraordinary phenomena. Furthermore, throughout these reports, and in every dispute about extraordinary phenomena, the events in question have been framed in particular ways, and discussed in ways that warrant that particular view about what was going on. We can therefore see directly how beliefs about extraordinary phenomena have been expressed and justified.

However, we can also make an argument about beliefs themselves, depending upon how we understand the relationship between beliefs and discourse. For example, we could argue that discourse about extraordinary phenomena reflects the beliefs we have inside our heads, though not in the simplistic way that questionnaires assume. As Billig has said, in *Arguing and Thinking* (1987), of views more generally, such beliefs are inherently argumentative, since they express one position rather than another. To believe in extraordinary phenomena, to exclude ordinary explanations, requires an awareness of an alternative point of view (as does, of course, a position of disbelief). To frame an ostensibly extraordinary event as real or not, or as one thing rather than another, requires some sort of internal argument (in the form of silent thought) that presumably resembles in some sense an external dispute about the event in question. We need not assume, as questionnaires do, that an individual who expresses a particular belief is expressing an ongoing mental state. We need only say that extraordinary beliefs are inherently argumentative, formed and maintained in the face of opposition, and that what goes on inside the head is like an argument with somebody else: one considers the options and comes to a conclusion, for whatever reasons. Few individuals will consider the matter to the same extent as an ongoing public dispute, of course, but the latter might be considered the rhetorical territory within which individuals might locate themselves, subject to interest and inclination. In that sense, individual views might be seen as subsets of the wider debate: the public discourse contains the available arguments, and individual positions reflect some of these.

Another option, if we wish to make an argument about beliefs based upon discourse, is to define beliefs as things that are not merely inside our heads. After all, attitudes were once defined as bodily postures, and as such could be observed directly. Later, about a century ago, attitudes came to be understood as mental phenomena and, as such, were considerably harder to see. When psychologists began to study attitudes, according to this definition, they had to rely upon self-reports, and take such expressions of attitudes as indications of (what were now considered to be) *actual* attitudes.[31] However, just as attitudes were relocated according to a change of meaning, so might beliefs be moved to somewhere we can see them more directly. Indeed, all manner of psychological processes can be seen as being beyond the skull. Philosophers have argued that an address in a notebook is a form of memory, that the writing down of a thought is a form of thinking, that a facial expression or bodily gesture is part and parcel of an emotion.[32] Thus, it could be argued that expressions of belief, rather than being indications of something else (i.e. *actual* beliefs), are part of what it means to believe. In this sense, beliefs about extraordinary phenomena can be seen as necessarily social and interactional, rather than as merely individual and internal. Whatever is going on inside individual heads, such beliefs are expressed and warranted in a social context that provides the wider controversy within which individual positions might be adopted (*in relation to* that wider controversy). They are necessarily accompanied by reasons that justify the position adopted, not only to oneself but also to others, based upon wider notions about what counts as an acceptable reason. Thus, it might be said, extraordinary beliefs are constructed and maintained in a discursive form that can be seen directly in the public arena.

Whether one sees expressions of belief as indications of belief, or as part of the beliefs themselves, depends upon how we define beliefs, as it does with any psychological category. Since my own view, following Billig, is that extraordinary beliefs are necessarily social and interactional, constructed and maintained in public discourse, and that the public discourse roughly resembles the sum of private views on the matter, it is tempting to talk of discourse as part and parcel of what it means to believe. However, the term 'belief' is so strongly associated with internal mental stuff that to define such discourse as *actual* belief, rather than as expressive of it, might be unhelpful at this stage. At the same time, however we define belief, we need to engage with expressions of belief. After all, even those who explore the neural bases of paranormal belief rely upon expressions of belief via questionnaires.[33]

For these reasons, the following chapters shall consider the discourse relating to extraordinary phenomena, as a way of examining in proper detail how beliefs have been manifested (expressed, constructed in argument) and maintained (defended in the face of opposition), regardless of what was going on inside people's heads. The advantage of talking of framing is that framing is an expression of belief about what is going on, and what we are dealing with in terms of evidence are forms of expression. We can see directly how people frame things in language (what they say is going on), but not what they believe (inside their heads). Hence the following chapters shall talk about how people have framed particular events, or expressed and justified beliefs about them, because it is a more direct reflection of the available evidence, based upon commonly understood meanings. Occasionally, in the interests of brevity, I shall refer to believers and disbelievers, but only as terms for those who express belief or disbelief in the phenomena being discussed.

Nevertheless, we are concerned at the end of the day with beliefs, as things that are thought as well as expressed. The problems identified with questionnaires are considered sufficient to doubt whether a particular expression about an abstract category (the meaning of which is not considered), given on a particular occasion (in a somewhat unnatural context), represents an ongoing internal mental state of an individual. However, by examining discourse over time, we can identify patterns in how beliefs (about the relevant events) have been expressed and justified (in the terms used by the relevant people), in many different contexts (the ones in which beliefs have arisen). We are concerned, then, not with individual mental states, but rather with the various ways in which extraordinary phenomena have been framed, with how beliefs have been expressed and justified in response to certain events that were observed and reported, disputed and defended. The relevance of all this to beliefs as mental states or, for that matter, as neural activity, shall be discussed again in the concluding chapter, after a number of arguments have been presented, based upon almost two centuries of evidence.

There are, of course, countless events that might be classed as paranormal, but the following chapters shall focus upon those that have been demonstrated by mesmerists, mediums and mind-readers, and which were the basis of mesmerism, spiritualism, psychical research and parapsychology. There are other kinds of phenomena, of course, notably individual private experiences, such as apparitions, out-of-body experiences and meaningful coincidences. Others have focused their attention upon these, sometimes as exemplars of paranormal belief. However, one of the advantages of analyzing shared experiences, rather than private ones, is that we can see how the same event can be framed in different ways by different observers. There is also the practical matter of locating real world discourse, and public demonstrations have been matters of public debate to an extent that private experiences have not. However, the relationship of these phenomena to other kinds of extraordinary phenomena shall be discussed briefly in the final chapter.

Meanwhile, extraordinary (e.g. paranormal) beliefs are dependent upon the exclusion of ordinary (e.g. normal) explanations for certain events. To understand such beliefs, we need to consider the events about which beliefs are held, and what is believed about them. In order to understand these events, we need to consider how they are made convincing, in demonstration and in report, since those who demonstrate and report such events do so in ways that are designed to be convincing. Whether and what is believed, of course, is ultimately a matter of reception, which is why we need to consider how such events are framed by those who see, read and discuss the evidence. In describing and disputing such events (as framing them as one thing or another), beliefs about them have been expressed and justified. As we shall see, this includes appeals to a range of contemporary matters, such as the conditions in which the event took place, the competence of the observers, and the adequacy of the available explanations at the time, not least in terms of contemporary scientific knowledge. By examining how extraordinary phenomena have been framed by those who demonstrate, report and dispute them, we can see how beliefs (as expressed views) take particular forms, and are maintained (as justifiable views) in the face of opposing opinions.

Such an approach, of course, does not in itself require a historical study, but what history offers is a perspective that allows one to consider a range of different contexts, in which what has been considered ordinary or plausible has differed in significant ways. And, despite these different contexts, what history shows is a significant degree of continuity; in short, as anyone familiar with the history of parapsychology knows, we have been having similar kinds of arguments about extraordinary phenomena for a very long time.[34] As we shall see, this provides a way of understanding extraordinary beliefs, not only in the past but also in the present. Furthermore, it reveals how the study of such beliefs by psychologists has itself been inextricably linked to the object of study. As such, it provides an example of how psychological knowledge is both constructed by, and constructive of, the subject matter that it seeks to explain.

Each of the following chapters considers extraordinary phenomena that have been associated with, respectively, mesmerism, spiritualism, psychical research and parapsychology. There is an obvious chronological order to these, though there are significant overlaps in terms of time, people and, of course, the phenomena themselves. However, considering particular phenomena (at a particular time and place) in relation to the wider debates about mesmerism, spiritualism, psychical research and parapsychology, is a useful way to understand how beliefs about them have been expressed and justified. The purpose is not to attempt a comprehensive historical survey, but rather to consider certain elements of continuity and change over time in order to better understand beliefs about such phenomena. This is, first and foremost, a psychological enquiry, which seeks to use historical evidence in order to make a number of points about beliefs relating to extraordinary phenomena, and about the psychology of such beliefs. Scientific psychology seeks knowledge about humans that is independent of time and place; history is necessarily chronologically – and geographically – specific. But history is about continuity as well as change, and the focus upon particular times and places, and on particular case studies, is in order to make a more general argument that I suspect is relevant beyond the specific British and American sources to which I have been restricted by time, monolingualism and a belief that this will be sufficient. I begin with mesmerism, or rather with demonstrations, reports and disputes about the phenomena of mesmerism, at a particularly relevant time and place in which continuity and change in the form of extraordinary beliefs, and the wider psychological implications of this, can be considered.

THREE

The making of mesmeric phenomena

In January 1844, William John Vernon gave a lecture in Greenwich that provoked 'extraordinary uproar'.[1] He placed a young woman into a trance, and doctors were unable to rouse her. She was not dead, but in a mesmeric coma, and seemingly oblivious to the strong ammonia that they were waving beneath her nostrils. Vernon then raised the woman's arm until it was horizontal to the floor, and it remained in position, in a state of catalepsy. He was planning to exhibit greater feats than these – demonstrations of phreno-mesmerism, insensibility to pain, and even clairvoyance – but that was when the 'extraordinary uproar' began, and everyone had to go home early. It is a minor episode in the history of extraordinary phenomena, but it is worth a closer look because it can tell us a great deal about the bigger picture. After all, the bigger picture is merely the sum of all the little episodes, and we are interested in what they have had in common. As we shall see, what happened in Greenwich was fairly typical (in certain key respects) of how mesmeric phenomena were demonstrated and reported.

How this was done matters because beliefs about mesmerism were responses to demonstrations and reports of mesmeric phenomena. If we wish to understand such beliefs, then we need to consider the reported events to which people were responding. The demonstrations themselves are long gone, of course, so our only access is through reports of them, and these reports did not merely describe the events, but described them in a particular way. By examining them, we can form a general idea of what happened at the demonstrations, and we can see in detail how they were framed by contemporary reporters for the wider public. In doing so, we can see how the performance and reporting of mesmeric phenomena were fundamental to beliefs about mesmerism, and we can begin to identify various patterns that have been part and parcel of extraordinary beliefs since.

In Britain, the early 1840s were the years in which the key threads were unravelled, and so provide the most useful domestic window into a considerably longer and more widespread dispute.[2] The origins of the dispute, of course, had been in late eighteenth-century France, when Mesmer and his followers had provoked a great deal of controversy over animal magnetism. According to Mesmer, all living bodies contained a magnetic fluid, the realignment of which could cure a range of illnesses. In Paris, he had gained a reputation for miracle cures, and a long list of patients who had shaken and swooned in his presence, and afterwards had said that they felt much better. Needless to say, he had divided opinion. In 1784, there had been a famous Royal Commission in Paris, chaired by Benjamin Franklin, and including such luminaries as Antoine Lavoisier. The aim of the investigation had been to test the existence of the magnetic fluid; its conclusion had been that it did not exist, and that the phenomena were the result of imagination and fraud. This report went on to be cited regularly by sceptics as evidence that mesmerism was a fraud, despite the fact that many of the phenomena had been described as real (caused by the subjects' imagination). Furthermore, a second commission, which reported in 1831, concluded that most of the phenomena of mesmerism, including lucid somnambulism (clairvoyance), were genuine.[3]

Mesmeric phenomena had arrived in Britain courtesy of travelling French lecturers, such as the flamboyant Baron Dupotet, who had not only given public lectures and demonstrations, but had also excited the interest of John Elliotson. Elliotson, a well-known professor of medicine at University College London, had begun his own investigations into mesmerism. He had conducted tests with different metals, and had concluded that animal magnetism could be stored in some metals, such as nickel, but not in others, such as lead. He had also given demonstrations of mesmerism, first in the wards for his students, then in the hospital's public theatre for a wider audience. His most successful subjects were two young Irish servant girls, Elizabeth and Jane O'Key, who would go into trance, and behave in various ways that servant girls were not supposed to, from flirting with the professor to demonstrating clairvoyance. All of this attracted public attention, of course, and was reported, among other places, in *The Lancet*.[4]

Thomas Wakley, founding editor of *The Lancet*, had been initially supportive, but had changed his mind. In a famous case of debunking, he had invited Elliotson and the O'Key sisters to his home, and in the company of other medics, had tricked one of the sisters into thinking she was being mesmerized. According to Elliotson's experiments, a mesmerized piece of nickel could be used to magnetize a subject, but a piece of lead could not. Wakley had taken a piece of lead, without saying which metal it was, and had applied it to Elizabeth O'Key; meanwhile, a stooge had audibly whispered not to apply the nickel too strongly. Elizabeth had immediately turned violently red, formed a squint, and fallen back in the chair. From our point of view, she was responding to suggestion, and the 1784 Paris Royal Commission had attributed similar behaviour to the imagination. Wakley, however, had concluded it was fraud, and ran a series of hostile letters that would appear in *The Lancet* over the following years.[5]

By the 1840s, then, one could appeal to a French Royal Commission in order to support the view that mesmeric phenomena were real, or the view that they were not, or the view that they were real but the theory was wrong. One could treat Wakley's tests as evidence of fraud, or as evidence of the power of the imagination, or as evidence of nothing more than the fact that some metals were inconsistent in their conductance of animal magnetism. In short, one could believe or disbelieve in mesmerism, whether that meant the theory of animal magnetism, or else some (or all, or none) of the phenomena, and any of these beliefs could be based upon available scientific evidence. However, it was during the 1840s that the controversy over mesmerism became significantly more widespread, as relevant evidence became more widely available, and more people argued about what it meant.

One reason for this was the appearance of specialist journals (in particular, Elliotson's *The Zoist*), which described many and varied phenomena, which, in turn, were reported elsewhere. Another was the growing awareness of the potential relevance of mesmerism to medicine, as accounts emerged of painless operations and successful mesmeric cures. In 1842, the first British painless surgery was reported, in which a mesmerized patient had his leg amputated. Numerous other cases were published by Elliotson in 1843, and the widely reported painless operations by James Esdaile in India began in 1845. By then, the well-known writer, Harriet Martineau, had very publicly claimed that mesmerism had cured her of a long and painful uterine disease, this being only the most famous of reported mesmeric cures.[6]

As Alison Winter has shown, the response of senior medics to the alleged efficacy of mesmerism in medicine was hostile. It was said that, since Martineau had received no medical education, she was not qualified to know whether or not she was cured. Indeed, Darwin suggested that her apparent cure was a symptom of madness, and noted that a 'tendency to deceive is characteristic of disordered females'.[7] Similarly, the painless leg amputation was greeted with deep scepticism by senior medics, as eminent surgeons claimed that the patient had been lying about the absence of pain. When ether emerged as a chemical anaesthetic in 1847, it was immediately proposed as an alternative to mesmerism, despite the risk to the patient initially being greater. Thomas Wakley hoped ether would destroy 'one limb of the mesmeric quackery', and Robert Liston, the most famous surgeon of his day, enthusiastically claimed that it had done so.[8]

We cannot understand what people made of mesmerism at the time unless we consider this context of controversy over the potential role of mesmerism in medicine: on the one hand, there were growing numbers of reports of mesmeric analgesia and cures; on the other hand, senior medical figures were declaring that these were not real. There were, of course, other relevant matters, such as the ways in which contemporary notions of class and gender were reflected in mesmeric demonstrations, and in who counted as an ideal subject, or the claims of certain clergymen that mesmeric phenomena were, in fact, the work of Satan. In other words, how extraordinary contemporaries found mesmeric phenomena, or particular explanations for them, would have been shaped by more general views about what was considered ordinary or plausible at the time. But whether or not they were real, and what that meant, was consistently disputed in terms of who was qualified to make a reliable assessment, and medical expertise was never far from the discussion.

The 1840s also saw the emergence of greater numbers of popular lecturers, the result being that demonstrations of mesmerism became more widely available, and more widely reported.[9] These kinds of demonstrations impacted not only upon general audiences and readers of newspapers, but also upon key scientific figures, whose interests were provoked by such demonstrations. This had been the case with Elliotson, and it was a demonstration in 1841 that provoked the interest of James Braid, the Manchester surgeon whose theory of hypnotism redrew the boundaries of what was real and ordinary in relation to mesmerism. By considering a number of such demonstrations, how they were reported and subsequently disputed, we can identify several themes that have become commonplace in the framing of extraordinary phenomena since.

Framing mesmeric phenomena (in performance)

We will begin by considering the demonstrations themselves, and do so by focusing initially on one of the key demonstrators at the time. W. J. Vernon was one of the most prominent lecturers in 1840s England, his lectures and demonstrations were widely debated, and he paid regular attention to their controversial nature. He is, therefore, an ideal introductory guide to how the various extraordinary phenomena of mesmerism were being demonstrated, reported and disputed, just as the boundaries of ordinariness were being redrawn.

His background is worth a look since, like many mesmerists, Vernon was initially interested in phrenology, and was not one to shirk from the public eye. We first hear of him in 1840, when he was giving lectures and demonstrations of phrenology in the south-west of England. He was then working with a colleague, the pair billing themselves as 'Professors W. J. Vernon and Adolphe Kiste', though their use of the title of 'Professor' was thought by some 'to throw around the proceedings an air of quackery'.[10] Nevertheless, in Exeter, their courses of lectures were 'numerously and respectably attended', and led to the founding of the Exeter Phrenological Society. In November, they proudly reported that a visit to the Exeter asylum for the deaf and dumb had greatly impressed the boys, despite the presence of the headmaster, Mr Gordon, who they described as a 'hereditary opponent, being a near relation of the late celebrated anatomist, John Gordon of Edinburgh, one of the earliest and most celebrated opponents of phrenology in this country'.[11] Over the next few months, Vernon continued to report on the excited interest resulting from his 'numerously and fashionably attended' lectures in Torquay, and a Dartmouth resident even wrote to the *Phrenological Journal* to give 'a flattering account of the skill of this "highly gifted gentleman" as a lecturer and manipulator'; alas, the journal declined to publish this letter, on the grounds that the author was one 'W. J. Smith, Solicitor' who, 'as the handwriting plainly shews [sic], *is no other than Mr Vernon himself*'.[12] Subsequent references to Vernon in the journal were treated with a degree of scepticism.[13]

By 1843, perhaps in need of an alternative outlet, Vernon was editor of the *People's Phrenological Journal*, more popular than its rival by inclination rather than circulation, and had become interested in mesmerism and phreno-mesmerism.[14] From around 1841, phreno-mesmerists had used magnetic influence to excite the phrenological organs, causing subjects to behave according to the corresponding faculty. In such performances, a young lady (it was invariably a young lady) would be mesmerised, then the mesmerist would influence one of the phrenological organs. If, for example, it was the organ of Veneration, she might go down on her knees and hold her palms together as if praying. The power of such performances was that they appeared to demonstrate the truth of phrenology as well as mesmerism. Rather than simply being told that phrenology was valid, a point that was regularly disputed by critics, the audience was being provided with direct observable evidence that distinct parts of the brain represented different aspects of character. As John Elliotson noted at the time, 'where formerly *one* had been converted to the truth of phrenology, now, through mesmerism, *one hundred* were converted'.[15]

However, Vernon really came to public attention when he agreed to give a lecture on mesmerism in Greenwich, one that is an excellent first case study of disputes surrounding extraordinary phenomena. The lecture was prompted by what was later known as the Deptford case. In December 1843, reports appeared in the press about a case in which one William G. Smith of Deptford had mesmerised his servant boy, James Cook, and that the latter had exhibited clairvoyant abilities. The controversy was fuelled by being denounced as a 'delusion' by one Mr Hope, a surgeon of the Dreadnought hospital ship at nearby Greenwich. According to the *People's Phrenological Journal*, the case 'has excited much interest and commentary, having gone the round of the newspapers, and... many inaccurate reports have been circulated'.[16]

In the midst of the controversy, Vernon went to visit the boy Cook, and arranged to meet with Mr Hope and 'several of the leading medical men of Greenwich and Deptford'. Hope did not turn up on the day, but those present observed the boy being placed into a mesmeric coma, and exhibiting muscular rigidity, and declared that 'any question of collusion or deception on this occasion was out of the question'. Their conclusion was that 'the subject appeared to be deserving further investigation'. Vernon described these events in a letter to the *Medical Times*, announcing that a lecture was to be arranged in Greenwich in order to illustrate the phenomena, and calling on Hope to attend so that he might 'acknowledge publicly the error he has committed in making assertions upon subjects of which he is evidently ignorant'.[17]

The lecture took place at Greenwich Literary and Scientific Institution on 4 January 1844, and attracted a large, varied and excited audience. The playbill promised 'striking instances of the Mesmeric Coma, – vital attraction in the waking state, – sympathy of taste and feeling, – Catalepsy, and excitement of the Phrenological Organs', and it 'earnestly requested' the attendance of 'Professional Gentlemen, who may wish to ascertain the truth or fallacy of the present Mesmeric Theory'.[18] According to the *Morning Herald*, the hall, which could hold 'upwards of one thousand people, was crowded to excess, amongst the company were a great number of ladies, several of the County magistrates, gentry and professional and scientific men'.[19] In the gallery, there were 'a number of medical students from the London hospitals'. Several medical men, including a Dr Oak and a Mr Sherwin, were on the platform with Vernon, along with three patients (the boy Cook, and a young man and woman).

Vernon began with a speech that shows the sort of rhetoric typically used by exhibitors of such controversial phenomena. He declared that he

> had no doubt that he should show effects which would convince any unbiased mind that mesmerism was not a delusion, but deserved to be ranked amongst the sciences... that it was the result and the law of Nature... He should only show that this law did exist, and leave it to the medical profession to sift out how it arose, and how it could be applied for the benefit of the human species.

He complained of those who avoided the facts 'because it would disarrange previous opinions', 'who resolutely supported theory against facts', and suggested a comparison between mesmeric influence and less controversial scientific phenomena (it was 'as difficult to explain as sound, motion and light', 'it was like the laws of gravitation, motion, and heat, only known to exist'). In short, the facts were demonstrable, and their explanation was a secondary matter, to reject unexplained facts was an act of prejudice (and out of line with scientific thinking), and the facts of mesmerism were not only real but also beneficial to humanity. Along the way, he also pointed out that mesmeric influence was not 'derived from Satan' but rather was a 'gift of God', and concluded with a declaration that his only aim was to discover the truth and 'follow it wherever it might lead' (this received 'general applause').

He then proceeded to the demonstrations, the details of which (if we accept them as generally accurate for the moment) give a sense of the atmosphere. The young woman was seated facing the audience, with Dr Oak, Mr Sherwin and other medical gentlemen nearby. Before he could start, however, one of the medics defied Vernon to mesmerise him, and 'seated himself in a chair amidst tumultuous applause'. Vernon objected, this not being part of the arrangement, and accused him of 'antics something amounting to mountebankism'. When a member of the audience cried out 'no shuffling', Vernon claimed that it 'proved he could not approach the subject as a matter of science', and if he was talking to him, 'he privately knew how to treat him'. When Sherwin complained that he and his colleagues had come 'at the invitation of the learned professor', Vernon responded: 'Don't call me a learned professor', provoking a cry of 'hold your tongue, don't quarrel, who can go to sleep in such a noise [laughter]', followed by further argument among the main parties, and 'hisses and much confusion' among the audience.

After calm had been restored, Vernon made the usual passes over the young woman, and a state of mesmeric coma was declared. Sherwin applied a bottle of strong ammonia to her nostrils and mouth for several minutes, yet 'the patient showed but very slight oppression'. He then 'unclosed her eyelids, and introduced his fingers into her mouth without visible effect'. When 'loudly called on to state his opinion' as to whether she was in a mesmeric trance, Sherwin gave some 'ambiguous answers', then suggested she was asleep. Vernon claimed that the ammonia test proved she could not be asleep, at which point Dr Oak maintained that 'it was evident she was hysterical', and another heated argument followed, leading to 'great uproar'. Vernon complained that such 'uproarious conduct . . . was more like that in the gallery of a theatre than of those met for the requirement of scientific knowledge . . . they were not capable of appreciating any scientific explanation'. He promptly escorted the young woman offstage amidst an ongoing mixture of cheers, jeers and heckles.

To the surprise of the audience, however, he returned, and order was again restored after the chairman announced that Vernon had attended for the sake of truth, and that he was to receive 'not a farthing' from the admission fees. Vernon continued with the young man, who was put into a coma, and his left arm placed into a state of catalepsy so that it 'appeared as unmoveable as a statue'. At that point, one Mr Harris, a cabinet-maker from Greenwich, suddenly and unexpectedly 'struck the patient a tremendous blow on the hand with a stick, the blow sounding above the buzz and noise of the meeting'. This provoked universal indignation, and there were cries of 'turn him out, police, shame, shame &c. and he was pretty roughly handled, several accidental collisions led to the exchange of blows, and for a few minutes the confusion was indescribable'. Once Harris had been taken into custody by police, Vernon explained that it was impossible to continue the lecture with 'so much excitement', and stressed the need for proper enquiry.

In the midst of all this, despite the claims and counterclaims, and the general pandemonium, those present and readers of the *Morning Herald*, and of the various provincial newspapers that copied the story, were nevertheless provided with evidence that mesmerism was real.[20] After all, the woman was reported not to have reacted to the ammonia test, the explanations of the medics were hardly conclusive, and as for the boy who was struck with a stick, it was reported: 'strange to say, the lad never flinched from the blow, nor did his hand show the least mark'.[21] Whether this was noticed in the midst of the uproar is, of course, another matter, but then Vernon was far from finished in Greenwich. He promptly arranged another lecture on the 18 January, which proved to be less eventful, but rather more successful.

On this occasion, according to the *People's Phrenological Journal*, 'no one was admitted except conditionally, and by ticket. Strict order was enforced, judges and a chairman appointed, and no one else was allowed to address the meeting, or even ask questions, except through the chairman.' The hall was nevertheless 'crowded, and numbers were unable to obtain admission'. The judges were three medical men, all of whom declared themselves to be hostile to mesmerism. In the first demonstration, Vernon placed a boy into a mesmeric coma, and raised his pulse from 80 to 140 beats per minute. 'This fact', it was reported, 'was unquestioned'. Vernon then offered to lower it to 12 beats per minute, but the judges 'considered the experiment far too dangerous. They were all opposed to Mesmerism, but their prudence on the occasion shewed [sic] that their scepticism had been shaken.' There then followed a test in which a young female subject attempted 'reading with her eyes closed. One of the judges held his fingers over the eyes in such a manner, that seeing in the natural way was perfectly impossible. In this condition she read the title page of a book held at a little distance in front of her.' This experiment, we are told, 'was unequivocal, and indisputable, and produced, naturally enough, a great effect upon the audience'. When asked to give comments about what they had witnessed, the first medical gentleman declared that he 'had come as a complete sceptic, but now he was satisfied that there *was* something in mesmerism'. The second was rather more ambiguous, conceding that he 'certainly thought that there was something in it, but that he should not wonder if, after all, it turned out to be nothing'. The final medic, it seems, was unable to express himself properly, making 'a very lame affair of what he said, and ultimately broke down'.[22]

Such a positive account from the *People's Phrenological Journal* was in itself hardly surprising, though accounts of sceptics being overwhelmed by the facts have been standard fare in the history of such disputes. Nevertheless, regardless of the extent to which particular accounts might have been one-sided, we can see that Vernon's Greenwich lectures illustrate several features typical of demonstrations of mesmeric phenomena, and of extraordinary phenomena since.

First, and perhaps most importantly, they were designed to exclude alternative explanations, most obviously the possibility that subjects were faking it. In this case, when Vernon placed his subject into a trance, various procedures were used to check whether she was pretending or asleep. Insensibility to pain was demonstrated by attempts to induce pain, and eyeless vision by the apparent elimination of normal vision. The ruling out of ordinary explanations (in this case, imposture) was a fundamental part of such demonstrations, though how this was done, and whether or not it was done adequately, was naturally a topic of dispute. We shall consider later what made particular demonstrations more convincing than others, but it was always the case that they were designed to demonstrate the inadequacy of various (ordinary) explanations.

Second, they were accompanied by particular arguments (made by Vernon here and later, and by countless others since) designed to address the extraordinariness of the phenomena. For example: that they were facts was something that could be observed by anyone; to reject the facts because they did not fit with existing knowledge was an act of prejudice; and comparisons were made with other (generally accepted) natural phenomena that were not yet fully understood. Thus, the existence of facts that could not (yet) be explained in ordinary scientific terms was presented as quite compatible with scientific thinking. Such arguments, of course, were designed to convince others that the phenomena were real, however extraordinary they might seem.

Third, the case for the phenomena also relied upon another line of argument, that in addition to being real, they were also a desirable thing. When Vernon argued that mesmerism would be beneficial to humankind, he was referring to its potential to remove pain and cure illness. That it was 'a gift from God' rather than 'derived from Satan', and that his was an honest, open-minded quest for 'truth, wherever it might lead', appealed to moral sensibilities rather than matters of fact. Whatever his audience made of this, such rhetoric was designed to convince them that his demonstrations, in addition to being displays of facts, were also illustrations of a good thing.

This makes perfect sense, of course, since these demonstrations were intended to succeed in a context of scepticism and indifference. In this case, there seems to have been a deliberate and premeditated attempt by some to debunk the demonstrations. Indeed, according to the *Morning Herald*, '[i]t was publicly stated, on the authority of some medical men, that the [medical] students had come down purposely to create a disturbance and stop the lecture'.[23] The hostility of scientific orthodoxy to extraordinary claims has, of course, been another consistent theme (though the reasons for hostility have varied somewhat), but it needs to be remembered that public audiences could be equally hostile in the face of controversial claims.[24] Furthermore, it was not only hostility but also indifference that lecturers faced. Just because people attended a lecture – indeed, even if they paid admission – it did not follow that they took a serious interest in the subject. As the theatrical atmosphere shows, their reasons for being there could be as much to do with entertainment as education.[25] Regularly faced with hostile and indifferent audiences, such demonstrations were designed to convince the public not only that the facts were real, but also that they mattered.

The form this took, of course, was in terms of the relevance of mesmerism to medicine. In 1844, when painless surgery was neither available (except through mesmerism) nor regarded as necessary (by surgeons), it was certainly an issue for any potential patient. When Vernon's subjects displayed insensibility to pain, they provided the public with direct evidence that mesmerism was indeed an effective analgesic. Similarly, when he demonstrated that mesmerized subjects could see without using normal vision, and that their bodies could be affected via magnetic influence, the possibility of diagnosis and cure of ailments must have seemed that much more plausible. Indeed, Vernon reportedly used mesmerism to provide painless tooth extractions, and his advertisements offered mesmeric treatments for 'medical and surgical cases'.[26] When Harriet Martineau's case became public, Vernon cited it in his lectures, and later he was reported in a letter published by Elliotson to have cured another woman of a similar uterine disease.[27] Vernon's stage demonstrations, then, were part and parcel of the contemporary dispute about medical knowledge and authority.

As a result, the matter of medical expertise was never far from any argument, though the way in which it was deployed in rhetoric was not as simple as one might expect. In Greenwich, Vernon presented the facts as observable to anyone, but acknowledged that it was up to the medical profession to explain the facts. In other lectures, he both challenged medical expertise (e.g. when he claimed that mesmerism could aid self-diagnosis) and appealed to it (e.g. when he noted the growing acceptance of mesmerism among the medical profession).[28] His playbills might announce that he was engaged in a 'public medical challenge', yet included on the bill one Dr Owens, RCS, whose name and credentials were in a larger font than his own.[29] Thus, while mesmerists were in many respects a challenge to orthodox medical expertise, they also actively appealed to such expertise when, to put it crudely, it suited them. This has been another regular thread in disputes about extraordinary phenomena, that in framing the phenomena as real, proponents have deployed the topic of expertise in the most effective way (e.g. by claiming to have adequate expertise, by citing the credentials of those who agree, by challenging the expertise of those who do not). As we shall see, critics have done the same, but in terms of the demonstration of extraordinary phenomena, the basic point is this: constructions of (what counts as) adequate expertise have been a means through which the phenomena have been made convincing.

So far, then, the case of Vernon the mesmerist has been used to illustrate a number of themes that were typical of mesmeric performances: the attempt to demonstrate the inadequacy of ordinary explanations; the deployment of particular arguments designed to address the extraordinariness of the phenomena; the claim that they were not only facts but also a good thing; and the construction of adequate expertise. These were recurrent themes in the lectures of Vernon (and, as we shall see, in those of other mesmerists too), which provided evidence and arguments upon which observers could form an opinion. The demonstrations were designed to be convincingly real and extraordinary, to be plausible unexplained facts that one would wish to be true. This is how they were framed in performance by professional lecturers, whose primary aim was to convince others, and whose careers depended upon sufficient public interest. One cannot understand beliefs in mesmerism without appreciating the ways in which demonstrations of mesmeric phenomena were designed to be convincing. Whether they were actually found convincing is, of course, another matter, and though we cannot know what people thought, we do know what they wrote in response to such demonstrations. Indeed, when we examine how others reported such phenomena, we can see how similar themes are present in the framing of them as one thing or another. In other words, they were central to how beliefs about the phenomena were expressed and justified.

Framing mesmeric demonstrations (in reports): reporting the facts

Reports of such demonstrations, like the demonstrations themselves, were ostensibly presentations of the facts. However, which facts were reported was a matter of choice, since a lecture of two hours might be reported in a couple of newspaper columns or less. And though we cannot know what was not reported, we do know that the reports described how ordinary explanations had been excluded, and repeated the arguments relating to the extraordinariness of the phenomena, adequate expertise, and the potential benefits of mesmerism. Thus, readers of newspapers, like those who attended, were faced with evidence of mesmeric phenomena, and with the arguments that accompanied them. In the process, a wider audience was provided with the case for mesmerism.

This is not to say that reporters sought to persuade their readers that mesmerism was true. On the contrary, many reports were couched in the language of neutrality, as reporters addressed the practical matter of having to report extraordinary events. Nevertheless, whatever individual reporters were thinking, they described particular facts, and did so in particular ways, and in the process they framed the phenomena one way or another. Furthermore, in disputing the facts, the language of neutrality can only get one so far, since disputes are hardly disputes unless different views are articulated and argued about. By examining how the demonstrations were reported and disputed, then, we can see how they were a means through which the phenomena could be framed one way or another, and through which different beliefs about mesmerism could be expressed and justified.

Framing the phenomena as extraordinary

Demonstrations of mesmerism were designed to exclude alternative explanations, primarily that the subject was pretending to be in a mesmeric state, and was faking her behaviour and abilities, perhaps in collusion with the mesmerist. Accounts of these demonstrations, then, reported various kinds of evidence suggesting that the subject could not have been faking it. A newspaper report of one demonstration reported that, while the subject was in a trance state, 'a pistol was fired without her previous knowledge, under the platform, but she did not start, or show the slightest indication of consciousness... A lighted cigar was held under her nostrils, into which the smoke entered freely, but without producing any perceptible effect.'[30] In other reports, the subject was described as having been insensible to the smelling of ammonia, or the application of pins to different parts of the body, and occasionally one read of surprise tactics, like those of the stick-wielding cabinet-maker of Greenwich, such as the 'brutal assault' by a surgeon who 'violently seized a sleeper's arm and shouted that the house was on fire'.[31]

Reporting how ordinary explanations were excluded did not necessarily involve an expression of belief, but the way in which they were reported could frame things fairly clearly. For example, changes in the rate and strength of the subject's pulse were often presented by mesmerists as direct proof that the mesmeric sleep was not feigned. Sceptical medics often rejected this, reports often commented upon this, and in the process an implicit position could be conveyed. Thus, on one occasion, it was reported that a surgeon taking part in a demonstration:

> contended that the sleep was natural sleep, and that the sleep would account for the difference in the action of the heart, but when asked how he could account for the natural sleep being induced in one minute in a young country girl agitated till she trembled from head to foot and in the face of a large concourse of people, he said it was 'the imagination'. The audience evidently thought the facts too strong to be so easily explained away.[32]

In demonstrations of phreno-mesmerism, one of the obvious explanations was that the subject knew which of her phrenological organs was to be excited, and then simply acted accordingly. Thus, mesmerists often had the audience choose the organ to be excited, and in a way that the subject could not know which organ had been chosen. Reports of phreno-mesmeric demonstrations noted that this was the case, that they 'were written on a black board, hidden from the patient', or that the lecturer insisted that 'they should be written by any individual and handed to him; there should be no contact between his hand and the organ to be excited; and all the conversation with the patient should be carried on by a gentleman chosen by the audience'.[33] Similarly, demonstrations of mesmeric catalepsy often included the hanging of a chair on the outstretched arm of a subject, and an invitation to members of the audience to check that the arm was truly rigid. These explicit attempts to exclude ordinary explanations were reported by the press, and often in language that left little room for doubt. Thus, for example, a 'gentleman stepped forward and having tried to bend the limb, declared most unequivocally that there could not be any deception, that the arm was stiff as a bar of iron'.[34]

In selecting which facts to report, accounts of such events included information that was directly relevant to the matter at hand. For example, a Maidstone newspaper described experiments with a retired servant 'of small stature, and of apparently very slight muscular development'. The relevance of her physical details soon became apparent, as the report continued to describe how, while her arms were held out horizontally, in a demonstration of mesmeric catalepsy,

> a medical gentleman then rather suddenly hung the top rail of one of the chairs on her hand. The limb sunk very little, but instantly recovered its position, and bore the weight of the chair, for three minutes more... To sustain a chair for three minutes on her extended wrist, appears scarcely possible, in a natural state, for so slight a woman.

During a subsequent demonstration of phreno-mesmerism, her organ of Tune was excited, and 'she sang a verse of a song, with great firmness and clearness of tone... without the slightest tremor affecting her voice, before an audience of musical critics and highly educated persons, [which] is equally improbable for a woman of her condition in life'.[35] Without the details about the woman's 'condition', the suspension of a chair for three minutes, and the singing of a song in public, would have seemed rather less extraordinary.

In addition to whether those involved in the demonstrations could fake it, there was also the question of whether they would do so. Thus, whether the subject was known to the mesmerist, or to the audience, was a regular matter of interest. After all, on the one hand, mesmerists preferred a subject whom they knew to be susceptible; on the other hand, audiences could be suspicious of a subject who seemed to be part of the demonstration. It was therefore common for lecturers to state, and newspapers to report, the extent of the relationship between mesmerist and subject. In Worcester, for example, collusion was ruled out in experiments 'performed by inhabitants of Worcester, upon residents of the city', and in Maidstone, it was noted that '[n]either of these parties had been seen by Mr B [the mesmerist] before that time'.[36] In Bristol, on the other hand, the mesmerist 'knew it would be objected that the patient was not from Bristol, and he knew he should be suspected of collusion with her'.[37]

If the individuals concerned were known to the reporter, however, a mesmerist might be described as a 'man of unimpeachable integrity', or as one 'whose honour and fairness Dr Riley expressed himself in the highest terms', or a subject as one 'whose character and station forbade the thought that she would lend herself to an imposition'.[38] References were made to successful experiments carried out 'in the presence of respectable persons', 'performed by one of the medical gentlemen of this town on a patient of his own at his own house', or by 'individuals who are actuated by no pecuniary motive – men of science and intellect, and of respectable positions in society'.[39] Much of this was naturally based upon contemporary notions of respectability, or contemporary notions of capability. Thus, despite the recent well-publicized case of the O'Key sisters, a rural servant girl might be deemed willing but unable to deceive her betters, and her background taken as unqualified evidence of the unlikelihood of fraud.[40]

By describing various ways in which mesmerists and their subjects could not, and would not, have faked the phenomena, newspaper reports regularly framed the phenomena as extraordinary. This did not mean that they expressed a belief in mesmerism – one could merely report 'the facts' – but in presenting particular facts, they also presented them in a particular way. Indeed, this was the case, even when explicit claims of neutrality were made. 'As our contemporary the *Guardian* says, we give these facts, and leave them with our readers', said one ostensibly neutral newspaper, though it described experiments 'under circumstances which seemed to preclude the very idea of collusion', and displays of clairvoyance by a young woman when 'it was evident to all she could not have known', and by some young men who 'could not possibly have seen'.[41] Another paper reported how the mesmerist 'applied the sharp point of a pin several times to the back of [a subject's] hand, her forehead, and her neck, without her showing the least sign of sensation', and described the mesmerist himself as 'obviously honest', yet noted that 'we do not feel called upon to hazard an opinion'.[42] Another, 'without offering an opinion on the merits of the system', concluded that normal awareness 'must have been physically impossible', and did not observe 'any attempt at imposition or deception by either of the parties'.[43] In other words, the lack of a conclusion on the reality of the phenomena did not prevent reporters from providing a version of events that could easily be read as having excluded ordinary explanations.

In addition to describing how ordinary explanations were excluded, reports included arguments about the extraordinariness of the demonstrations. For example, there were regular accounts of how initial scepticism had been overcome by the weight of the facts. A 'scientific gentleman, himself a sceptic as to mesmerism, prejudiced against it', had nevertheless become convinced, as had a subject who had been cured, even though he 'did not believe in the efficacy of mesmerism'.[44] Vernon was reported to have claimed (somewhat optimistically) that 'although at the first there had been considerable opposition, there was not one now who would dare come forward and deny the fact that there was truth in that science'.[45] For those who witnessed and reported demonstrations, the extraordinariness of the phenomena was regularly addressed by notes of initial scepticism, then appeals to the need for open-mindedness rather than prejudice: 'With such facts as these before our eyes it is impossible for us to deny or question the existence of an agency or influence which is called "Mesmeric" and on such a subject, we are content to be classed with the credulous few than with the prejudiced multitude'.[46] Reports regularly juxtaposed the reluctant believer with the prejudiced sceptic who, unlike the 'scientific gentleman' above, refused to believe the facts (who were 'still not satisfied', 'no evidence, though strong as holy writ, will ever convince them').[47]

They also often made the point that such prejudice against the facts was unscientific, either by repeating the words of the lecturer ('As men of intelligence and science, it became them to investigate the subject – not to denounce it without enquiry'), or else by commenting on the tactics of critics (such as 'a medical gentleman of this town, who exhibited not only a want of courtesy but also a species of ignorance and prejudice on the subject of the lecture totally at variance with a regard for science').[48] Yet such prejudice was to be expected since, according to the *Kentish Independent*:

> every new science (it may be laid down by axiom) has to contend with opposition... It is said that the science of mesmerism is ridiculous because its results are opposed to the present condition of science. Of course, they are, and perhaps the wiseacre, who makes this assertion, will tell us what new science the world has ever witnessed, the development of which has not appeared contrary to the ideas of the age.[49]

Elsewhere, the names of Galileo and Harvey were cited as examples of scientists whose facts had also been met with initial hostility, but which nevertheless had been shown to be true, and the facts of mesmerism were compared with those in other areas of established science that were not yet fully explained.[50]

In short, whether or not an explicit expression of belief was included as part of the account, reports of mesmerism conveyed the arguments concerning the extraordinariness of the phenomena: facts were facts, however extraordinary, believers had once been sceptics too, but resisting the facts was an act of prejudice, and unexplained facts (unlike prejudice) were quite compatible with scientific thinking.

They also, like the demonstrations themselves, appealed to different versions of expertise. As mesmerists claimed to have personal expertise, challenged the expertise of scientific critics, and cited scientific authorities who were sympathetic to mesmerism, so this was regularly reported.[51] Even when reporters stuck to the language of facts, the reporting of extraordinary facts involved describing how ordinary explanations had been excluded, and some sort of assessment was typical.[52] And, however extraordinary the facts might be, that they were facts was invariably presented as a matter of simple observation. Indeed, even when the facts were described as 'impossible to doubt, yet almost as difficult to believe, even on the evidence of our own senses', it was concluded that the evidence of the senses was sufficient: 'Let every man see, and judge for himself.'[53]

It was a point made on countless occasions, that extraordinary facts had to be seen to be believed, and even when seen, were hard to believe.[54] Nevertheless, those who saw and judged for themselves invariably reported both observations and judgements. If, in doing so, their judgements conflicted with medical experts, they could, like mesmerists, both challenge medical expertise and, at the same time, appeal to it.[55] General scientific expertise could be appealed to in the same way: opponents of mesmerism could be described as '[w]ithout one particle of scientific attainment... utterly unpracticed in the science of reasoning', whilst, at the same time, the phenomena could be described as having 'baffled the penetrations of men of science', 'men of science and intellect'.[56]

Reporters of such demonstrations, like the demonstrators themselves, presented themselves as personally competent (if only to observe the facts), and whether directly or indirectly via the arguments of the mesmerists, questioned the experts who opposed mesmerism and cited the expertise of those who did not. And, in the process, they conveyed to their readers the benefits of mesmerism, including references to recent cases of painless surgery, to the reported cure of Harriet Martineau, and describing mesmerism as 'applicable to the important subject of performing surgical operations without pain to the patient', as a science that could 'alleviate human suffering', that could 'allay the sufferings of our fellow creatures' and that 'promised to be beneficial to mankind'.[57]

If the purpose of the demonstrations was to display the facts, the ostensible purpose of the reports was to report them. In describing what they saw, of course, reporters also made judgements about what they saw, if only in deciding which facts to report, and how to report them. Whatever they were thinking, they described the attempts to exclude ordinary explanations they had seen, and the claims of the mesmerists they had heard, and did so in particular ways that often lent credence to both the phenomena and the claims. Those who expressed a belief about the phenomena, if only in the reality of the facts, engaged in the same sort of rhetoric as the mesmerists – and why not? The arguments had been designed to be convincing by those whose aim and living depended upon convincing as many people as possible, and those who had attended the lectures had been made familiar with them.

To summarize for the moment, then, by describing how mesmerists and their subjects could not, and would not, have faked the phenomena, newspaper reports regularly framed the phenomena as real. In doing so, they made the arguments (whether as their own views, or as those of mesmerists) that facts were facts, however extraordinary, that believers had once been sceptics too, that resisting the facts was an act of prejudice, and that unexplained facts (unlike prejudice) were quite compatible with scientific thinking. Like the demonstrators, they presented themselves as competent observers of the facts, questioned the expertise of those who opposed mesmerism, and appealed to the expertise of those who did not. And, like them, they conveyed the idea that if mesmeric phenomena were true, this would be a good thing.

These recurring arguments were ways of making mesmeric phenomena more convincing and, whatever the reporters actually believed, they were regular features of their reports. Anyone who wished to form a view, about what they had seen or read, was provided with a range of arguments that were designed to influence that view. As for anyone already leaning to the view that mesmeric phenomena were real, they were provided with ammunition with which that view could be sustained, either in thinking about it themselves, or else in discussion with others. In short, such arguments provided a basis upon which belief in mesmerism could be constructed and maintained.

Framing the phenomena as ordinary

A month after the uproar provoked by Vernon in Greenwich had subsided, locals were treated to another lecture on mesmerism. This time, however, it was delivered by John Quilter Rumball, anti-mesmerist. J. Q. Rumball was a member of the Royal College of Surgeons, an advocate of phrenology but an active critic of mesmerism. His lectures on 'The Fallacies of Mesmerism' were designed to be antidotes to those of Vernon and others. In February 1844, Rumball gave a lecture in Greenwich at the same venue in which Vernon had spoken, which was an explicit attempt to debunk his earlier lecture. Indeed, Vernon found him to be rather a nuisance, later complaining that he 'was continually following him about from place to place, wherever he lectured'.[58]

Rumball's lecture included a range of arguments that were typical of those used by critics of mesmerism. He claimed that mesmerism was a delusion, and rejected the facts as the product of deception and self-deception. In rejecting the facts, however, he denied prejudice ('he had placed faith in it for some time'), but the claims of mesmerists were not in line with natural law (they 'do away with the laws of nature'). He challenged the expertise of mesmerists (not only Vernon but also 'gentlemen of still higher talents and intelligence') including 'great men of the scientific world' who had claimed that mesmerism was real, and whom he dismissed as a 'set of incapable imbeciles'. His was a disinterested quest for truth ('he had taken up a position in the front ranks of truth', and 'had suffered much in pursuing truth'), and mesmerism was, in his opinion, 'one of the grossest impositions ever attempted to be palmed upon the public'.[59]

The arguments of critics, like those of proponents, were always open to dispute, of course, and, unfortunately for Rumball, Brookes the mesmerist was in the room. Brookes, who was almost as well known as Vernon, immediately challenged the speaker, by claiming that those whom he called 'imbeciles' had a good deal more scientific credibility than him. This provoked a heated debate, until some of the crowd became restless, and began to call out for 'experiments'. At this point, an exhibition of clairvoyance began, in which a boy in a mesmeric trance was blindfolded, then was asked to name various playing cards. When the boy succeeded, 'Mr. Rumball said he was convinced some of the audience had communicated with him'. In order to exclude this ordinary explanation, a tablecloth was then used to hide the boy from the audience view. When the boy succeeded again, 'Mr Rumball said he was convinced it was an imposture and abruptly quitted the hall'.[60]

As he continued to suffer in the pursuit of truth, Rumball must have decided that words were not enough, as he was soon demonstrating his own experiments, along with rather more detailed explanations of how they were done. For the moment, however, he provides an initial example of how critics of mesmerism disputed the reality of mesmeric phenomena, by claiming that ordinary explanations had not been excluded, by making their own arguments about the extraordinariness of the phenomena (the facts were inadequate, the claim was extraordinary, they were not prejudiced but displaying proper scepticism), by disputing the expertise of proponents and by taking the moral high ground themselves. And, if all else failed, by simply walking away.

In claiming that ordinary explanations had not been excluded, critics appealed to all manner of possibilities. As one debunker put it, with a sense of sarcasm that was common in such disputes: 'it is well known that an elderly parson, with a tedious sermon, would soon send his hearers into a profound coma!'[61] For another, it was hardly surprising that an effect was produced by a mesmerist 'roughly grasping the throat and thrusting his two thumbs into the orbits of his patients, frightening them by intently and sternly gazing at them'.[62] Rumball himself, when asked to deny that he had been mesmerized and 'had felt some effects... did not deny this, but said no wonder, when a fellow kept poking his fingers in his eyes for nearly half an hour'.[63] Others suggested that the subject was pretending, and alluded to the possibility of collusion. For example, it was noted that Vernon's subject was 'no new patient [but] one who is a practiced hand, who has rehearsed the part over and over again'.[64] And there was always a last resort, that whatever was going on was somehow explicable, that was 'if real, evidently a form of deranged nervous action', or that 'any state produced by mesmerism may be produced by other means'.[65]

As for more impressive feats, such as demonstrations of clairvoyance, these could always be dismissed as trickery, as 'a clever piece of jugglery', or references could be made to similar feats that were a 'proved case of fraud', such as a recent case of a clairvoyant boy in which, it transpired, 'the father was a ventriloquist, and the boy never spoke at all'.[66] Thus, in rejecting any particular event, critics could appeal to other more dubious cases of mesmerism where, it was claimed, fraud had taken place. That fraud was a common feature of mesmeric demonstrations 'has been proved, in a numerous series of phenomena', and it was 'an acknowledged fact that much clever deception has been practiced by gentlemen of Mr Brookes' profession'.[67] For critics, it was a fact that mesmerists and subjects could and would engage in deception, and any particular case could be considered as one more example of this. After all, the nature of successful fraud is that it is not detected. And, if asked to explain what happened on a particular occasion, a critic could simply point out that there were limits to how much time one could spend on the matter: as Rumball himself put it, 'he could not pledge himself to find out every case of delusion'.[68]

Critics also discussed the extraordinariness of the claim in relation to the facts and their compatibility with scientific thinking. Of course, prejudice in the face of facts was undesirable and unscientific, but not in the face of extraordinary claims backed by unconvincing facts. 'We disclaim any prejudice, except in favour of common sense and against humbug. Prove by a set of well regulated experiments', a medical journal challenged, 'and we will be among its most strenuous advocates'.[69] In the absence of adequate facts, however, such claims deserved to be treated with scepticism, they were 'contrary to all rational belief', 'exceptions to the general law of nature', and critics 'had a right to doubt everything contrary to the natural course of nature'.[70] '[W]e are not to reject facts because of our inability to comprehend them, nor is it consistent with true science', agreed a sceptical surgeon, however, '[t]here is, Sir, a limit to human patience, but there seems none to human credulity'.[71] Thus, critics argued that the extraordinariness of the claim required not prejudice but adequate scepticism, and open-mindedness but not gullibility.[72]

The construction of neutrality, which was part and parcel of both demonstrations and reports of mesmeric phenomena, was also part of critical discourse, and was similarly bound up with the question of expertise. Far from being prejudiced, it was argued, scientists had already examined the matter, 'its merits were tested and thoroughly sifted by scientific men... it was weighed in the balance of scientific investigation but was found sadly wanting'.[73] Disputes over what counted as scientific expertise included other matters that we shall consider later, but one of the regular themes was the need for an absence of bias. Thus, for example, in rejecting the charge of ignorance of the subject, a medical critic could claim: '[t]hat we have no *practical* acquaintance with the subject of mesmerism we candidly allow, and consider this very circumstance renders us more capable of forming a correct opinion of the experiments of others'. Unlike mesmerists who were 'anxious for the success of their experiments... we, having no theories to support and anxious only for the elucidation of truth, look on with the most perfect calmness, if not indifference'.[74]

Others, of course, were less concerned with portraying a neutral position, and dismissed the phenomena as obvious nonsense, not worthy of serious consideration. When a medical journal reviewed a book by an advocate of mesmerism, it described it as 'trash', and complained of 'old tales and cases that have been over and over again proved to be falsehoods and deceptions'.[75] The only example cited by the reviewer, however, was the Deptford case, in which Vernon had been involved, and for which no evidence of deception had emerged. Nevertheless, the lack of detail provided on this by the reviewer suggests that the case, if not the details, would have been known to readers, and would have been regarded as an obvious deception. Similarly, when a *Times* journalist reported on a Vernon lecture in London, he assumed that the demonstrations were fake, and focused his attention on the speaker's lack of eloquence. 'Mr Vernon', he wrote, 'with that spirit which so distinguishes men of genius and persons gifted with original powers of thinking, courageously bade defiance to those grammatical rules which shackle men of vulgar understandings'.[76]

For all the appeals to the need for unprejudiced scientific enquiry, the sarcastic dismissal of extraordinary phenomena, and those who believe in them, has been another regular theme. Its rhetorical power, of course, is in its ability to confirm rather than to convert, as those who adhere to a similar view can agree that such things are not to be taken seriously. In terms of belief, the dismissal of the silly reinforces the boundary around common sense. That, no doubt, is why it has been so popular, not only with critics but also with proponents, who have deployed similar tactics in portraying the enemy as beyond the pale of common sense (though the audience for sneering at the extraordinary, rather than the ordinary, has tended to be larger).

Nevertheless, in form if not in frequency, the dispute has been symmetrical. Just as mesmerists had presented the phenomena as beneficial, and their mission as a quest for truth, so critics framed mesmerism as harmful, and their own response as a quest for truth. They were performing a 'duty to the public', and combatting 'an act of violence to our reasoning faculties' by those 'whose only object can be to extract money from the pockets of the public, under pretence of the pursuit of truth'.[77]

In summary, then, by framing the phenomena as the result of ordinary explanations that had not been excluded, critics argued that mesmeric phenomena were not real. Far from being prejudiced in the face of extraordinary facts, critics claimed that the facts were inadequate to support such an extraordinary claim, one that required a proper degree of scepticism. It was the proponents who were prejudiced, and the critics who were competent, because a disinterested scientific enquiry was needed. It was the critics who sought truth, and fought the good fight against imposture on the one hand, and credulity on the other. Thus, any evidence of mesmeric phenomena could be rejected as inadequate, and a position of disbelief could be maintained, even in the face of unexplained phenomena.

The construction of a new boundary between ordinary and extraordinary

All of the arguments made at this time, whether by proponents or critics, have been common themes throughout the history of extraordinary phenomena, but this period is of particular interest because it is when a new frame emerged by which mesmeric phenomena could be defined. It was in 1841 that James Braid witnessed the demonstrations of Lafontaine, and became convinced that mesmeric phenomena were real, but not so extraordinary after all. From his first publication, in 1842, and throughout various subsequent writings, Braid drew a boundary between the extraordinary claims of mesmerists and the blanket rejection of critics, by offering an alternative explanation for many, but not all, of the phenomena. In distinguishing between particular phenomena, and between the facts and theory of mesmerism, he had to engage with the arguments of both proponents and critics.

Braid excluded the standard ordinary explanations. According to him, subjects were not sleeping in the ordinary sense, they were neither acting nor seeking to deceive, and the imagination theory was quite inadequate to explain what was going on. Instead, the hypnotic sleep was the result of intense concentration, best induced by fixing attention on an object. While in the deeper stage of sleep, catalepsy and insensibility to pain could indeed be displayed, and through hypnotic methods, certain ailments could indeed be cured. But no invisible physical fluid was involved, and the higher phenomena of mesmerism were not real. In making his argument, Braid drew a new boundary of ordinariness within which some, but not all, of the phenomena could be included. The boundary was, of course, constructed in discourse, and presented to both colleagues and the public.

His lecture to the Royal Institution was typical of his boundary-work. In relation to the lower phenomena, he echoed the views of proponents of mesmerism. He had been initially 'quite sceptical', yet found 'some of the phenomena unquestionable', and argued that they were 'reconcilable with well-established physiological and psychological principles'. He challenged the expertise of those who dismissed the facts because of the theory, accusing them of ignorance and misinterpretation. For example, referring to the first French Royal Commission, he explained that there had been 'no attempt here to deny the phenomena; on the contrary, they actually confirm their reality, and yet this is the celebrated decision that has continually been referred to [by critics] ever since as a complete death-blow to mesmerism and all its pretensions'. As for Wakley's experiments, though well conducted, they had been wrong in their conclusion of imposture, which was 'equally erroneous [and] far more heartless and unwarrantable'.[78]

As he criticized the critics, he also positioned himself in the centre, by distinguishing between his views and those of others who believed in all the phenomena of mesmerism. Indeed, he had introduced the term hypnotism 'to prevent my being confounded with those who entertain these extreme notions', those *'ultra mesmerists . . .* with extreme views'. And, when it came to the higher phenomena, he echoed the views of critics of mesmerism: these were 'feats which far transcend the laws of all known philosophy', and thus in need of 'far stronger evidence, and a more extensive series of experiments, and those subjected to more searching scrutiny than hitherto, before being received as facts'. He also criticized the expertise of the mesmerists, by pointing out the sources of fallacy that had misled them, and the flaws of their experiments in clairvoyance. As he drew a boundary between mesmeric phenomena that were ordinary and those that were extraordinary, so he positioned himself between the prejudice of those who had thrown out the baby with the bathwater, and the credulity of those who had swallowed the lot.

In Braid's view, the facts that were real had an explanation that was in line with scientific knowledge, while the rest could be rejected as error and imposture. He too had been sceptical, but not prejudiced, unlike those whom he accused of incompetence, along with the mesmerists who had made their own mistakes. As he provided ordinary explanations, redefined the limits of extraordinariness, and constructed his own expertise in relation to that of others, he also spoke of the benefits of hypnosis, and of the harm associated with conducting regular experiments in public.[79]

This was how Braid sought to convince others of his own position, which amounted to a new way of framing mesmeric phenomena, even if it was not entirely new.[80] Nevertheless, his theory gained gradual acceptance, and the boundary-work in which he engaged – which included the appeal to scientific expertise over that of public lecturers, and the active debunking of clairvoyance – no doubt made his position more palatable to many in the medical establishment. According to one letter to *Medical Times*, which praised Braid's scientific credentials and lack of prejudice, he had shown that 'many of the marvels of mesmerism are capable of rational explanation'.[81] With an ordinary explanation now available, many of the observable facts were now easier to believe.

Braid also highlights a more profound theme in the history of extraordinary beliefs. While countless others had witnessed similar demonstrations, the kernel of Braid's new theory was based upon an alternative interpretation of observed behaviour. In short, he saw the same facts in a different way. This is important because proponents and critics were often arguing about different events. Critics might frame one demonstration as fake on the grounds that other demonstrations were fake, while proponents might play down the importance of a particular demonstration by appealing to others that were more convincing. However, it was often the case that people could observe the same demonstration, yet come to radically different conclusions. And while this, in itself, is hardly surprising, this was not simply a case of disputing the details of what happened. Certainly, there were disagreements about precisely what happened, but even when the observed facts were agreed upon, what they meant in terms of evidence could be fiercely disputed.

This was most obviously the case with observable changes in the subject's behaviour, which could easily be dismissed by critics as imagination or pretence. Demonstrations of insensibility to pain might be dismissed as 'hysteria' (something of a catch-all term in the case of female subjects), or else one might choose to accept Braid's theory. But Braid had no room in his theory for clairvoyance, which remained as extraordinary as ever. The importance of framing such demonstrations, either as real or else as fraud, remained part and parcel of the debate about mesmerism, since most proponents and critics continued to group all the phenomena of mesmerism together. Furthermore, disputes about the higher phenomena of mesmerism were the parents of disputes about spiritualist and psychic phenomena, and the form that they took reveals how extraordinary beliefs have been disputed since. By examining how mesmeric clairvoyance was disputed, we can see more clearly how extraordinary beliefs have been maintained.

We have already seen how, in disputing mesmeric clairvoyance, both sides described themselves as sceptical but open-minded, and appealed to the facts as the basis of their views. In doing so, of course, they constructed the facts in different ways, either as evidence of extraordinary phenomena, or else as examples of error or fraud. However, there was more to the debate than demonstrations such as those above. What is often forgotten is that mesmerists regularly failed in their attempts to display clairvoyance, others performed similar feats and claimed that these duplications were the result of trickery, and those who claimed to be clairvoyant were sometimes reportedly exposed in fraud. Such events might seem to be self-evidently negative kinds of evidence, and certainly that was how critics treated them. However, just as critics had been able to dismiss any demonstration as the result of some ordinary explanation, so proponents were able to argue that failures, duplications and exposures were evidence of something more extraordinary. By examining how this was done, we can see how the dispute about mesmerism was not about the facts of observed phenomena, but rather about how any demonstration could be framed as a fact of one sort rather than another. And we can see how, in the process, beliefs could be made impervious to any observation.

Framing a failed demonstration of mesmeric clairvoyance

We have considered responses to mesmeric demonstrations, and how they were framed in different ways. Particular events could be framed as the product of extraordinary processes, or else they could be framed as the result of ordinary ones. More generally, mesmerism was disputed in terms of whether or not the evidence was adequate.

When proponents appealed to the best evidence, critics claimed that even this was inadequate support for an extraordinary claim. But the dispute was not always about the best evidence; indeed it was often about the weakest. Demonstrations often failed, and when they did, these could be framed not only as evidence against mesmerism but also as evidence in favour of it.

Take, for example, the minor but revealing episode that occurred in 1843, when W. H. Weekes, a surgeon from Kent, claimed he had discovered a boy who could demonstrate lucid somnambulism. A sceptical medic, one Dr Smethurst, heard about this, and went to witness a demonstration in which the boy was blindfolded, then attempted to identify objects that were placed before him. According to Smethurst's account, published in the *Medical Times*, controls against fraud were inadequate, and the boy was able to peek beneath the blindfold. At one point, he recalled, 'the delusion was unmasked, for I particularly noticed that everything to be distinguished by the boy was invariably placed before the light, just under his nose, so that he could not fail of seeing them in that position'.[82]

Smethurst interrupted the demonstration to suggest a more stringent test, at which point the boy became anxious and cried out in terror. Weekes then ended the demonstration, told Smethurst that he had 'alarmed the boy by speaking', which was contrary to the rules of the society, and announced that the meeting was dissolved. Smethurst asked for a further test, and when his requests were declined, he 'then, without the slightest hesitation, denounced the boy an impostor'. Smethurst's conclusion, which was subsequently described in the same letter to *Medical Times*, noted that mesmerism, 'invariably, when properly investigated, terminated in an exposure of their nefarious and barefaced attempts to impose upon the credulity of the weak-minded'. Thus, though Smethurst's theory about how the boy was cheating amounted to no more than a suspicion (according to his own account), the failure to adopt more stringent controls was presented as proof that mesmerism was a fraud.

Smethurst's letter to *Medical Times* provoked a response from Weekes, who presented the events in a quite different manner. Though he disputed certain details, he did not deny that the test in question had been a failure, but rather denied that this was evidence of fraud. On the contrary, he presented the boy as an example of 'a genuine and beautiful instance of clairvoyance or lucid somnambulism'. Weekes' reframing of the incident as evidence of the reality of clairvoyance involved two key elements. First, it was presented as merely failure on this occasion by citing prior successful tests of a similar kind. The validity of these tests was, in turn, warranted by an appeal to the stringency of the conditions, the scientific expertise of others who had witnessed them, and to Weekes' own experience of having been 'upwards of thirty years disinterestedly engaged in promoting the objects of free and unprejudiced inquiry and scientific truth'. Second, this particular failure was attributed to Smethurst's interruption, by noting that he 'did not remain silent, *agreeably to the conditions at starting*', and adding that had he remained silent, he would have seen experiments 'which, I think, must have put aside the most inveterate of your doubts'.[83] By describing the incident as one failure among countless successful trials, and as the result of conditions that were known (by those who had studied the subject) to be unfavourable, Weekes' account of the same incident was constructed as evidence of the reality and nature of clairvoyance.

A similar incident was reported a few months later, when Vernon gave a lecture at Southwark Literary Institution in south-east London, and several members of the London Medical Society made a point of attending. As Vernon prepared to demonstrate clairvoyant reading with several young female subjects, a medical gentleman produced a 'full face mask' that was lined with black velvet, and 'so contrived as to render vision impossible'. Vernon 'at first objected to its use, as the mask would render the face very hot; the slit for the mouth was very small, and there would not be a sufficient degree of lucidity'. Nevertheless, he agreed for it to be tried, several subjects were tested, but they were 'utterly unable to read'. Vernon explained the failure 'by attributing it to want of sufficient lucidity'. The failure was discussed a few days later at the London Medical Society, where one medic 'looked upon these exhibitions as utter deceptions' and another, who admitted to having attended deliberately in order to expose the deception, 'considered Vernon to be a thorough impostor, and one who ought to be exposed.' This discussion was also published in *Medical Times*, and was reprinted in other medical journals.[84]

Like Weekes before him, Vernon wrote a letter to the journal, appealing to his right to reply to personal accusations of dishonesty. Admitting that the experiments had indeed ended in failure, he asked: 'is it sufficient to justify medical gentlemen in imputing to me a desire to impose upon the public? Is it not a notorious fact that scientific experiments, which are universally allowed to be true, often fail in consequence of attendant circumstance?'[85] He then, like Weekes, described several similar experiments that had been conducted previously, in which he stressed the stringency of conditions and the medical credentials of the witnesses, such that two medical gentlemen had declared 'that clairvoyance is a fact they can no longer resist', and another had gone from being 'one of my strongest opponents' to one who 'expressed his firm conviction of the truth of clairvoyance'. Vernon also framed this particular failure as the result of conditions that he had expected to be unfavourable, pointing out that he had 'stated at the time that the mask might so far interfere as to prevent the manifestation of the faculty, but did not object to the experiment being tried'.[86] Thus, while critics might frame individual failures as exposures of the fallacy of mesmerism as a whole, proponents could reframe them as one failure among many successes, and as the expected outcomes of particular conditions that were expected (by those with expertise in the subject) to be unfavourable to the phenomena, thereby constructing an account of failure as evidence of the reality and nature of the phenomena.

Indeed, the description of such phenomena as prone to failure in certain conditions would have made perfect sense to many. As Vernon himself argued, that certain experiments sometimes failed in certain conditions was quite compatible with scientific work. Furthermore, failure could actually reinforce the view that such phenomena were not the result of trickery. After all, the alternative explanation for feats of this sort was some form of collusion between mesmerist and subject, a method that logically would work every time. That this was the case was reinforced by contemporary performers of very similar demonstrations of blindfolded vision, who relied upon codes to communicate information and framed what they did as entertainment. These performers, who will be discussed in a moment, were often reported as never failing. Whatever observers may have known about how such feats might be done, therefore, the occasional failure was something that did not fit with the attribution of trickery, and did not look like contemporary performances that were more generally assumed to be trickery. Thus, for some, failure could be seen as evidence that what they were watching was not a trick. For example, when one observer of a mesmeric clairvoyant reported that the subject failed on occasion, he stated that '[t]hose exceptions to his general accuracy were, however, to me proofs of the absence of all collusion'.[87] Such an argument was by no means unique, and as we shall see, proponents of extraordinary phenomena would continue to argue that the occasional failures of mediums and psychics demonstrated that they were not employing trickery.

Framing a successful demonstration

Just as accounts of a failed demonstration could be constructed as evidence in favour of mesmerism, so could successful demonstrations be framed as evidence that the phenomena were merely trickery. At the same time as the proponents of mesmeric clairvoyance were demonstrating the ability of subjects to see while blindfolded, others were entertaining the public with very similar performances.

Indeed, already in 1831, there had been Louis M'Kean, 'the double-sighted Scotch phenomenon'. M'Kean was an eight-year-old boy who performed with his father at Egyptian Hall, a popular venue for entertainment in Piccadilly. The boy stood in a corner of a room, his back to the audience and his eyes covered with a handkerchief. His father collected items from the audience on a slate, and held them up one at a time, asking short questions about what they might be. The boy described the objects in detail, including the dates and types of coins, and also discerned messages that the audience wrote on the slate. He then went next door, while members of the audience were asked to whisper softly. On his return, the boy repeated precisely what they had said.

Presented as a Highland youth and dressed in impressive tartan regalia, the 'double-sighted Scotch phenomenon' was billed as being possessed with something resembling the Highland gift of second sight. According to his playbills, he possessed a faculty that 'has defied the research of all the Medical men'.[88] Early reviews suggest that the double-sighted Scotch phenomenon could be taken seriously. In a review of the performance, the London *Morning Advertiser* noted with astonishment that 'even when an attempt was made to mislead him, he instantly detected it'. It pointed out that 'he never made any mistake', that he answered 'without a moment's hesitation', and that there 'could certainly be no collusion'. As a result, the paper declared, he 'excited the very highest degree of wonder'.[89] According to the *Morning Chronicle*, the performances

> differ widely from all the traditions that have reached us concerning the marvellous talent of second sight. He deals with things present, both as to time and space... There can be no doubt that the answers proceed from the boy. By what means he is enabled to give them is a mystery... If all these feats are genuine the lad is equally a prodigy for knowledge and discrimination... If all these performances are the

result of art, it is managed with such dexterity that it deserves the patronage of all seers of sights who find a pleasure in visiting the exhibitions of human ingenuity.'[90]

Nevertheless, the nature of the mystery (if not the details) became more apparent. In December, M'Kean performed for the royal family, at which point he and his father may have felt a need to be clearer that this was mere entertainment. By then, after all, the royals had savoured the ingenuity of Don Carlos, 'the Double-Sighted and Beautiful Dog', whose 'acquirements consist chiefly of Performances with Cards, wherein he displays the greatest precision. He will also select the handsomest Lady in the Room, according to his judgement (which is seldom questioned) . . . and the Gentleman most partial to the Ladies.'[91] Don Carlos also moved on to Egyptian Hall, where any comparison between a double-sighted dog and a double-sighted boy must have led many spectators to conclude that nothing particularly mystical was going on.[92]

If the press is anything to go by, the general view seems gradually to have become an assumption that the performance was no more than a display of 'amusing and curious feats'.[93] By January of 1832, the previously mystified *Morning Chronicle* noted rather more condescendingly that M'Kean had proved a 'most attractive amusement during the past week, particularly to the rising generation about to take their departure for school'.[94] In May, when the *New Monthly Magazine* described the 'extraordinary exhibition, that puzzles the public not a little', it recommended their 'readers to see him and try to discover his secret, or rather his father's secret, for he, of course, communicates with the boy, in some way or other, although we have failed to ascertain how'.[95]

Nevertheless, the extraordinary feats remained unexplained, and though some kind of code may have been suspected, this was no more than an assumption. Indeed, when J. C. Colquhoun translated the report of the second French Royal Commission on animal magnetism, which had concluded favourably on mesmeric clairvoyance, he included a reference in the appendix to the young M'Kean, and strongly recommended that his power be investigated.[96] A few years later, and at the same time that Vernon was claiming to demonstrate genuine clairvoyance, a performer called the 'Mysterious Lady' was performing very similar effects to M'Kean, describing 'minutely objects which are placed in such a situation as to render it wholly out of her power to see any portion of them'.[97] Some spectators, at least, attributed her abilities to mesmerism.[98]

This was despite the fact that her performances were billed in the contemporary language of rational recreation, being 'interesting, surprising and instructive', and the show included 'some sleight of hand tricks, performed with dexterity', and was written up in the 'Entertainments' section of newspapers.[99] Indeed, she was sometimes advertised in direct competition to those who claimed to do it for real. In March, as Vernon was publicizing his demonstrations of 'Mesmerism and Clairvoyance', the Mysterious Lady was advertising (on the same front page of the same newspaper) her performances, which threw 'completely into the shade the wonders of Mesmerism and Clairvoyance'.[100] Furthermore, medical critics of mesmerism encouraged others to witness such performances on the grounds that they were just as impressive as the feats of mesmeric clairvoyants.[101] Thus, while such performances were not self-evidently trickery, and precious few seem to have been able to discover how they were done, they were nevertheless framed by both performers and medical critics of mesmerism as evidence that the real thing was not real at all.

What is significant here is that, so far as they were framed as evidence that mesmeric clairvoyance was fraudulent, this was not on the basis of observable evidence. Neither M'Kean nor the Mysterious Lady ever showed or explained how they could see while blindfolded, nor did they explicitly state that what they did was trickery. They may have framed what they did as entertainment, described it as superior to 'the wonders of Mesmerism', and been viewed by certain critics of mesmerism as demonstrable proof that such feats were the result of trickery, but it is evident that at least some observers were not at all clear on this point. Thus, successful demonstrations of feats that were very similar to those of Vernon and other mesmerists, and which were clearly capable of being seen as the result of mesmerism, could also be framed as direct evidence against mesmerism.

There were also the lectures and demonstrations of the antimesmerists, such as J. Q. Rumball, RCS, who had been giving lectures in venues previously used by Vernon. After his failure to convince the people of Greenwich, he had learned some of the tricks of the trade, and soon he was not only debunking but also demonstrating eyeless vision. In Bristol, shortly after Vernon had been exhibiting there, he provided a demonstration of a boy being able to read while his eyes were covered, claiming that this was identical to demonstrations of mesmeric clairvoyance, but that, in this case, it was done by trickery. 'We were not present' reported the *Bristol Mercury*, 'but have been informed that the lecturer exhibited, by means of his pupils, all the phenomena said to attach to mesmerism, and which were avowedly effected by collusion, but the operation of which was beyond the discovery of his audience'.[102] The audience, who left the theatre without any explanation of how the feats were done, were expected to view the demonstrations as fraudulent because the demonstrator said so. Thus, again, what was clearly observable as a successful demonstration of mesmeric clairvoyance could be framed as evidence that mesmerism was a fallacy.

Framing an exposure of mesmerism

When critics claimed that mesmerism had been exposed, they were normally referring to failures or duplications. When a mesmerized subject failed to perform successfully in particular conditions, or when individuals like Rumball performed similar feats while disclaiming any extraordinary powers, these were often described as exposures of mesmerism. However, even when individuals were caught cheating, and proponents of mesmerism agreed that fraud had taken place, this could be constructed as evidence of mesmerism.

The most famous case of this was that of George Goble, a former subject of both Vernon and Brookes, who became something of a household name as a result of being tested by John Forbes. Forbes was editor of the *British and Foreign Medical Review*, the most widely read medical journal at the time. By the time he tested George Goble, Forbes had already tested others, including Alexis and Adolphe Didier, the celebrated French somnambulists. In the case of Alexis, his journal had noted that 'all persons who witnessed the investigations at the house of Dr Forbes... considered [them] to be proof of downright imposture', adding somewhat cannily, 'in our extreme caution, we do not go so far'.[103] In the case of Adolphe, who was then working with Vernon, the experiments also ended in failure. Indeed, in reading Forbes' reports, it is hard not to see his experiments as typical of so many that would subsequently follow: clairvoyance was displayed in uncontrolled conditions, but began to disappear as the controls tightened up.[104]

The significance of such a narrative should not be missed. For example, in an early experiment, Forbes seemed to rule out ordinary explanations. At one point, Adolphe was handed

> a folded paper (not many times folded, and unsealed)... This he twisted about, looking earnestly at it, placed to his chest, mouth, &c. and then, though still declaring he could not see, began to announce, by fits and starts, and with great seeming carelessness, some of the letters of the word enclosed. He first said the word contained two L's (ll), then the letters 'shall', then 'marshall', or something like it. I watched the paper while in his hands, and saw that he did not unfold it. The paper was then opened, and was found to have written on it 'Maschalla'.[105]

By stating that Adolphe did not unfold the paper, and by not considering any other method, this might easily have been read as evidence of clairvoyance. But not so easily in the context of Forbes' report of his experiments, which was a narrative about the use of increasingly tight experimental controls, and how the deployment of proper scientific conditions gradually displayed the inadequacy of the facts. Thus, later in the narrative, Forbes explained how, when

> some dozen articles were placed before him, all carefully prepared, and all thoroughly enclosing printed words (French), so that it was *impossible* for ordinary vision to reach these [i.e. the messages were inside small wooden boxes, nests of envelopes, or written on paper that was folded several times and sealed] . . . Adolphe took up some of these, and handled and twisted them about, placing them to his breast and mouth, but almost immediately declared that he could not see.[106]

Thus, the earlier successes were framed as the result of inadequate controls.

When we consider the case of George Goble, we see a similar theme of initial success and subsequent failure, as scientific investigation revealed the limits of lay conclusions about extraordinary phenomena. While others were claiming to see through blindfolds, or through folded paper, George Goble rose to fame by claiming he could see the contents of a closed box. He was not the first do so, but he seemed to some to be more proficient. 'Unlike any other patient we have seen', *The Critic* observed, 'he has never failed in a single instance'.[107] For some, of course, this alone might have been cause for suspicion.

Having left the employment of Vernon and Brookes, Goble was now working as a clerk for a barrister. At some point, George had managed to convince his employer that he possessed clairvoyant powers, and the latter had written to Forbes, inviting him to put Goble to the test. Goble's technique was, at best, idiosyncratic. On receiving a box containing a written message, he would lie on the sofa, and hold the box beneath a pillow with both hands. After several minutes, he would place his head beneath the pillow. He would then reveal the message by putting the box under someone's foot, placing his head on top of their foot, and calling out the message in a burst of excitement. As he did this, he would open the box, unfold the message and tear it into pieces.

Forbes, it seems, was taken aback, but impressed. Indeed, William Benjamin Carpenter, the psycho-physiologist and scourge of spiritualist mediums would later recall how Forbes had written 'in some excitement after the first of them [the experiments], that at last he seemed to have got hold of a genuine case of clairvoyance'.[108] Nevertheless, when Forbes came to describe the experiments, his story was that he had been less than impressed, and had simply assumed that Goble had opened the box beneath the pillow, sneaked a look, then destroyed any evidence of tampering.

If these were Forbes' initial suspicions, they were confirmed over a series of experiments in which boxes were used that Goble could not open so easily. On the first two experiments, he simply gave up. On the next, he took a chance, and said he saw the letters 'har' or 'hart', but the actual message turned out to be 'insane'. On the fourth experiment, Goble was successful, but only after a 'snap was distinctly heard from under the pillow', and later the box was found to be broken. And then on the fifth, in a remarkable display of 'bold confidence', Goble 'selected one of the best secured' boxes. He 'proceeded to a desk standing in the room, placed the box within it, locked it, and gave [Forbes] the key!' After placing his head on the desk 'for some time', he wrote down six marks (to indicate six letters), then the letters 'cas' twice. Had the message been 'cascas', it would have been a miracle. Unfortunately for George, the message was '1787'.[109]

Forbes was 'perfectly satisfied with the results' (satisfied, that is, that Goble was a fraud), and planned no further experiments, but the barrister, still convinced, invited him back. So Forbes once again accepted the invitation, being 'desirous to go further... and to establish, if possible, not merely George's failure... but the positive fact of his roguery'. So a box was prepared with small bits of cork positioned inside, so that if it were opened, their repositioning would be impossible. During the trial, as George's head was beneath the pillow with the box, he was seen 'hurriedly and repeatedly putting his fingers to his mouth', and 'small fragments [were seen] falling on the floor beneath the sofa'. When, on examination, bits of cork were found in George's hands and mouth, and on the floor, he finally 'confessed his roguery and implored forgiveness'.[110]

For Forbes, this was the end of the matter, but not for the still unnamed barrister, who wrote again to Forbes, urging yet further investigation. According to him, George had been in a mesmeric state throughout the entire proceedings, including his cheating and confession. It was only after Forbes had left that the barrister had discovered this, and George had awakened 'in an agony of tears, quite unconscious of what had passed'. The barrister, while conceding that fraud had indeed been detected and admitted, nevertheless insisted that George had genuine powers. George had assured him that, though he had cheated before, he had done so 'only occasionally, when his powers failed him'. Thus, his cheating had been provoked by the unreliability of his mesmeric powers and, in this case at least, was due to the mesmeric state itself. In short, the exposure was framed as the result of mesmerism, rather than as evidence against it.

Regardless of even the agreed upon facts, those who wished to do so could frame any event as evidence either for or against the reality of mesmerism. Just as any demonstration could be framed as the result of imposture, any failure, duplication or exposure could be framed as evidence in favour of the nature and reality of mesmerism. This is not to say that nobody changed his or her mind; indeed, if we take the countless claims to prior scepticism (or prior belief) at face value, then we would have to conclude that conversion was fairly typical. However, if we consider the form of rhetoric in its own terms, rather than as a reliable indicator of what people were actually thinking, then the function of an avowal of prior scepticism (or prior belief) can be seen as a means of displaying critical thinking (or open-mindedness) in the face of extraordinary facts. Whether such statements actually represent a change of mind is beyond our ken, but the form they took can be seen as having a relevant function in this context. Similarly, by framing failures, duplications and exposures as evidence for, rather than against, the reality of mesmerism, those who had expressed belief in such phenomena could maintain their position, even in the face of ostensibly negative evidence.

The case of George Goble would later be cited as an exemplar of the credulity of folk.[111] Indeed, the reframing of an exposure as evidence that supports one's belief is easy to dismiss as a desperate attempt to cling on to deeply held beliefs, though the same might be said about those who dismiss any evidence that they cannot explain. But the point being made here is rather different: that while both sides appealed to the facts, and claimed to be sceptical but open-minded, nobody needed to change their position on the basis of even the agreed upon facts. There were always arguments that could be made, either to oneself or else to others, in order to maintain a particular position. As we shall see, similar arguments have been made regularly since.

From a critic's perspective, such arguments might be the product of credulity and a desire to believe, but from the proponent's perspective, such matters were covered. The exclusion of ordinary explanations, at least in the case of some phenomena, the compatibility of unexplained phenomena with scientific thinking, and the adequacy of the expertise of those who had investigated the matter, made such phenomena as plausible as any other scientific phenomenon that was not entirely understood. The benefits of mesmerism being real made the investigation worthwhile, and could be compared to the prior cases of Galileo and Harvey, and of other scientific theories that had been thought implausible once, but had since been shown to be both true and useful. What critics dismissed as gullibility and wishful thinking could be seen as no more than a difference in the perceived plausibility and value of mesmerism.

The name of the anonymous barrister would be revealed years later, and he would play a crucial role in the framing of spiritualism and psychic phenomena. And, as we shall see, the arguments about spiritualism would be very similar to those about mesmerism, and would include the framing by spiritualists of failures, duplications and exposures as evidence for, rather than against, the reality of spiritualism. For the moment, however, Forbes published his experiments into mesmeric clairvoyance, in what was an early Victorian example of scientific debunking of extraordinary phenomena. Such debunking narratives are typically seen as attempts to change beliefs, but they invariably do much more than that. By taking a closer look at the form of Forbes' rhetoric, we can see how the debunking of extraordinary phenomena could be designed to be constructive as well as destructive.

Constructing a psychology of error

When Forbes published his experiments into mesmeric clairvoyance, they were more than a disinterested description of scientific investigation. They were originally published in *Medical Gazette*, but he went on to publish a small book for the public, *Illustrations of Modern Mesmerism from Personal Investigations* (1845). It was a collection of his previous articles on the experiments with Alexis and Adolphe Didier, George Goble, and on the Martineau case, and the fact that he republished these to make them more widely available suggests a desire to reach a larger audience. In the preface to the book, he framed the collection of his articles in terms of public education, and his journal, the *British and Foreign Medical Review*, though it formally declined to 'offer any opinion of the merits of this little book', nevertheless published extracts from the preface. In any case, the form of the preface deserves a closer look, as it is an exemplary case of boundary-work in the rhetoric of debunking. In the preface, he explained the purpose of *Illustrations*:

> If received simply as specimens or illustrations of the sort of things which mesmeric professors daily hold forth to the world, and which the world receives, as marvels of the highest order and as truths admitting of no question, they must surely give rise to reflections that may lead to some beneficial results... If the professors do not condescend to supply the public with evidence of a more satisfactory kind, the public must cease to be satisfied with the evidence they do supply... If they refuse to adopt the rigid system of observation required in the sciences, and repudiate all the ordinary rules of induction and rational inference deemed essential to establish facts on other departments of knowledge, they have no right to quarrel with those who persist in disbelieving [things] which, for the most part, have no other evidence in their favour than the bare assertions of ignorant, interested and, it may be, very unprincipled persons... It is also hoped that the perusal of the exposures contained in this little book, may teach a useful lesson to those numerous unscientific persons, who are accustomed to attend mesmeric exhibitions... Such persons, it is believed, must now feel convinced that no reliance whatever is to be placed on the results presented at such exhibitions, as evidencing the truth and powers of mesmerism. As these results are witnessed by the ordinary visitor, it is quite impossible to discriminate the true from the false.[112]

These extracts from the preface, which ostensibly explain the purpose of the book, display a number of discursive themes that deserve consideration, because they have been part of debunking discourse ever since. First, and most obviously, the author presents the book as an attempt to show that the facts of mesmerism are false: the evidence is less than 'satisfactory'; the rules 'deemed essential to establish facts' have been repudiated; and the reader should place 'no reliance' upon them. Second, in doing so, he presents mesmerists as lacking basic scientific expertise: they are quacks ('professors', the term then having been used regularly to refer to itinerant lecturers with no formal qualifications); they do not use the 'rigid system of observation required in the sciences'; they are uninformed ('ignorant') and biased ('interested'). Third, in his rejection of both the facts of mesmerism and the expertise of mesmerists, the author presents himself as scientific: as one who can assess whether evidence is 'satisfactory', can recognize whether scientific procedures have been employed, and can 'teach a lesson' to 'unscientific persons'. Fourth, the author presents his own expertise as superior to not only the mesmerists but also the public: who receive such facts 'as marvels of the highest order and as truths admitting of no question'; and who, as 'ordinary' people, cannot 'discriminate the true from the false'. Thus, as he draws boundaries between the true and the false, he also does so between his own scientific expertise and that of both mesmerists and the public.

It is also notable that the false beliefs of the public in mesmerism are attributed not only to the mesmerists but also to the limits of ordinary thinking and observation: to the gullibility of the world (which accepts marvels without question) and to the unreliable observation of the 'ordinary' witness. Furthermore, the challenging of such beliefs is presented as having wider social and moral value: they are based on evidence presented by those who are not only 'ignorant' and 'interested' but also 'it may be, very unprincipled'; and more critical reflection is described as being 'useful' and liable to produce 'beneficial results'. Thus, the author rejects the phenomena in question by constructing what might be called a 'psychology of error' (i.e. beliefs in such phenomena are the result of errors in observation and thinking), displaying the superiority of his own scientific expertise over that of mesmerists and the public, and warranting its deployment as necessary and valuable.[113]

In the process of framing the phenomena as imposture, Forbes also made a comparison with the feats of contemporary conjurors, who could deceive the untrained passive observer. 'The coarsest jugglery may pass with the honest spectator, seated at a distance from the scene of action, for mysterious and awful truths. If Herr Dobler and Monsieur Phillipe [two of the most famous contemporary conjurors] can puzzle and perplex a whole theatre, surely George Goble may bamboozle the erudite captain and the six ladies on Mr Vernon's back seats!'[114]

These same themes of public credulity when faced with unexplained feats, of the unreliability of testimony (even in the case of honest, respectable, and educated observers), and of the need for scientific expertise in assessing phenomena that puzzle unscientific people, would reappear with remarkable regularity in the debates about spiritualist phenomena throughout the decades to come. There would also be countless more comparisons between those who claimed they could do it for real and those who made a living from openly faking it. Having framed the phenomena as imposture, and having appealed to particular versions of expertise and the respective benefits and harm associated with the matter, Forbes went on to address the question of prejudice in the face of extraordinary facts: 'I have not denied their possibility or even their existence as matters of fact. I still profess myself ready to believe them on obtaining sufficient proof of their reality.' Like everyone else, then and since, Forbes was sceptical but open-minded, but what counted as 'sufficient proof' would remain a matter of endless dispute.

Forbes' tests went on to be cited by a wide range of opponents of mesmeric clairvoyance, from James Braid to those who rejected all kinds of mesmeric phenomena.[115] According to the *Monthly Journal of Medical Science*, it was an exemplar of 'real scientific investigation'.[116] But it is worth noting that this was not the only way to interpret Forbes' results, since both critics and proponents of mesmerism rejected his claim to open-minded enquiry. On the one hand, some critics of mesmerism dismissed the idea that testing individuals like Goble might establish the existence of clairvoyance. According to the *Athenaeum*, for example, even if they had been successful, it 'would have proved only that George was a cleverer fellow than the doctor supposed, and able to outwit a doctor and two professors. Why, we have known common conjurors who would have been more than a match for the whole College of Physicians.'[117] Thus, no matter the results of his experiments, disbelief could always be maintained by dismissing them as the product of undetected trickery. On the other hand, proponents of mesmerism wrote even more scathingly of Forbes' experiments, accusing him of ignorance and narrow-mindedness.[118]

Thus, Forbes' view was by no means self-evident, and was disputed by both critics and proponents of mesmerism. It did, however, provide a means of engaging in useful boundary-work, as Forbes was able to construct a psychology of error that placed scientific expertise above that of mesmerists and the public, and to present such expertise as valuable. Furthermore, by framing beliefs as the product of (what we would now call) cognitive deficits, he was doing much more than providing an explanation for beliefs. His argument, and the active dissemination of it to the public, was both an expression and a justification of his own beliefs about mesmerism, as well as an attempt to reduce beliefs. In short, the crude psychology of belief he presented was a direct reflection of, and a deliberate attempt to change, the kinds of beliefs it purported to explain. As we shall see, the 'psychology of error' has regularly been used since, ostensibly to explain beliefs, but also to construct expertise, to reduce belief, and to warrant an alternative view about extraordinary phenomena.

Mesmerism and the constructive powers of psychological knowledge

In Chapter 1, this study was located within a much wider argument about the nature and relevance of psychological knowledge, in short that it is both constructed by, and constructive of, people. Knowledge about mesmerism was psychological in that it concerned human thoughts, feelings and behaviour, and that it was constructed in a variety of ways should be apparent by now. But knowledge relating to mesmerism was also constructive, since it can be seen to have transformed psychological phenomena in a number of ways.

In the most obvious sense, application of such knowledge provided striking illustrations of how significant changes in individual thoughts, feelings and behaviour could be brought about. Moreover, such demonstrations also affected the attitudes of the wider public. After all, they were not only displays of psychological change but were also illustrations of psychological traits deemed characteristic of certain social groups. In 1840's Britain, for example, demonstrations of power over the minds of various subjects could be treated as evidence of the inherent mental inferiority of women, the working class or the Irish.[119] More generally, they were illustrations of the powers of the human mind, and changed how people thought about themselves. The wider influence of mesmerism was in how it shaped views about what the mind was and what it could do, particularly in its power to change people.

Indeed, for all the disputes over the validity of mesmerism, that it involved some kind of psychological change was largely accepted. For example, the 1784 Paris Commission, in its dismissal of the theory of animal magnetism, had explained observable changes in the behaviour of subjects as the product of their imagination, and the English translation of the report had noted that this reframed mesmerism as a mental rather than a physical phenomenon.[120] Indeed, disputes over the validity of various mesmeric phenomena were regularly disputes over the mental condition of subjects.

After all, when subjects displayed overt changes in behaviour, medical critics maintained they were not in a trance state. When patients reported feeling no pain during surgery, critics maintained that their testimony was unreliable and that they did, in fact, feel pain. And when Harriet Martineau claimed that she had been cured by mesmeric treatment, critics dismissed her as hysterical. Such was their psychological reality according to orthodox scientific knowledge in early Victorian Britain, just as Braid was proposing his theory of neurypnology. As his theory gained acceptance, however, an alternative scientific view came to be established. According to this new scientific knowledge, the mental condition of subjects was quite different: subjects were in a trance state after all; surgical patients did not feel pain; and Harriet Martineau was no longer hysterical.

Of course, such a change in understanding was neither immediate nor universal, and was only one of several changes in the theory and practice of those who came after Mesmer. Indeed, Braid's historical significance may have been exaggerated, not least by those who have presented him as the champion of science over pseudoscience. Nevertheless, Braid's theory and the new terminology he employed, much of which has continued to be used, was an explicit attempt to distinguish between his view and previous ones.[121] And it is clear that many of his contemporaries recognized his view as a distinct departure from that of both the mesmerists and the sceptics. On the one hand, he provoked the hostility of both John Elliotson and Thomas Wakley.[122] On the other hand, some previously sceptical medics began to distinguish between animal magnetism and hypnotism, as the latter was seen to provide a more plausible theory according to contemporary medical thinking.[123]

The shift in thinking that Braid's theory represented involved a change not only in how certain psychological phenomena were described and understood, but also in the experience of those being understood in this way. In one sense, to view these phenomena according to Braid's theory was to observe a quite different psychological reality, and observations according to this new understanding would, of course, inform psychological theory and practice. This would, in turn, shape how others thought, felt, and behaved in a variety of ways. However, what 'hypnosis' provided was not only a new way of understanding psychological phenomena that would shape new practices, but also a new kind of experience. After all, according to Braid, the mental state of his subjects was due neither to the will of another nor to their own imagination, but rather was the result of intense concentration of attention on their part. It required the consent of the subject, indeed it could easily be self-induced, and did not require the person who 'put' them in the state to arouse them from it.[124] The hypnotic experience itself, therefore, depended upon the subject understanding what was going on in a quite different way from someone who was being mesmerized. Indeed, William Gregory distinguished between the two processes in terms not only of the induction process, but also the character of the sleep produced and the kinds of phenomena that might occur.[125] In short, the experience of the hypnotized subject was different from that of the mesmerized subject. Braid's hypnosis, then, was a new form of psychological knowledge and practice that brought into being a new experience, that of being hypnotized.

While the hypnotic experience shared certain features with the experience of being mesmerized, it was the same for neither facilitator nor subject. It could be argued, then, that hypnosis amounted to a new psychological reality, in the same sense that multiple personality disorder and post-traumatic stress disorder shared certain features with, but were not the same as, previously understood psychological conditions, and in turn produced not only new understandings but also different kinds of experience for those who were treated, and who understood their conditions, according to these categories rather than previously available ones.[126] In the same sense Richards has claimed that 'nobody prior to Freud had an Oedipus Complex, that nobody before Pavlov and Watson was "conditioned" and that nobody before about 1914 had a "high IQ", nobody prior to Braid was "hypnotised"'.[127] Without this new psychological concept, one could not discuss, observe or even experience 'hypnosis'.

Discussion

So what can we say about beliefs in mesmerism? As Alison Winter has shown, mesmerism was a topic that permeated early Victorian

Britain. Among other things, it reflected academic and professional rivalries, power and authority, and more general attitudes relating to class, gender and race, and religious and political hopes and fears. It worked for some as a metaphor for the nature of power and the possibility of change, and as such must have been thought by many to be not only plausible but also desirable. In short, there were all sorts of contextual reasons that would have shaped beliefs about mesmeric phenomena: the fact that power was invariably being exercized by a man over a woman or child (rather than vice versa); the implications for medicine (and the obvious challenge to medical authority); and the wider implications for religion and society (could Jesus' miracles have been mere mesmerism?; if we can change individuals so easily, what about society as a whole?). These, and countless other specific considerations, would have made mesmeric phenomena seem more (or less) plausible or desirable.

Similarly, though we have been concerned with Britain, mesmerism was obviously an international affair. The early lecturers and demonstrators had come from France, and had travelled elsewhere in Europe and to North America, and while such demonstrations were similar, there were obviously differences in context. For example, historians have suggested that American attitudes to mesmerism may have been more open because professional authority, including the medical profession, was less established than in Britain, and there was a greater tendency towards independent thinking and personal autonomy.[128] In France, animal magnetism had been publicly debated for longer, and more thoroughly, though its rejection by the medical establishment had not dampened enthusiasm, even among (provincial) medics. Political and religious circumstances in other European countries would have influenced access to demonstrations and reports, the perceived authority of those who offered competing explanations, their desirability or not, and so on. Meanwhile, in India, mesmeric cures could be viewed as very much in line with indigenous healing methods.[129] In other words, a variety of cultural differences in beliefs about how the world worked, and who were trustworthy authorities on this, no doubt shaped levels and forms of belief.

But even in relation to contemporary scientific knowledge in Britain, the influences were ambiguous. On the one hand, new knowledge of electricity and physiology may have made the theory of an animal magnetic fluid seem increasingly implausible (to those who took an interest in such matters). On the other hand, manifestations of this new knowledge made possible things that must have seemed impossible. If thoughts could be communicated through invisible forces, as in the case of the electric telegraph, how plausible must have seemed the claims of mesmerists?[130] Thus, in relation to new science and technology, mesmeric phenomena did not necessarily seem so extraordinary for the majority. And this was not a simple matter of believers misunderstanding scientific truth, since critics rejected facts that would now be accepted, and in ways that would now be considered unscientific. Indeed, just as mesmerism was once dismissed as a pseudoscience, more recent historians have stressed its role as a predecessor to scientific psychology.[131] There was, to put it crudely, something in it, and so no wonder that people believed that certain mesmeric phenomena were real.

If we wish to understand why people, at a particular time and place, believed in mesmerism, there are plenty of reasons from which to choose, which would have made some people more inclined to believe, and led others to be more reluctant to believe. In considering various social, cultural, religious, political and scientific matters, there would have been individual psychological differences, though what these might have been is far from clear. After all, before we could begin to consider them, we would need to be clear about what we mean: belief in what?; belief that what? And this is where beliefs about mesmeric phenomena can inform us about extraordinary beliefs today, because despite the many changes over time, there have also been significant continuities in how extraordinary phenomena have been demonstrated, reported and disputed.

We have seen that demonstrations of mesmeric phenomena were designed to be convincing: by displaying the inadequacy of ordinary explanations; by backing their claims via appeals to particular versions of expertise; by deploying arguments designed to address the extraordinariness of the phenomena; and by pointing to the benefits of the phenomena being real. Reports of these demonstrations reflected these same themes, providing a wider audience with the case for mesmerism and, therefore, a basis for belief in the phenomena. Meanwhile, critics countered: by appealing to the possibility of ordinary explanations; by rejecting the facts as inadequate in relation to the extraordinariness of the claim; by questioning the relevant expertise; and by arguing that such demonstrations, and beliefs in their reality, were harmful. Such arguments allowed any evidence to be framed as the result of ordinary processes, and therefore provided a basis for disbelief.

But belief or disbelief in what? If we wish to understand beliefs about extraordinary phenomena, then we need to consider the objects of belief, and what has been believed about them. There were, of course, a wide range of mesmeric phenomena, but to believe in mesmerism was to frame at least some of these phenomena as real (i.e. not the product of fraud). However, this was not the same as attributing such events to animal magnetism. On the contrary, those who framed the phenomena as real made regular distinctions between facts and theories. People expressed belief in the facts when, and in ways that, they did not express belief in the theory of animal magnetism. If we take such expressions as evidence of beliefs (i.e. as what people actually thought), then a belief that certain mesmeric phenomena were real was not the same as a belief in mesmerism.

And whether one believed that either the facts or the theory were compatible with science was yet another matter, since proponents argued that they were, and critics claimed that they were not, and even if we rely upon the hindsight of current (mainstream) science, some of the reported events were real and compatible with science, and others (most would say) were not. This matters for understanding extraordinary beliefs today for the simple reason that, if certain paranormal phenomena were real and compatible with science, then they would not be classed as paranormal, and nobody would be wondering why people believe in them. The meaning of paranormal is based upon its relationship to orthodox science, and unless we understand beliefs about that relationship, we do not understand paranormal beliefs.

In the case of mesmerism, one might believe that mesmerized subjects felt no pain, but reject the existence of animal magnetism. Or else, one might believe in animal magnetism, and that it could induce clairvoyance, despite the clashes with scientific knowledge. Both represented belief in mesmeric phenomena, but these were different kinds of beliefs; indeed, according to present definitions, the latter would count as paranormal belief, but the former would not. Beliefs about the reality of the phenomena, what might explain them, and their compatibility with science, were three different threads in disputes about the phenomena of mesmerism. So far as these represented what people thought, they represented different forms of belief. As we shall see, this has also been the case in disputes about extraordinary phenomena since, and remains essential to understanding paranormal beliefs today. Meanwhile, the first point is simply this: in short, belief that an event is real, that it is due to a particular cause, and that this cause is not compatible with science, are not the same thing.

Second, whatever one believed about mesmeric phenomena was based upon particular phenomena, not only different kinds of phenomena but also particular examples. This is worth stressing, because it is easy to view the response of believers to failures, duplications and exposures as evidence of a more general kind of belief, as if believers are so gullible that they simply believe in anything. However, such responses actually illustrate the dependence of beliefs upon particular phenomena: failures did not challenge beliefs because beliefs were based upon successful demonstrations; duplications may have been similar, but were not identical, to the demonstrations upon which beliefs were based; exposures might be accepted as evidence of fraud, but beliefs were based upon other demonstrations being considered real. Beliefs could be maintained in the face of failures, duplications and exposures precisely because beliefs were based upon particular (i.e. other) events. It was on the basis that certain events were real that failures illustrated the unreliability of the phenomena, that alleged duplications might actually be real, and that exposures (of someone already considered genuine) could be attributed to the nature of the phenomena.

Third, extraordinary beliefs may depend upon the exclusion of ordinary explanations, but one has to be competent to exclude them. To frame an event as extraordinary, to exclude ordinary explanations for it, is to assume that the observer (whether oneself or someone else) is competent to do so. And to frame such events as ordinary, to decline to believe those who have excluded such explanations, is to question either the honesty or the competence of those people. Disagreements about the reality of such phenomena are bound up with disputes about honesty and competence, not simply because disputes often involve accusations about such matters, but because disagreements about whether ordinary explanations have been excluded actually depend upon them. After all, as we have seen, appealing to the facts did not settle the matter, so competence to assess the facts was a necessary component of any position.

Since one cannot debunk such phenomena without accusing others of incompetence, and it is difficult to assume such a position without assuming greater competence, the construction of special expertise has been an inherent part of the debunking process. However, claiming that one is better than those with whom one disagrees is, in itself, an unattractive position. Hence, debunkers have invariably appealed to the harm of such beliefs and, therefore, the value of debunking and the expertise that backs it up. The construction of oneself as a useful expert has its own rewards, of course, but the point is that this is, in any case, an essential part of the debunking process. One cannot reject the exclusion of ordinary explanations by others without appealing to superior expertise in such matters, and this can be made more convincing by presenting it as a good thing.

As we have seen, the debunking of mesmeric clairvoyance by Sir John Forbes, in addition to framing the phenomena as fake, was also designed to construct scientific expertise over that of both mesmerists and the public. It did so by deploying what has been called a 'psychology of error', in which lay observation and thinking was presented as inadequate, and beliefs as harmful, hence the need and value of scientific expertise. This has been an ongoing pattern in disputes about extraordinary phenomena, though the construction and negotiation of what counts as scientific expertise is a considerably larger topic. However, what I am arguing here is merely that such arguments, so far as they have been deployed in disagreements about the reality of extraordinary phenomena, can be seen as part and parcel of beliefs about such phenomena. Whatever else they may have been doing, disputants were warranting their views by appeals to adequate expertise, and the construction and deployment of special expertise was a necessary aspect of debunking. Opposing views could not persist without claims and counterclaims about who was best qualified to assess such things. Thus, different beliefs were dependent upon different claims to expertise.

Finally, Forbes' 'psychology of error' was more than an appeal to ordinary explanations based upon a construction of his own superior expertise. It was an expression of belief about the phenomena, and an explanation for the beliefs of those with whom he disagreed. And, of course, it was a debunking text, which argued that such views were not only wrong but also harmful. In short, he was expressing a belief, explaining beliefs and (at the same time) attempting to change them, a combination that has continued to date, and which shall later serve as a clear illustration of the reflexive nature of psychological knowledge.

Meanwhile, Braid's theory of hypnosis provides a more immediate example. The exclusion of ordinary explanations depended not only upon adequate expertise but also upon what one regarded as ordinary, in relation to wider scientific knowledge. By drawing a new boundary, Braid created a new way of seeing some of the facts as compatible with science and, as a result, a new kind of experience. Braid's thinking would influence later psychologists in their understanding and treatment of others, which would in turn provoke those others to think, feel and behave in different ways. Wider views about the power of the mind would also be shaped by popular dissemination, in literature, on stage and in the emerging self-help movement.

To summarize for the moment: in a given social context, beliefs in extraordinary phenomena, that they are not only real but also extraordinary (subject to what counts as ordinary at any given time and place), depend upon the exclusion of ordinary explanations, in relation to particular events, based upon the competence of those who have excluded them. This, at least, is what can be seen in the discourse surrounding the phenomena of mesmerism, and we shall see that similar themes have pervaded the discourse on extraordinary phenomena since. The particular events would be different, of course, if not in what was observed, then in how they were framed, and there would be different ordinary explanations, and different versions of expertise, based upon different views about what was now considered ordinary, and what now counted as adequate expertise.

Some of the phenomena of mesmerism had been transformed into something less extraordinary, but physical fluid theories persisted. Such theories, along with the higher phenomena of mesmerism, became part of modern spiritualism, which attracted many proponents of mesmerism, and the animosity of many of its critics. Though spiritualism was a radically different affair, the disputes that followed were remarkably similar, as indeed were some of the phenomena. Just a few years after the methods of mesmeric clairvoyants had been tested and exposed, one could find spirit mediums performing very similar feats, but now as proof of an afterlife.

FOUR

The making of spiritualist phenomena

In 1862, Charles Foster sat in a room with some very respectable ladies and gentlemen, and demonstrated what had quickly become his trademark feat. His audience wrote down different names on different slips of paper, which were then rolled into pellets so that the writing could not be seen. The paper pellets were placed on the table, so that Foster did not know which was which. Nevertheless, moments later, he began to announce, letter by letter, one of the names. He then picked up one of the pellets; it was the one with that very name written on it.[1]

Like the lucid somnambulists of some years earlier, Foster demonstrated the ability to know what was written on folded up slips of paper. This was no demonstration of mesmerism, however, but rather a spiritualist séance, in which this extraordinary feat was seen as proof of life after death. What could easily have been seen as a demonstration of mesmerism was presented as an instance of spirit communication. The framing of such things in performance was fundamental to beliefs about spiritualism because, at the vast majority of séances, nobody actually saw a spirit. A rap was heard, a table moved, the medium conveyed certain information; all of this was taken as evidence of spirit communication, but (rather like the table movements) this did not happen by itself. What was true of Foster's feat was true of every phenomenon in which spiritualists believed: they had to be framed in demonstration, and framed in a very particular way, because spiritualist beliefs were beliefs that what happened at séances was the work of spirits. How this was done in such a way that they became the objects of spiritualist belief shall be discussed below.

Foster's pellet phenomenon may have resembled the feats of the somnambulists, but it was different from what most mediums did at the time. Indeed, it was a feature of spiritualism that novel kinds of phenomena regularly appeared, and Foster was only one of several pioneers. Thus, though not the most famous of Victorian mediums, he gained a significant degree of celebrity, not only in his successes but also in his failures, both of which exemplify the wider dispute about spiritualism. What was said of Foster was said of countless other mediums, and reveals the ways in which beliefs about spiritualist phenomena were expressed and justified.

However, to begin a chapter on spiritualism in the 1860s may seem like arriving at a séance late, discovering that the spirits arrived earlier and that one is in the dark. There are advantages to walking in at this point, since events are already in full flow and we can better appreciate what is going on. Nevertheless, what was now happening was understood in terms of recent developments, which had led to a context in which the strange dimly lit goings on could be demonstrated, reported, defended and disputed as evidence of spiritual beings. Some of the phenomena may have been similar to those that had been demonstrated by mesmerists, but the available explanations were not the same, and neither were the beliefs.

The origins of this, according to the standard version, had been New England in 1848. It had been there that Modern Spiritualism had appeared, announcing its arrival with some mysterious knocks, in the company of the young Fox sisters. Such rappings were not new, but these particular raps attracted significantly more interest than earlier ones, and led to the emergence of a spiritualist movement that has survived ever since. The story has been told many times, and others have noted the links to mesmerism in terms of both the phenomena and the personnel, and the various contextual factors that made spiritualism of particular interest then and there.[2] Some of these shall be discussed later, but whatever the other relevant factors, the foundations of spiritualism were the various phenomena that seemed to demonstrate communication with the dead. At first, there were the unexplained raps, which seemed to communicate information from the spirits. Belief that such things were from a spiritual source depended upon the exclusion of ordinary explanations: first, that the raps had a mundane source; second, that the information came from the medium. The rejection of these options, in relation to certain events, was the basis of spiritualist belief.

Nevertheless, it was not very long before ordinary explanations appeared. In 1851, an explanation for the raps was provided by three professors from Buffalo, who claimed that the Fox sisters were clicking their knee joints. In a public demonstration, with the Fox sisters on stage, they demonstrated this to be the case, at least to the satisfaction of many. Two months later, an in-law of the Fox sisters by the name of Mrs Culver announced that the Fox sisters had confided in her. She confirmed the theory of the professors, that the raps had been produced by the joints of the knees and the feet, and revealed how the medium could obtain the information needed to communicate on behalf of the spirits. The messages that appeared were simple enough, spelt out by pointing to letters of the alphabet, the correct letter being identified by a rap. Whatever the information, however esoteric it might be, somebody present clearly had to know the answer. And providing the person pointing to the letters knew what they were looking for, it was a simple matter to 'watch the countenance and motion of the person'.[3] An eager sitter, anxious to hear what they wanted, would usually inadvertently pause at the correct letters, thus prompting the timing of the rap.

Modern Spiritualism soon came to Britain. In 1853, Mrs Hayden arrived from the United States, set up shop in London, and attracted some very impressive clients, such as Robert Owen and Robert Chambers, both of whom were very impressed. By then, table-tipping and table-turning were also becoming rather popular, as fingers were placed lightly on top of small tables, which then tipped back and forward, or turned around, seemingly of their own accord. For some, this was evidence of a mesmeric force, for others it was the work of Satan, but many expressed a belief that the table was being moved by the spirits.[4] Thus, in the absence of an ordinary explanation, there were a number of extraordinary ones from which to choose.

Once again, however, an ordinary explanation appeared, this time courtesy of William Benjamin Carpenter, the eminent psycho-physiologist whose various sceptical endeavours means that we shall be meeting him more than once. Carpenter provided a new 'ideo-motor' theory with which to explain the movement of tables according to unconscious muscular movement.[5] The theory was tested by Michael Faraday, who placed moveable boards on top of the table, then fingers were placed upon the top board, and when the board moved before the table, it was considered proof that people were unconsciously pushing. It was also considered newsworthy, and was announced very publicly indeed.[6] Meanwhile, Mrs Hayden was publicly debunked by the philosopher George Lewes, who had heard of Mrs Culver's claim that the raps were produced by the medium, based upon watching the sitter for cues. The philosopher had reasoned that, if this was the case, he could provoke the medium to provide any message he wanted. So he went along to a Hayden séance, and had her spirits communicate that she was a fraud. This bizarre spirit conversation was then published in the press, and widely discussed with sceptical mirth.[7]

From even this briefest of glances, then, it should be clear that ordinary explanations were not only available, but were being actively disseminated. And yet, despite this, spiritualism grew, with increasing numbers of mediums emerging, and the publication of the first spiritualist journals in Britain from 1855.[8] There seems to have then been a brief decline, but the 1860s saw a further growth in spiritualist publications and groups, and much wider discussion in the periodical press. How, then, does one explain such beliefs when ordinary explanations were so freely available?

Many thought then, as many think now, that it was a simple matter of gullibility, as credulous folk wandered into séances unarmed with the necessary critical faculties. Like sceptics today, they understood that people were superstitious in the past, but despaired at their modern contemporaries who were guilty of such primitive thinking. It has been one more theme in the history of extraordinary beliefs, that every generation has wondered how, in this day and age, such credulity is possible. Nevertheless, though we might find it easier to understand such beliefs in the past than in the present, we nevertheless feel a need to find reasons for them. Thus, instead of gullibility and wishful thinking, we might consider what made spiritualism plausible or desirable.

Some historians have pointed to overlapping interests, as spiritualism offered new opportunities for women, or ideas that were attractive to the working class.[9] Further up the social ladder, respectable ladies could play hostess to the most fashionable medium in town, and eager guests knew that one had to be open-minded.[10] Meanwhile, serious scientists could see links between the phenomena of the séance room and new discoveries in electricity and magnetism, while anyone else could marvel at the rapidly changing world of technology, one in which an electric telegraph could allow communication with unseen others at a distance, and wonder whether anything was possible.[11] Meanwhile, the rise of scientific knowledge and authority was accompanied by a more sceptical attitude, which challenged the historical accuracy of the Bible and threatened the fundamental tenets of Christianity. In the face of biblical criticism, geological findings and evolutionary theory, as some Christians suffered a 'crisis of faith', spiritualism provided ammunition against the rising tide of materialism, and support for belief in the supernatural.[12]

There were, then, a variety of reasons why individuals would have found spiritualism a plausible and desirable thing, and many of these were articulated by spiritualists at the time. Nevertheless, whatever else was said, beliefs were always expressed in terms of the evidence, because spiritualist beliefs were beliefs that the phenomena of the séance were the work of the spirits, based upon the exclusion of alternative explanations. Thus, spiritualists continued to believe, despite the existence of ordinary explanations, because they viewed such explanations as inadequate. As the dispute continued, ordinary explanations might become available, but the rise in the number of mediums and spiritualist journals was a matter of supply as well as demand. Significantly more phenomena were now being demonstrated and reported and, within this growing body of evidence, some of it was more impressive than many critics seemed to realize. The very idea that all spirit raps were the product of clicking joints, or all spirit messages the result of reading facial expressions, or that all the table movements they had seen were caused by unconscious pushing, were dismissed, and often with disdain.[13] Such explanations might be regarded as interesting, and might even explain some of the phenomena, but they were, it was argued, inadequate explanations for all that had been observed. As always, beliefs were based upon particular events, associated with particular mediums, and the variety of phenomena and mediums was considerable. By considering some of these, we can see more direct reasons for various beliefs about spiritualist phenomena.

For example, there were the Davenport brothers, the most public of mediums in the 1860s, who sold tickets to their stage performances in theatres around the country, and provoked an astonishing range of reactions, from sincere belief to physical violence. On the other hand, there was Daniel Home, the most private of mediums, though still the most famous, who conducted séances in the private drawing rooms of celebrities and monarchs. Home never charged a fee, but he still provoked everything from devotion to death threats, including a verbal thrashing from Dickens and a near physical thrashing from Browning.[14] Between these poles lay other mediums, including Charles Foster and countless others, most of whom were women. But Home and the Davenports provoked more controversy in the 1860s than other mediums, and so will serve as useful examples for the moment.

Spiritualists continued to believe, then, despite the emergence of ordinary explanations because, according to them, they found such explanations inadequate. This might easily be dismissed as stubbornness – indeed it has frequently been dismissed as such – but it was not such an unreasonable position if we consider the case of Daniel Home. Home arrived in London in 1855, and attracted the attention of some important people. One was David Brewster, co-founder of the British Association for the Advancement of Science and author of *Letters on Natural Magic*. In other words, he was an eminent scientist and an authority on natural explanations for seemingly supernatural events. He attended a séance with Daniel Home (in Brewster's own words) 'to assist in finding out the trick', and could afterwards (in his own words) 'give no explanation'.[15]

A few years later, Home was in Amsterdam, having been invited by a group of rationalists, who had challenged him to produce phenomena in front of their sceptical gaze. According to them, as they chatted in candlelight in a hotel room, the table around which they sat, large enough to sit more than a dozen people, rose in the air. They looked under the table and on top of it, and failed to find any apparatus, and then the table began to descend, despite their best efforts to prevent it from doing so. The rationalists stated that they could not explain what they saw, and nobody has done so since.[16] Now, whatever else one wishes to make of this, one can hardly blame anyone for excluding ideo-motor action as an explanation.

It was a point often made by spiritualists, and by believers in extraordinary phenomena since, that however many fraudulent cases there might be, it only took one genuine case for spiritualism to be true. And despite the best efforts of critics, there was always something that remained unexplained, certainly to the satisfaction of spiritualists, but also to many others who expressed no belief in the spirits. This was not simply a dispute between the rational and the gullible, or so far as it was, it was not always clear who was on which side of the argument. It was a dispute about what was going on in the séance room, because the phenomena were the basis of Modern Spiritualism, in theory and in practice. These were the objects of belief for spiritualists, and of disbelief for others, and one cannot understand beliefs without considering the things in which people believe. And these were not physical objects but events, demonstrations by other people, with whom the observer sat and interacted. Not surprisingly, how this was done was fundamental to how such phenomena were framed.

Framing séance phenomena (in performance)

The phenomena of spiritualism, like those of mesmerism, were demonstrated in ways that were explicitly designed to exclude ordinary explanations, and in far subtler ways than has often been appreciated. This was the case regardless of whether they were real, but in order to appreciate them now, we need to do what every spiritualist did, and consider the possibility of trickery.

When Charles Foster demonstrated his pellet phenomenon, the basic effect was simple enough: he displayed, apparently via the spirits, knowledge of what was written on the pellets. If we consider how this might have been done, without recourse to the spirits, then the basic method is obvious enough: somehow he knew what was written on the pellets. Since one did not need to be a conjuror to consider this, the extraordinariness of the demonstration depended upon this possibility being excluded. And this is precisely what he did in performance, regardless of whether it was genuine or fraudulent. By appearing not to touch the pellets, by allowing sitters to write down names in private, in some cases before they arrived, his demonstrations were designed to exclude the possibility that he could know the contents.[17]

The Davenport brothers performed in a spirit cabinet, a large wardrobe with a bench inside, to which they were tied with ropes. The phenomena that followed – musical instruments were heard to play, and objects were thrown – happened while the boys were (supposedly) tied up. The idea that they released themselves from the ropes in order to produce the phenomena was such an obvious possibility that they had to address this directly. Thus, the cabinet was inspected, as were the ropes, the knots being tied by strangers, and often those who had some knowledge of knots.[18] When, at the séances of Daniel Home, tables moved and spirit hands appeared, he invited sitters to check under the table, even as the phenomena were occurring, precisely in order to exclude the possibility that he was responsible for what was happening.[19] Regardless of whether any of this was real, the demonstrations of mediums openly sought to exclude the possibility of trickery, and did so by addressing precisely the sorts of methods that were relevant to the phenomenon in question. For all the talk about the gullibility of spiritualists, one needs to bear in mind that beliefs were based upon the exclusion of such explanations, not the lack of consideration of them.

As mediums sought to exclude the possibility of trickery, they also presented themselves as the sort of people who would not engage in fraud. American mediums arrived in Britain with letters of recommendation from respectable gentlemen, the Davenports were accompanied by the Revd Dr J. B. Ferguson, a well-respected man of God, and Home quietly claimed to be related to Scottish aristocracy.[20] Later mediums, such as Florence Cook, Mary Showers and Anna Eva Fay, might have played the role of the frail and innocent young woman, incapable of such dishonest behavior, at least until they were caught cheating, but could also appeal to social status as an indicator of innocence.[21] Thus, in a range of ways, mediums sought to exclude the possibility that they could, or would, engage in trickery.

However, demonstrations of séance phenomena were as much about framing the phenomena as spiritual as they were about excluding the possibility of trickery. This was fundamental to beliefs about spiritualism because, without such framing, the objects of extraordinary belief had no meaning. After all, Foster's pellet phenomenon was only extraordinary because he could not have known what was written on the pellets, and the ability to know what was written down beyond the vision of the performer had been displayed by Louis M'Kean and the Mysterious Lady, and by mesmeric clairvoyants such as George Goble and the Didier brothers. In the former case, it had been predominantly framed as entertainment, in the latter, as evidence of the powers of mesmerism. As we shall see, the feat has been framed in a variety of ways since. However, Foster framed this effect as spiritual, by having his sitters write down not random words but rather the names of deceased friends and relatives, and by revealing the information in the form of spirit raps. Advertised as a spirit medium, in the context of a private séance, the same basic effect was firmly framed as evidence of spirit communication. The exclusion of trickery might make it seem real, but it was the framing of the performance that made it seem supernatural.

Similarly, the Davenports' spirit cabinet might have been framed in several ways. On the one hand, the Davenports avoided explicit claims about the source of the phenomena, and the Revd J. B. Ferguson made a similar disclaimer in his opening remarks. However, both the Davenports and Ferguson were explicit that the phenomena were real, strenuously denying the charge of trickery, and Ferguson publicly stated that he believed the boys to be spirit mediums.[22] Advertised as a séance, and introduced with a lecture on spiritualism by a sincere man of God, even the public antics of musical instruments in a wardrobe could be framed as something of spiritual significance.

But the public stage demonstrations of the Davenports were hardly typical of most séances, which looked and felt quite different from what one might have seen in a theatre. Private séances were held either in the premises of the medium, or else in the home of a respectable spiritualist, and the latter were generally deemed the most convincing, if only because the venue was less open to suspicion. Thus, the space in which most séances took place was radically different from those associated with theatrical performances. For anyone who compared the feats of mediums to those of stage conjurors, and this was almost everybody, the comparison was supposed to be unsatisfactory.

It was true that conjurors did similar kinds of things, and gradually the feats of mediums became standard tricks within the conjuring repertoire. Initially, however, most séance phenomena were novel in effect or presentation, and even after they were adopted by conjurors, the séance experience was rather different. Mediums did not use entertaining patter, and were not in control of what was going on. Unlike the conjuror, who could perform his feats twice nightly, mediums had to rely upon the spirits, and the spirits did not always do as requested. Evidence of this was provided by mediums, who not only explained that this was the case, but also behaved accordingly, struggling to summon up their guests, displaying great effort and appearing exhausted.[23] Sitters had to wait for something to happen, and sometimes they had to wait in vain, as it was not uncommon for nothing to happen.[24] In the process, mediums would have given the impression of humility and sincerity, since if they were genuine, this would have been natural, and if they were faking it, this would have been effective. Conversations no doubt involved mediums' biographical details, which if published writings are anything to go by, would have included descriptions of how they had first experienced the phenomena, and had come to realize that they were the work of the spirits.[25] All of this made it look and feel quite unlike any conjuring performance, and such personal interactions would have been crucial to convincing sitters. Indeed, as we shall see, they were regularly cited as reasons for having been convinced.

As with mesmeric phenomena, demonstrations were also framed in ways that made them matter. There was nothing inherently spiritual about a knocking noise, a moving table or, indeed, any of the physical phenomena of spiritualism. From the perspective of demonstration, then, this needed to be provided. The framing of the phenomena as the work of the spirits, rather than something more mundane, required mediums to present not only the phenomena but also themselves as part of a serious quest to communicate with the departed.

This was the case, regardless of whether the phenomena were genuine or not, but if they were not, such framing provided particular advantages for the deceiver, and even spiritualists conceded that there were a few of them. By attributing the phenomena to the spirits, the attention of observers was directed away from the medium, giving the latter more scope for trickery. Indeed, so far as observers found the spirits to be a plausible explanation for the phenomena, there was no need for them to seek an alternative method for what was going on.[26] In this sense, the spirits acted as a pseudo-explanation, rather like Robert-Houdin had attributed the suspension of his son to the mysterious powers of ether. However, unlike an audience of a conjuring show, who sat at a distance from the performance, sitters were active participants in an event that was ostensibly about seeking contact with the spirits. By presenting himself as a fellow enquirer, not in control but trying hard to succeed, the medium could align himself with the audience and direct their attention accordingly. This apparent lack of control over events also allowed the medium to choose his moment. If suspicious eyes were upon him, he could simply wait until they were not, and since he was ostensibly not in control, he could wait indefinitely. Unlike the professional entertainer, there was no obligation to maintain levels of attention, and boredom could be usefully exploited. And, of course, there was always the option for the medium not to risk detection, by blaming the spirits for non-cooperation. None of this was available to the stage conjuror, and when such techniques succeeded, the phenomena were made that much more convincing.

Nevertheless, whether genuine or not, the séance experience made the phenomena seem less extraordinary, as sitters sat in the presence of sincere believers, and were asked by their hosts to be open-minded. The natural tendency to be polite, or the social pressure to behave appropriately, forced a degree of compliance upon even sceptical observers. Asked only to observe, and to believe the facts, they heard the spirits being asked to move the table, and then they saw the table move. Scepticism was not overcome so easily, but neither was it easy to believe that one was being deceived by apparently respectable and sincere folk. And if one was not being deceived, then the facts were real, and the facts were that the spirits had been asked to move the table, and then the table had moved.

However plausible the spiritual explanation, the facts themselves were observable to anyone, as séance demonstrations, including the various options for checking against trickery, were based upon the understanding that sitters were competent observers. And the benefit of this being real was made explicit in communications from the beyond, which provided not only personal messages but also the possibility of a new conviction in life after death. Like the demonstrations of mesmerists, those of mediums explicitly sought to exclude ordinary explanations, framing the phenomena as not so extraordinary, observable facts that anyone could see, and that most would want to be true. The details of what was said during private séances may not be available, but we shall see from the public dispute that these were central themes in the framing of séance phenomena, and all of this was in response to demonstrations by mediums who framed what they did in very particular ways. Thus, whether or not any of these phenomena were real, and whatever individuals made of them, beliefs were the product of the complex social interactions of the séance. The form in which such beliefs were expressed, and the ways in which they were maintained in the face of opposition, can now be seen in the more public social interaction of disputes about the phenomena of spiritualism.

Framing séance phenomena (the reception): reporting the facts

When the journalist S. C. Hall attended a séance with Foster, he excluded ordinary explanations as follows: 'it would have been so utterly impossible for him to have fraudulently done that which he did do, as to convert a diamond ring into an inkstand'.[27] He was not alone in his confident dismissal of trickery as a possibility at a Foster séance. According to the essayist, William Howitt, 'I conjecture that nothing in the shape of evidence can be made more complete, not even, if an angel stood visibly before us, and provided the truth of these facts with a trumpet'.[28] A committee investigating the Davenport brothers 'formally and unanimously admitted that the manifestations...were...free from all suspicion of trickery'.[29] Similarly, Home's witnesses were 'convinced' that no fraud had been present, that it would have been 'impossible', of this they were 'certain'.[30]

That mediums simply could not have cheated was a standard theme in accounts of séance phenomena. The claim was regularly justified by appeals to careful observation, and to conditions that either prevented fraud, or else in which it would have been detected. It was regularly pointed out that a séance took place in the presence of people unknown to the medium, or in the home of a respectable party, often a house to which the medium had never been.[31] Tables that moved were frequently described as large and heavy.[32] Observers described how they were given the opportunity to check for trickery, or control against fraud, such as looking under the table, or holding the hands of the medium.[33] In countless more specific ways, whether relating to the Davenports being tied up, or to the absence of special machinery that might explain a Home levitation, witnesses excluded the possibility of fraud by appealing to critical observation and the adequacy of the conditions.[34]

There was, of course, something potentially suspicious about such things happening in darkness, but this was also addressed. On the one hand, witnesses invariably reported what light there had been in ways that stressed its adequacy. Thus, for example, while the room had been 'comparatively darkened, light streamed through the window from a distant gas-lamp outside', or 'contrary to the assertions so constantly made that the manifestations are always in the dark, the whole of the phenomena of which I have spoken were manifested in a room light with gas, and a bright fire burning'.[35] On the other hand, darkness was described as a necessary condition of some phenomena, comparisons being made with biblical miracles and, indeed, with photography.[36] Presumably, one spiritualist pondered, photographs must be developed in light 'or the sceptic would reject the fact of the portrait before him'.[37]

The exclusion of the possibility of deception was accompanied by references to information that suggested the medium would not deceive.[38] In terms of motive, the most obvious matter was that almost all mediums worked for money. When they did not, most famously in the case of Daniel Home, this was cited as evidence that he was 'beyond suspicion'.[39] Indeed, when Home was accused of taking money for séances, this was vigorously denied by spiritualists, and when he was on trial for fraud, Dr Gully pointed out that he had never known Home to accept money for his séances, but had known him to 'repeatedly refuse offers of as much as 20 guineas for a single séance'.[40] As for those who took money for their work, it was noted that there was little difference between a medium and a Church of England minister, who was also paid for his services.[41]

By excluding the presence of deception, by describing conditions in which it would have been impossible, and by countering suspicions about a medium's willingness to deceive, witnesses described events in ways designed to exclude fraud as an explanation.

Unlike public demonstrations of mesmerists, or those of the Davenport brothers, the events of a private séance were open to another explanation, at least by those who had not attended, namely that they did not really happen. Indeed, though mesmerism had been a common route into spiritualism, it had also led to a new awareness of the power of subjective experience and, therefore, an alternative interpretation of the evidence. Thus, observers regularly denied that they had been mesmerized, hypnotized, 'psychologized' or 'biologized'. 'I never was biologized', one stated bluntly, 'I have biologized others. I therefore feel that what I saw, I saw, and what I heard, I heard, really and truly; and if you say I was biologized, the friends I see before me do not exist, and the scene before me is biological'.[42] 'We were neither asleep, nor intoxicated, nor even excited', explained another, 'We were complete masters of our senses'.[43] An editor of a London newspaper reported that the medium 'did not fix his attention upon us, or we might have imagined ourselves under mesmeric influence', adding that he was sober and that, while tea and coffee had been served, he had not accepted a drop.[44]

As they dismissed the various possibilities that what they reported had not really happened, witnesses also denied the charge of insanity and dishonesty. The accusation that they were 'knaves or madmen' was, it was said, to be expected, though when a spiritualist noted that some 'thought that he was a fit subject for a lunatic asylum', it was most likely read as a jest.[45] There was little sense of irony in denials of dishonesty, however, as witnesses pointed out that they were not lying, or employed pseudonyms such as 'Verax', 'Honestas' and 'A lover of truth'.[46] Thus, the exclusion of ordinary explanations was not only for one's own benefit — after all, nobody had to convince themselves that they were telling the truth — but were designed to anticipate every imaginable accusation. However, if we accept that what they reported was what they thought, then their beliefs depended upon the rejection of deception and self-deception. And even if we remain agnostic as to what they were really thinking, by countering potential accusations of deception and self-deception, witness accounts were designed to establish the events as having really happened, and what happened as being real.

Managing extraordinariness

When David Brewster had left his séance with Daniel Home in 1855, he had privately confessed to being unable to provide an explanation. However, in public, he had expressed a quite contrary view, and in the midst of various attempts to explain what he had seen, he had stated that the table 'had appeared' to rise from the ground. 'Appeared to rise from the ground?', responded one spiritualist, 'Did it rise? Why make a question of so plain a fact?'[47] According to the Revd Dr Maitland, Brewster (an expert on optics) had 'place[d] himself before the public as a person who really could not tell whether a table, under his nose, did or did not rise from the ground'.[48] 'Whether a table does so rise', stated another witness, 'is a question of fact to be determined upon evidence'.[49]

Throughout the 1860s, witnesses continually stressed that, however one tried to explain them, the phenomena themselves were facts that had been obtained through the normal means of observation, and the spiritualist press regularly made the same point. Every issue of the *Spiritualist* newspaper stated its aim of supplying facts to non-spiritualists. The *Spiritual Magazine* pointed out the materialist 'clamours for facts which his senses can take note of. Spiritualism meets that demand in the most simple and direct way. It gives him the very kind of evidence he needs – plain, palpable facts, and plenty of them.'[50] In a public debate with the radical reformer and atheist, Charles Bradlaugh, the spiritualist publisher James Burns began his argument by stating that he argued not as a philosopher but as an observer of facts, and ended the evening by stressing 'we must succumb to FACTS'.[51] Time and again, witnesses, whether or not they expressed a belief in spiritualism, pointed out that they were merely describing facts, not drawing conclusions.[52] As one anonymous witness put it, 'the phenomena of Spiritualism I cannot but believe, if I am to take my five senses as my guides in this as in other matters... When, however, I pass from facts to theories, and I am asked to account for these facts, then I hesitate.'[53] By making an explicit distinction between facts and theories, extraordinary facts were presented as real, however extraordinary they might seem.

In the process, avowals of prior scepticism were remarkably common. Spiritualists frequently described how they had been 'forced' to accept the facts, and spoke of a 'hardened sceptic mind, which, I am free to confess was, until recently, my own state'.[54] In doing so, one did not have to express a belief in spiritualism: 'We went to Mr Jones' house disbelieving his statements of fact: we saw phenomena which were significant to show us that all he has related could occur by the same power, whatever that power may be'.[55] Just as their own prior scepticism had been overcome by the facts, so they criticized as prejudiced those who continued to deny the facts. Regular complaints were made about those who displayed ignorance and narrow-mindedness, who were 'blinded' by prejudice, who 'seem determined to deny' the facts, who were unwilling 'to look an unwelcome fact in the face'.[56] Such prejudice reminded some of the story of the King of Siam, who refused to believe that water could turn so hard that an elephant could walk on it, because he had never seen it for himself.[57] For Robert Chambers, another self-proclaimed sceptic turned believer, it was as though 'facts are in cases nothing, and a scientific theory everything'.[58]

Yet, as others regularly stressed, such denial of the facts was unscientific, and prompted comparisons with those who had denied the novel facts of Copernicus, Galileo and Harvey.[59] In the words of William Gregory, Professor of Chemistry at the University of Edinburgh, '[o]ur duty is to study nature as she presents herself and to take the facts as we find them'.[60] When Michael Faraday wrote that, prior to any scientific investigation, 'we should set out with clear ideas of the naturally possible and impossible', he was promptly criticized by the mathematician, Augustus de Morgan, who 'stared when we first read this... We thought that mature minds were rather inclined to believe that a knowledge of the limits of possibility and impossibility was only the mirage which constantly recedes as we approach it'.[61] Indeed, the seemingly endless possibilities of Victorian science and technology were cited as evidence that, to paraphrase a popular quote, there were more things in heaven and earth than were dreamt of.

Those who reported séance phenomena, whether or not they expressed a belief in spiritualism, deployed the same arguments as those who had reported mesmeric demonstrations: the facts were facts, however extraordinary, believers had once been sceptics too, but to reject the facts was an act of prejudice, and out of line with scientific thinking.

Nevertheless, for all the talk of sticking to the facts, the ostensible cause of the phenomena was a regular theme of accounts. And, unlike mesmerism, spiritualism had, by definition, an obvious religious significance. Thus, while the phenomena were framed as compatible with science, they were also framed as compatible with mainstream Christian thinking. Countless comparisons were made with religious miracles past and present, as examples of how such facts were not so extraordinary after all. Rhetorically speaking, the most effective comparison was with those in the Bible, upon which (virtually) all Christians could agree, and biblical authority was regularly cited in support of the possibility of miraculous phenomena.[62] Furthermore, spiritualists argued, and many others had to agree, that the evidence for séance phenomena was rather better than for biblical miracles, having been observed by hundreds of contemporary witnesses and reported immediately after the event. It was a common argument that, if the miracles of the Bible were subjected to the same criteria expected of séance phenomena, they 'would soon crumble in our hands under the application of such a test'.[63] In short, to reject the phenomena of spiritualism was tantamount to rejecting the central miracles of Christianity.

There were, however, a variety of positions expressed in terms of the relationship between Christianity and the phenomena of spiritualism, and there were also a remarkable number of witnesses who expressed the view that the phenomena were real, but not the work of spirits. These diverse positions shall be discussed later, when considering the wider reasons for belief. Meanwhile, belief in the facts, however extraordinary they might seem, and whatever theory might account for them, depended upon the exclusion of ordinary explanations. This, in turn, required a belief that those who excluded such explanations were competent to do so. Thus, beliefs were invariably expressed and warranted by references to what counted as adequate expertise.

Constructing and deploying expertise

It was essential to any spiritualist claim that the observer was deemed a competent witness. Thus, those who reported what they saw invariably did so in ways designed to present themselves as reliable observers. Disputes over scientific expertise were part of this, of course, but there were many other ways of presenting competence. Indeed, one way was by rejecting the need for any particular expertise at all. Time and again, witnesses appealed to sensory evidence, regularly pointing out that 'it was impossible to disbelieve the evidence of my own senses'.[64] Many explicitly rejected the need for scientific expertise in simple matters of observation, and resented the idea they were, in the frustrated words of Benjamin Coleman, 'not qualified to judge of plain matters of fact made patent to our senses, because, forsooth, we are deficient in scientific training! You insult our practical common sense, and earn our contempt for your scientific nonsense.'[65] Like the demonstrations of mesmerists, such facts could be observed by anyone.

At the same time, personal competence was cited, as remarkable numbers of witnesses described themselves as being particularly good observers.[66] Many appealed to the social or intellectual status of witnesses as evidence of their competence; as one put it, beliefs in spiritualist phenomena were 'not incompatible with the largest calibre of intellect and the highest culture'.[67] Many witnesses cited professional credentials, whether lawyers, journalists or doctors who, like Dr Gully, were 'all working in callings in which matters of fact, and not of fancy, especially come under observation'.[68] As observers stressed their observational skills, so they presented themselves as the sort of people who would not be deceived. 'I presume to say', noted S. C. Hall, in the process of excluding the possibility of trickery at a Foster séance, 'that the persons present were such as must have detected fraud in any one who dared to practise it'.[69] 'Those who know me', remarked a fellow optimist, 'may perhaps give a guarantee that I am not very easily deceived'.[70]

In excluding the possibility of deception, conjuring expertise was often cited. E. L. Blanchard, the playwright and amateur conjuror, claimed to be 'thoroughly acquainted' with conjuring techniques, and yet had been unable to detect 'the slightest attempt at imposition' by Foster.[71] Professional conjurors were also cited as having been unable to detect trickery at séances. It was said that conjurors were unable to duplicate the feats of the Davenport brothers, and that Daniel Home had been scrutinized by the most famous conjurors in Europe, and that

> the most accomplished professors of the 'Herr Frickell and Robert-Houdin' order... assert, not only that they have not detected any contrivances by which he could accomplish the manifestations they witnessed, but that it was impossible he could have any without their

having detected them, and they accordingly affirm their belief in the ultra-mundane cause of the phenomena.[72]

As we shall see, the expertise of conjurors was also appealed to by critics, when the former began to perform duplications of séance phenomena on stage, and offered possible explanations for what happened at a séance. When this happened, spiritualists challenged their expertise, claiming to have greater expertise themselves (having investigated the phenomena properly) and thus being better qualified to judge. Like the proponents of mesmerism, they claimed that they had adequate expertise, appealed to experts whose views supported their own, and challenged the expertise of those whose views did not.

This was the case for expertise in deception, and was also the case for expertise in observation. As witness accounts excluded the possibility of deception and self-deception, they described themselves as having competent observational skills, and this frequently included the language of science. Séances were described as 'experiments', having taken place in 'test' conditions, and references were regularly made to the scientific expertise of witnesses.[73] Such expertise may have been described as unnecessary by some, in the observation of plain facts, but it was nevertheless a frequent theme in accounts. On the one hand, the scientific credentials of witnesses were cited in support of the reality of the phenomena.[74] On the other hand, the scientific expertise of critics was challenged. Thus, for example, an unsuccessful investigation by sceptics was deemed 'very unscientific', and Brewster was described as 'not the most learned and scientific man of his age'.[75]

As we shall see, when the formal scientific investigation of séance phenomena began, disputes over what counted as proper scientific expertise were a fundamental part of the dispute. However, by then, this dispute over scientific expertise was part of an ongoing dispute over the reality of the phenomena, based upon the construction of what counted as proper expertise. What has always counted in the reporting of extraordinary facts is that one is deemed a competent observer and, as we have seen, scientific expertise was not the only kind of competence that mattered. Beliefs about the extraordinary phenomena of spiritualism, like those associated with mesmerism, were expressed and warranted by appeals to different versions of expertise, whichever ones might be most effectively deployed in argument.

The phenomena of mesmerism had also been framed as real by appealing to potential benefits, and this was the case with the phenomena of spiritualism, though the benefits were rather different. Since the benefits of rappings and moving tables, or musical instruments that played by themselves, were not self-evident, this also had to be constructed in argument. Mediums framed such things as the work of spirits, and many witnesses became convinced, but their spiritual relevance remained unclear, hence the need for discussion. When spiritualists asked 'Cui bono?', a regular question in spiritualist periodicals, their answers tended to be that such phenomena proved that souls survived, that miracles were possible, and so provided evidence in support of Christian faith. There were also occasional references to spiritual cures, or to having received useful advice from the spirits, but more common were claims that witnesses had had their Christian faith restored, and how Modern Spiritualism was a refutation of the creeping materialism of the age.[76]

This, of course, is very much in line with the theory that beliefs in spiritualism can be understood as a response to the crises of faith suffered by many Victorians in the light of geological discoveries, evolutionary theories and growing scepticism about the literal truth of the Bible. But there are several reasons why this is an inadequate analysis, which we shall discuss below. Meanwhile, we have seen that witnesses of séance phenomena ruled out deception and self-deception, based upon competent observation, argued that the facts were real, however extraordinary they might seem, that this was in line with both science and religion, and that it provided the benefit of support for belief in an afterlife. In doing so, like earlier mesmerists, they provided arguments upon which to base beliefs in extraordinary phenomena. Yet despite all their efforts, most contemporaries disagreed, and how they did so shows how the very same events that were the objects of belief could be framed as objects of disbelief.

Framing séance phenomena as not real

If one wished to argue, in 1860s Britain, that extraordinary phenomena were not real, one did not have to look very far for possible ordinary explanations. There had recently been a widespread debate about mesmerism, and a new theory of hypnosis was available to explain how people might experience something that was not really there. There was also enormous public interest in optical illusions, with a variety of popular optical devices that were being sold commercially, and professional performances that relied upon visual illusions.[77] One could buy a zoetrope, stroboscope or kaleidoscope (invented by David Brewster), or visit the Royal Polytechnic Institution to view a range of larger optical illusions, including the remarkably popular 'Pepper's Ghost', which allowed audiences to see the projection of an actor dressed as a ghost on stage.[78] Just because one saw a spirit, this did not mean the spirit was real.

And then there was the problem of insanity, a perennial topic of concern for the Victorians. As contemporary periodicals continued to express concern about the apparent increase of lunacy, the preoccupation with insanity was evident in the popular literature of the period. Insanity was, according to Nenadic, one of the 'Victorian nightmares'.[79] And, for those who took an interest, contemporary mental science texts explained how delusions, illusions and hallucinations could be experienced by otherwise sane and educated people.[80] Indeed, this point was made to non-specialists who simply read the periodical press.[81] In short, it would have been very easy in the 1860s to believe that people might see things that were not really there.

It is in this context that the relative scarcity of such arguments becomes significant. Despite the option of appealing to hypnosis, optical illusion or madness, there is a noticeable lack of critics offering these as explanations for the reported phenomena, despite the fact that many prominent critics were experts on such matters.[82] Not even avowedly sceptical witnesses suggested that they had been mesmerized, or the victim of an optical illusion (and confessions of insanity were rarer still). That witnesses denied such things suggests potential criticisms, yet there was precious little suggestion in the periodical press of the 1860s that this might be what was going on. Comparisons might be made between Pepper's Ghost and the spirits observed in the séance room, third-hand rumours of mass hallucination might appear in the popular press, and links between mesmerism and spiritualism were made in terms of their relevance to mental science, but the view that the phenomena were a wholly subjective experience does not appear to have become a common argument until later.

Indeed, the link between spiritualism and insanity was generally expressed in the opposite direction, as many claimed that spiritualism was the cause of insanity. John Henry Anderson, the conjuror debunker, publicly claimed that spiritualism was 'a delusion that has driven ten thousand persons mad in the United States', and the periodical press spoke of 'lunatic asylums, filled with maniacs on the subject of Spiritualism', and noted that 'it is a fact, that many of the persons who constitute the circles of the spiritualists... are either insane or on the verge of insanity'.[83] In turn, of course, spiritualist periodicals disputed the idea that spiritualism led to insanity, but the idea that séance phenomena were the product of insanity, that was another matter.

When a critic suggested that believers should be 'pointed to the lunatic asylum', few would have read it as literal advice.[84] Nevertheless, the language of mental science was common enough. Critics could refer to the 'intellectual condition' of a witness, possible 'mental defects', 'excited imagination', 'weak nerves' or even the 'verge of insanity', without crossing the line.[85] Even when the phenomena were attributed to delusions, illusions and hallucinations, it was pointed out that these could be the product of a sane mind.[86] Indeed, the language of madness was common enough elsewhere. Mackay's *Memoirs of Extraordinary Popular Delusions* (1841) had included chapters on the 'South Sea bubble' and 'Popular admiration for great thieves', and such topics were referred to as 'epidemic maladies' in both the *Journal of Mental Science* and the *Westminster Review*.[87] Thus, spiritualism might be described as an 'epidemic delusion', but the term could mean no more than 'popular error'.

The ambiguity with which the language of mental science was used is understandable, not least in terms of the implications of accusing individuals of being insane. Thus, when such language was used, it was rarely in reference to a specific individual. The same was the case for more general appeals to the problem of testimony. As *Fraser's Magazine* put it,

> it is a complete mistake to imagine... that the respectability, honesty, and good faith of a witness are in any way a sufficient guarantee of his accuracy in reporting a matter of fact. Great allowances must be made for want of observation, for credulity, and the many other mental defects which more or less incapacitate [most] persons of average ability and information.[88]

There was, then, a critical view that, despite all the talk about facts, testimony was not wholly reliable, and that somewhere between the facts and the report, the observer had somehow got it wrong. But it only became a major thread in the dispute after 1870, for reasons we shall shortly consider. Meanwhile, the overwhelming way of framing séance phenomena as ordinary was to accept that what was reported had actually happened, but to attribute events to trickery.

Framing séance phenomena as trickery

As we have seen, Brewster had left the séance with Home in 1855, admitting in private that he could not explain things, yet he had nevertheless attempted to explain them in public. In the process of this, he had included a statement that the table 'appeared' to rise from the floor, and this suggestion that it may not have done so, as we have seen, provoked a response. For the most part, however, Brewster had attempted to explain events as the result of trickery, claiming in the press that the phenomena 'could all be produced by human hands and feet'.[89] This also provoked a lengthy dispute, in which demands for more details emerged, and critics took to appealing to the authority of conjurors. When John Henry Anderson decided to join in, he claimed that mediums relied upon electromagnetism and, at other times, 'the skillful adjustment of levers and cleverly arranged horsehairs'.[90] Whatever this was supposed to mean, it clearly did not convince everyone. One correspondent demanded, on behalf of 'the anxious public', a proper explanation.[91] A few days later, having received no reply, he wrote, 'I again ask for a straightforward answer or explanation to the cause of the phenomena'.[92] A more direct request is hard to imagine, yet no such explanation was forthcoming. This was common of expressions of the view that séance phenomena were not real: appeals to trickery as an explanation, with insufficient detail to satisfy those who took a proper interest in the subject.

This was most obvious in the case of Home, who defied the debunkers more successfully than any other medium. In 1860, following the publication in the *Cornhill* magazine of an account of a séance in which Home had levitated to the ceiling, there was a considerable debate in the press about how this might be explained. However, there was precious little by way of detailed explanation.[93] Indeed, throughout the 1860s, explanations for Home's phenomena were primarily of two forms: first, there was an appeal to the possibility of fraud in such conditions, particularly because they took place in the dark; second, there was an appeal to the authority of conjurors who, it was assumed, would know what was going on.

As observers had stressed the adequacy of the conditions, critics stressed their inadequacy. Thus, *Fraser's Magazine* claimed, in direct contradiction to what had been stated in the *Cornhill* account, that Home's phenomena 'were only enacted in special conditions. It was always in Mr Home's own house or in that of some person who, if not an accomplice, was at all events an implicit believer in his supernatural powers, and allowed him free scope for his preparations.'[94] Others referred to the suspiciousness of darkness, and to the expertise of stage conjurors, who could no doubt shed light on those 'strange things done in the dark'.[95] Nevertheless, what is evident is that detailed explanations of how it might be done were hard to find, and those who took the view that séance phenomena were not real had a limited number of options. If the public dispute is anything to go by, they depended upon the view that conjurors would know what was really going on.

The appeal to conjurors' expertise took various forms. Mediums were described as no better than conjurors, or not as good, since they relied upon darkness.[96] Conjurors were portrayed as knowing how mediums did it, by claiming that mediums would not, or could not, produce their phenomena in the presence of conjurors, or that they were caught in the act when they tried.[97] It is probably worth noting, if only to avoid confusion, that such claims (much like those made by spiritualists that conjurors were unable to explain the phenomena) were often unfounded. For example, spiritualists claimed that Robert-Houdin had been unable to explain what happened at a Home séance, and critics claimed that Home had refused an invitation to perform in front of Robert-Houdin.[98] There is, however, not a shred of evidence for either of these claims. Nevertheless, the claims were made publicly, and few would have known the details.

It is also worth noting that, despite the regular argument that conjurors knew how mediums did it, conjurors rarely explained the details. However, on the rare occasions that they did, we can gain some insight into what might have gone through people's heads at the time. For example, in 1860, *Once a Week* published an article entitled 'Spirit-rapping made easy', under the name 'Katerfelto', which explained how one might produce spirit raps, and make a small card table seem to float in the dark by using one's legs to lift the table. Subsequently, the well-known writer and spiritualist, William Howitt, wrote to the *Morning Star*, challenging Katerfelto to explain Home's phenomena as described in the *Cornhill* account. That same month, 'Spirit-rapping made easy, no. II' appeared in response to Howitt's challenge. Katerfelto stated at the outset that he intended to explain 'how Mr Home floated about the top of the room . . . and all the other wonders mentioned in the "Cornhill" narrative'. He then explained certain simple mediumistic tricks, but did not begin to deal with Home's phenomena, and ended by referring to 'the performances of Mr Home, which I am about to examine, [are more impressive, but the secret] when I have explained it, will be found to be ridiculously simple in proportion to its effects on the bewildered and mystified spectators (to be continued)'.[99] It was not until later, in the final installment, that Katerfelto finally revealed 'the secret' of Home's levitation, and it is hard not to imagine further disappointment among his readers.

According to Katerfelto, Home had a lantern and a slide of himself, and had used these to project an image of himself onto the curtain, giving the illusion that he was floating in the air. In order to do this, however, he would have had to smuggle the lantern into the room, light the candle in an otherwise dark room without being noticed, and project the image of himself over the heads of everyone there, without a single person turning round to see where the overhead beam was coming from. This was Katerfelto's 'ridiculously simple' secret, one that had 'bewildered and mystified spectators'. When it was brought to Home's attention, he was bewildered at its ridiculous simplicity, and the spirits (we are told) playfully destroyed a copy of the magazine at a séance that evening.[100]

No doubt there were those who glanced at the article, or heard about it second hand, and got a vague impression that all had been explained. But anyone who took an interest in the subject, or knew any of the individuals involved, or simply compared it to the original account, would have almost certainly concluded that this was an inadequate explanation. Thus, one could reject the reality of the phenomena on the basis that conjurors knew what was going on, but there must have been many, and not only spiritualists, who regarded their explanations as unsatisfactory; in which case, they might have had the opposite effect, as evidence that even conjurors could not explain what was going on. Nevertheless, the appeal to the authority of conjurors remained a standard argument for those who wished to reject the reality of the phenomena, but did not feel they had an adequate explanation themselves.[101]

There was, however, another line of argument based upon the question of expertise, namely that those who observed the phenomena were not sufficiently competent observers. The need for scientific observers had been stressed by critics earlier, for example by the zoologist and Fellow of the Royal Society, E. R. Lankester. He had concluded that 'the evidence of Prof Faraday was of more value in reference to Table Turning and Knocking than is the testimony of large numbers of persons not so well practised in observing'.[102] This, of course, was disputed by spiritualists, and the need for scientific expertise, and what precisely counted as such, became a major thread in the dispute.

This was, in part, because of the extraordinary nature of the phenomena, something that was also stressed by critics from the start. As

Chambers' Journal had stated in 1856: '[i]f this be a world of natural law, as most enlightened persons believe it to be, it is impossible that such things can be realities: they can only be some form of delusion or fallacy'.[103] Others expressed greater anxiety over the implications of such phenomena. The *Saturday Review* admitted that not all the reported facts had been explained, and noted their conflict with the known laws of nature, stressing that '[u]nless such laws are absolute . . . all confidence in cause and effect vanishes . . . Chaos has come again. The reign of Chance is inaugurated'.[104] Some years later, the *Athenaeum* noted that '[u]p to this time, the efforts of scientific men have been directed to explain an orderly world; but . . . [this] will certainly result in a great universal Bedlam. Incoherence and inconsistency will be the rule.'[105]

Thus, like critics of mesmerism, critics of spiritualism highlighted not only the extraordinariness of the claim, but also its potential dangers. In the process of doing the former, they stressed the inadequacy of the evidence, and the need for proper scepticism in the face of such extraordinary claims. In relation to the latter, spiritualism posed a threat not only to the sanity of individuals but also to rational thinking more generally, with regular comparisons being made to witchcraft. Appeals to ordinary explanations, to the need for particular expertise, to the extraordinariness of such claims and to the harm that they could do, continued to be made by critics of spiritualism, as they had been made by critics of mesmerism, and as we shall see, this has continued since.

Meanwhile, it is sufficient to note that anyone who wished to argue that the phenomena were not real could simply appeal to some kind of trickery, even if they were unable to provide a method. In doing so, disbelief could always be maintained in the face of unexplained phenomena. And, as in the case of mesmerism, beliefs that séance phenomena were real could also be sustained, even in the face of evidence that they were the result of fraud. When mediums failed to produce any phenomena, when conjurors duplicated what mediums did, and even when mediums were exposed in trickery, beliefs in the reality of the phenomena could nevertheless be maintained.

The framing of failures, duplications and exposures

Mediums often failed to produce any phenomena, but this could be treated as the result of conditions that were not conducive to the spirits. Séance phenomena were sensitive not only to light, but also to a range of other variables. There were, William Gregory pointed out, 'innumerable causes of failure', from the 'health of the subject' to 'the state of the weather', but particularly the influence of those present, and 'above all, if they be skeptical, prejudiced or excited by controversy'. Thus, when mediums failed to produce phenomena in front of critics, it was due to the latter insisting upon 'improper and absurd conditions, such as no one who is acquainted with the phenomena, or has any conception of the numerous sources of error and failure, can think of accepting'. In such cases, failure was 'highly probable'.[106]

Like the failures of mesmeric clairvoyants, then, the failures of mediums could be attributed to the ignorance and prejudice of investigators. In doing do, the need for proper acquaintance with the true nature of the phenomena was reinforced. Failures could be framed as evidence not only of the elusive nature of the phenomena but also of their reality, since (like failures in mesmerism) they pointed to the unlikelihood of fraud. Mediums were not in control of the spirits, and so could not, like stage conjurors, simply demonstrate such feats at will. Thus, for example, the fact that Home was not in control of the phenomena, and therefore often disappointed his sitters, was presented as evidence of a lack of trickery.[107]

Séance phenomena were also regularly duplicated by stage conjurors. John Henry Anderson performed spirit-rapping exposes from 1855, and John Nevil Maskelyne, who took over from Anderson as the most famous conjuror-debunker in Britain, began his career in 1864 when he began to duplicate the Davenport brothers' spirit cabinet.[108] These, and several other conjurors, explicitly framed their shows as evidence that séance phenomena could be produced by trickery, a strategy later used by Houdini and many other conjurors since.

The main response of spiritualists was to claim that these were not accurate duplications. One witness pointed out that the raps he heard at Home's séances were 'very unlike the Great Wizard's [Anderson's] raps, and occurred indifferently, as I said before, in all places and corners of the chamber', adding that the medium operated 'without any paraphernalia which would characterise a wizard's art'.[109] It was repeatedly said that the conditions in which mediums worked were different, with neither stage apparatus nor opportunities for preparation, and with controls against trickery permitted throughout, and that conjurors would not be able to duplicate the phenomena in the same conditions.[110] 'No conjurer permits you to hold his hands while he is performing his tricks', said one witness, who challenged Anderson and Robert-Houdin to perform their normal repertoire while their hands were held by members of the audience.[111] Comparing Anderson's performance to the events of the séance room, the extremely popular *Family Herald* stated, 'there is no more resemblance between his rapping and theirs than there is between the lowing of an ox and the song of a titmouse'.[112]

That such distinctions were made not only by spiritualists but also non-spiritualists and the press suggests there might have been something in this. Indeed, when periodicals framed the phenomena as trickery, and cited conjuring performances in support, they cited straightforward conjuring effects more often than pseudo-spiritualist demonstrations, suggesting that the latter were not as effective as intended.[113] And, some years later, when a former fraudulent medium revealed the methods he and other mediums used, he noted that '[t]here is absolutely no resemblance of any kind or description, to the séance of the "medium", in these alleged exposes of the professional magician'.[114] In other words, rejecting such duplications as invalid was not such an odd thing to do, but regardless of whether or not it was warranted, it was a means of maintaining the position that séance phenomena were not the result of trickery.

On the other hand, duplications could be accepted as similar to the real thing, and therefore as evidence of the real thing. For example, when Benjamin Coleman saw Maskelyne perform the spirit cabinet, he was so impressed that he concluded that Maskelyne was a genuine medium.[115] And when the comic actor, Edward Sothern, performed duplications of the phenomena of Daniel Home and the Davenports, they were regarded as so similar that some spiritualists claimed the phenomena were genuine.[116] Reports of Indian jugglers being able to escape from ropes, a traditional feat of street conjurors, were similarly framed as real (to the amusement, it seems, of the jugglers themselves).[117] Thus, the duplications of conjurors could either be rejected as inadequate duplications, or else be reframed as evidence of genuine phenomena.

Similarly, when it was claimed that mediums had been exposed as frauds, this was also denied. The reported exposures of the Fox sisters, or Mrs Hayden, were dismissed as invalid early on, as were those of countless others later.[118] On one occasion, the medium Mrs Marshall claimed to have contacted the lost missionary explorer, David Livingstone. When asked what had happened to him, the spirit (Dr Livingstone, presumably) said that 'savages had boiled his body and ate it'. Following the subsequent discovery of Livingstone, who was alive and well in Tanzania, a witness was asked what he thought of this. He answered that, clearly, the spirit had been lying. He was then asked how he could tell the difference between a lying spirit and a lying medium. 'You cannot tell', he replied, 'but in this case it was the spirit that was lying'.[119]

Even when spiritualists accepted that mediums had cheated, they were nevertheless framed as genuine mediums. This was the case with Charles Foster, who (it will be remembered) had been seen by witnesses who regarded trickery as 'utterly impossible', and who were 'not very easily deceived'. Nevertheless, Foster was subsequently caught cheating by spiritualists on more than one occasion. When this happened, the *Spiritual Magazine* declared: 'We believe Mr. Foster to be a medium... of remarkable powers, but we know him also to deceive and to cheat, noting that we believe it to be lamentably common that real mediums will occasionally "help the Spirits".'[120] Like George Goble, Foster was genuine but cheated when necessary (after all, he was not in control of the spirits), and his genuineness was warranted by appeals to other séances (in which trickery had been ruled out).

The same happened with Colchester, a medium who demonstrated similar feats to those of Foster, and about whom one witness had said: '[q]uerelous sceptics may save themselves the trouble of speculating on whether or not I may have been deceived by a sleight-of-hand trick. There was no trick in the case. It was broad daylight, and no possibility of deception'.[121] A few months later, when Colchester was caught cheating, the *Spiritual Magazine* stated: '[w]e do not agree that Mr Colchester is not a medium, for we know him to be one, and have seen remarkable phenomena in his presence'.[122] Like Foster, he was denounced for 'mixing fact and fraud', but the facts remained evidence of genuine phenomena. Indeed, spiritualists took credit for having detected fraud, something that, the *Spiritual Magazine* noted, others had failed to do.[123] In this way, the existence of fake phenomena could be used to argue for the existence of genuine phenomena, providing that one was competent to distinguish between the two. Nobody doubted that some phenomena were fake, but this had no bearing on the real phenomena. Spiritualists made analogies with counterfeit money, or pointed out that 'wigs do not prove that there are no genuine heads of hair, sets of false teeth that there are no natural sets'.[124] Indeed, the analogies suggested more, since the production of such counterfeits followed from the existence of the genuine article. Nevertheless, what mattered was that one could separate the wheat from the chaff.

Thus, exposures could be framed as evidence in favour of the reality of the phenomena. They demonstrated that witnesses were competent to detect trickery, which made those séances in which it had been ruled out that much more convincing. The occasional need to resort to trickery was an unfortunate result of the nature of the phenomena, over which the medium had no control. And sometimes fraud was framed as the work of the spirits themselves. For example, when a witness reported seeing the figure of Ira Davenport walking around the room when he was supposed to be tied up, this was explained as evidence not of his having escaped from the rope, but rather of a spirit double.[125] The 'spirit double' theory was later used to explain why other mediums were seen moving freely when they were supposed to be tied up.[126]

One of the attempts to expose the Davenports was to smear ink or paint on a 'spirit hand' that appeared during the séance. Afterwards, the mediums' hands could be checked for ink or paint. However, when it was reported that ink had been found on the hands of one of the Davenport brothers, it was suggested that the ink had somehow been transported from the spirit hand to the hand of the medium.[127] The same argument was made when a boy medium was found with black marks on his hands after a 'spirit hand' had pulled the blackened hair of a sitter. 'Instead of proving the boy an impostor, it indicates the existence of a [magnetic] law', the witness argued, 'it should be taken as evidence of the genuineness of the manifestations, rather than as proof of trickery'.[128]

On the other hand, when it was accepted that mediums had indeed been caught cheating, this could also be framed as evidence of the phenomena, by arguing that their behaviour was caused by the phenomena. A cheating medium might be in a trance, and the cheating the product of 'conscious somnambulism', or else she might be under 'bad spiritual influence'.[129] As one witness of the Davenport brothers put it, '[s]pirits made the boys do what they were unconscious of doing of [sic] themselves'.[130] And even when the mediums were held responsible for having deliberately faked the phenomena, the argument that genuine mediums occasionally cheated could apply, and indeed was used in relation to the Davenports and several other mediums.[131]

Thus, while many expressed the view that such exposures were clear examples of fraud, there was always a way to frame them as supportive of one's beliefs. As we have seen, the same could be done for failures and duplications. In this way, beliefs were maintained in the face of (what for most was) obvious evidence that the phenomena could be produced by trickery. Such arguments may seem like stubborn attempts to cling onto beliefs in the face of the facts, as if spiritualists were reluctant to give up on their newly found conviction. Extraordinary beliefs have long been explained as the product of wishful thinking, and in the case of Victorian spiritualism, the link has been made with the contemporary 'crises of faith'; in short, people believed in spiritualism because it provided a much-desired crutch in support of an increasingly challenged Christian faith. When we see what seem like desperate attempts by spiritualists to reject evidence of fraud, it is easy to attribute these to a need for faith in God, or in life after death, rather than to rational thought. However, the inadequacy of this explanation is clear when we take a more detailed view of extraordinary belief, as we shall now discuss.

Discussion

Spiritualist beliefs were responses to demonstrations and reports of the phenomena of the séance. These were designed to be convincing, even if they did not convince everyone, and provided a basis for various beliefs about séance phenomena. The arguments that followed were very similar to those that had been deployed in disputes about mesmerism, including all the ways in which failures, duplications and exposures could be framed in support of the reality of the phenomena. Thus, whatever one makes of these arguments, religious concerns did not have to be present in order to make them. Neither was religious belief sufficient, of course, since almost everyone involved was a Christian, and the vast majority expressed no belief in the phenomena of spiritualism. This included the most prominent critics, such as Brewster, Faraday and Carpenter, all of whom expressed their Christian faith as they expressed disbelief in séance phenomena. Indeed, when Brewster dismissed all manner of miracles as natural phenomena, yet made a special place for the ones in the Bible, he was making a point that many others would continue to make, and have continued to make since.[132] Just as one could believe in mesmeric phenomena without being religious, one could reject the phenomena of spiritualism while believing in the (equally extraordinary) miracles of the Bible. One could do so because beliefs in extraordinary phenomena are based upon particular events.

No doubt some Christians found solace in spiritualism, and certainly this is what some of them said, but there were also many (perhaps the majority of) Christian ministers who described séance phenomena as real, but as the work of the devil.[133] Furthermore, there were non-Christian spiritualists, and countless others who framed the phenomena as real, but not as supernatural.[134] The genuineness of the facts, whatever the theory, was a more common theme than one might imagine, since many of those who framed the facts as real declined to frame them as the work of the spirits. One witness had 'not yet found a place in my system for the phenomena, but that they were genuine phenomena, is settled in my mind'.[135] Another 'left it for science to explain', while another 'express[ed] no opinion as to the cause', and others made similar disclaimers.[136] William Gregory told spiritualists in 1856 that he inclined towards the spiritual hypothesis, but was not entirely convinced, and repeated this position in 1863.[137] Another witness wrote to Home, explaining that 'while admitting the extraordinary character of the phenomena that occur when you are present, I never could feel convinced that they emanated from the volition of the spirits'.[138] Some witnesses explicitly stated they did not accept that the phenomena were spiritual, others were not yet convinced.[139] According to Home's widow, several others were convinced that the phenomena were genuine without admitting spiritual agency.[140] Indeed, a study of Home, the most convincing of Victorian mediums, suggests that, while almost all of his witnesses framed the phenomena as genuine, about half of them did not frame them as the work of spirits.[141]

All of these people framed the phenomena as real, but not as supernatural, and this was not a rejection of the supernatural per se. If spiritualist beliefs were the result of a crisis of faith, one has to wonder why the overwhelming majority of Christians declined to believe in spiritualism, including so many of those who expressed belief in the reality of the phenomena. It has been argued previously that reports of séance phenomena, rather than being understood in terms of a crisis of faith, are better seen in terms of a crisis of evidence, in which widely reported unexplained phenomena provoked a dispute about what counted as reliable evidence.[142] However, as we have seen, this was not new to spiritualism, nor, as we shall see, has it gone away.

In terms of understanding beliefs, however, the variety of positions one could hold, about séance phenomena or biblical miracles, or for that matter more recent Catholic miracles, shows again that extraordinary beliefs were based upon particular phenomena. It also shows the range of beliefs one could hold about the same phenomena. One could attend a séance, and believe that the phenomena one observed were real, but not supernatural, or that they were supernatural, but not the work of spirits. One could believe that they were fake, but that other phenomena were real, whether natural or supernatural, spiritual or diabolical. Or one could believe that all séance phenomena were fake, regardless of what one thought of biblical miracles, and despite not being able to explain what one had seen. In short, like beliefs about the phenomena of mesmerism, there were several different beliefs that one could have about the events in question, which cannot be captured by a simplistic dichotomy between belief and disbelief.

Then, of course, there was the question of what one believed about such phenomena in relation to science, since already, by the end of the 1860s, some scientists were arguing that such phenomena were not incompatible with scientific knowledge. With the emergence of formal scientific investigation into séance phenomena, the dispute was about to become more concerned with scientific matters. In the process, beliefs about extraordinary phenomena would continue to be expressed and warranted as before, but increasingly in terms of formal scientific discourse, and with a greater dependence upon scientific expertise, and what scientists regarded as extraordinary. Spiritualist phenomena were about to be reframed as natural rather than supernatural, as the world was told of the first psychic phenomenon.

FIVE

The making of psychic phenomena

The birth of psychic phenomena

In 1871, Daniel Home sat in a room with some very respectable gentlemen scientists. William Crookes was a Fellow of the Royal Society, and William Huggins was its vice-president. In front of them, and three other observers, Home caused an accordion to float inside a cage, and altered the weight of a plank of wood, without (apparently) touching them. Unable to provide an ordinary explanation for what happened at these strange experiments, Crookes announced that he had discovered a 'psychic' force.[1]

The meaning of the term 'psychic' was ambiguous, since no theory was attached to it; indeed, it did little more than frame the phenomena as natural rather than supernatural. Nevertheless, this was enough to place its investigation within the remit of science, which was fundamental to the meaning of psychic phenomena, and to psychical research since. It was, however, no less problematic than the attempt to frame earlier phenomena as compatible with science. Crookes may have been a Fellow of the Royal Society, the chemist who had discovered the element thallium and editor of the *Quarterly Journal of Science*, but such scientific credentials were not in themselves sufficient. Thus, from the moment that Crookes went public about his investigations into the phenomena of spiritualism, he made the case in ways that were designed to be convincing.

It is worth being clear that, from the start, Crookes (whatever else he was doing) was expressing belief in the reality of séance phenomena, based upon the exclusion of ordinary explanations. In the introduction to his initial announcement that he was investigating the phenomena, he stated:

> That certain physical phenomena occur under circumstances in which they cannot be explained by any physical law at present known, is a fact of which I am as certain as I am of the most elementary fact in chemistry... I have both seen and heard, in a manner which would make unbelief impossible, things called spiritual, which cannot be taken by a rational being to be capable of explanation by imposture, coincidence or mistake.[2]

Similarly, his experiments were demonstrations of the reality of the phenomena, designed to exclude ordinary explanations. The phenomena might have been produced by Home, but they were demonstrated within a frame of formal scientific experiment, designed by Crookes to rule out every possible alternative explanation. In the process, like so many before him, Crookes provided standard arguments concerning the extraordinariness of the phenomena: he had been a sceptic too, but had been forced to believe in the facts; these were facts, regardless of what theory might account for them, and were compatible with scientific thinking, while rejecting the facts due to prejudice was not. And, of course, it was a quest for truth and, therefore, a good thing too.[3]

Crookes' reports are particularly interesting, however, for the ways in which they constructed scientific expertise. Framing séance phenomena as natural rather than supernatural, their investigation was presented explicitly as a scientific matter. Crookes described science as a process based upon accurate observation and a complete lack of preconceptions about what facts were possible. This allowed him to present himself as an ideal scientist, that is as one who was trained in exact observation and who had no preconceived notions about what was possible. He also used this definition of science to engage in clear boundary-work, by arguing that scientists (not the public, and certainly not spiritualists) were the ones best qualified to observe accurately such phenomena. However, most scientists were prejudiced against such phenomena, and science was also based upon a lack of prejudice. Thus, Crookes' presented himself as more competent than either spiritualists or scientific critics of spiritualism.[4]

Crookes' reports, then, were expressions of belief and a means of constructing his own expertise, and the construction of adequate expertise was, as it had been for mesmerists and spiritualists before him, a means of warranting his belief in the reality of the phenomena. That said, this could be seen as a more formal scientific project than anything previously, accompanied by formal scientific language and described in a recognized scientific journal by a Fellow of the Royal Society. Naturally enough, it provoked a response, one that was in line with prior criticisms of extraordinary phenomena, but also one that engaged directly with specific matters of scientific expertise.

The main response was from William Benjamin Carpenter, and it was (whatever else it was) an expression of belief about séance phenomena. According to Carpenter, such phenomena were the product of deception and self-deception, extraordinary in relation to natural law, and a danger to be guarded against.[5] In terms of what counted as scientific expertise, Carpenter accepted Crookes' description of science as being based on accurate observation and a lack of preconceived notions, but argued that it was he, not Crookes, who best exemplified these ideals. He questioned the scientific credentials of Crookes and his fellow observers and, like earlier critics of extraordinary phenomena, denied the charge of prejudice. '[I]t was only after [repeated failure in investigating such phenomena] that we, and our scientific friends associated with us, abandoned the pursuit, as involving a waste of time that might be profitably employed upon worthier objects of investigation'.[6] And, like earlier critics, he accused Crookes of being the prejudiced one.[7]

In the process, as Richard Noakes has shown, Carpenter engaged in his own boundary-work, by appealing to a particular version of expertise. While Crookes had stressed the primacy of technical expertise and the use of apparatus as a reliable means of observation in a scientific investigation of this sort, Carpenter stressed the importance of psychological processes that might mislead the senses, and argued that general scientific rather than specialist technical training was necessary, including proper mental training.[8] For Carpenter, spiritualists had been victims of their own prepossessions and expectations, and a prejudice in favour of such phenomena, of which he also accused Crookes, was a sign of a lack of expertise in such an investigation.

As Forbes had done in his debunking of mesmeric clairvoyance, Carpenter rejected the phenomena by deploying a psychology of error, in which erroneous beliefs were the result of mental fallacies, including the inclination to believe. 'There are *moral* sources of error', he explained, and 'one of the most potent of these is a proclivity to believe in the reality of spiritual communications, which places those who are not constantly on their guard against its influence under the two fold danger of deception – alike from *within* and from *without*.'[9] As Carpenter's psychological expertise made his own beliefs more authoritative, his psychology of error equated an inclination to believe with inadequate expertise in observation. Thus, beliefs in séance phenomena were the result of incompetent observation due to a lack of scepticism.

By deploying a psychology of error, then, Carpenter could warrant his own beliefs and construct his expertise in such a way that each supported the other. On the one hand, he had the necessary expertise that others (such as Crookes) did not, and such expertise made his views more reliable. On the other hand, his sceptical views made him a more competent observer than those inclined to believe, and so his beliefs enhanced his expertise. A similarly circular argument applied to believers in séance phenomena, whose beliefs were the result of insufficient scepticism, which made them incompetent observers, and led to erroneous observation. With the emergence of scientific Psychology, a psychology of error would continue to be deployed in order to debunk extraordinary phenomena, to deploy the concept of belief in order to warrant one belief and explain away another, and to construct the worth of psychological expertise in the process.

If one wishes to understand the dispute surrounding paranormal phenomena today, one could do worse than start by examining the dispute surrounding the alleged discovery of a 'psychic' force. The kinds of arguments, which themselves were not new, sound remarkably familiar to anyone involved in parapsychology today. Every possible ordinary explanation that one might imagine was proposed by critics, from suggestions that Crookes lied, or was hypnotized by a werewolf, to the idea that Home relied upon a trick accordion, or a special plank of wood.[10] All of these theories were excluded by Crookes, some more patiently than others, along with an invitation to fellow scientists to observe the experiments for themselves. Since these were, for the most part, declined by those who suspected there was nothing in it, the bulk of the evidence came from those who could be seen as being inclined to believe. And, as we have seen, those who were inclined to believe could not be trusted to report believable facts, even if one was a Fellow of the Royal Society.

There was, of course, much more to it, but the particular result of this episode was that nobody has yet provided more than a generic explanation for what actually happened, and subsequent sceptics have had to resort to indirect evidence of Crookes' lack of competence. Thus, it has been noted, that Crookes also endorsed the phenomena of other mediums, such as Florence Cook, Mary Showers and Anna Eva Fay, all of whom were reportedly caught cheating.[11] Whether one regards this as an adequate argument is, of course, a subjective matter, and the fact that Crookes went on to become President of the Royal Society suggests, if nothing else, that his views about such phenomena were not generally regarded as indications of scientific incompetence. However, the exposure of Showers, and Crookes' endorsement of Fay, provide links to other relevant matters.

For example, Showers was caught cheating during a séance, while she was faking a spirit head, in the home of Edward Cox. Cox was a barrister whose legal training made him as keen an observer as everyone thought themselves to be. He was also, as it happened, the same barrister who had endorsed the unfortunate George Goble, and had maintained that Goble had genuine powers even after he had confessed to cheating.[12] More recently, Cox had been one of the other observers at Crookes' experiments with Home. Indeed, it had been Cox who had suggested to Crookes the term 'psychic' to describe the new force in natural rather than supernatural language. Cox went on to found the Psychological Society of Great Britain, which sought to investigate a range of phenomena that included what would today be seen as both psychological (e.g. memory and consciousness) and psychic (e.g. thought-reading and supersenuous perception). Cox's inaugural address of the society, as it stressed, among other things, its focus upon the facts, however extraordinary they might seem, and their compatibility with other areas of science, was a call for a science of psychology.[13] At the same time, Cox, a lawyer not a scientist, suggested that the application of the rules of evidence in law might be a more appropriate way of assessing psychological facts.[14] The society lasted only four years, with the death of Cox in 1879, but it was both the first psychological society in Britain, and a precursor to the Society for Psychical Research (SPR).[15]

The establishment of the SPR in 1882 was itself, in a sense, an expression of belief not only in the reality of (what were now) psychic phenomena, but also that this could be demonstrated to the scientific world. When one reads the inaugural address of its first president, the philosopher Henry Sidgwick, one finds the usual themes (the inadequacy of ordinary explanations, the facts being independent of theory, the competence of witnesses and the incredulity of critics, and so on) yet only one explicit expression of belief, and that is in thought-reading.[16] While the interests of the SPR covered a wide range of extraordinary phenomena, it was thought-reading that was of primary interest and, many felt, best supported by the evidence. It was also less controversial, in the aftermath of several well-publicized exposures of physical mediums. Indeed, it was the one phenomenon for which Sidgwick felt conclusive evidence had been obtained.

It is the phenomenon of thought-reading to which we now turn, and in particular to its most notorious exponent. He received only scant attention from the founders of the SPR, but he is nevertheless a useful case study that allows us to consider, and hopefully clarify, some of the confusion surrounding extraordinary beliefs.

The problems of framing mind-reading: the case of Washington Irving Bishop

In 1877, not for the first time, Charles Foster sat in a room with some very respectable ladies and gentlemen. This time, however, he was in New York, awaiting a performance of Washington Irving Bishop. Bishop, a young man of 21, was presenting an exposure of spiritualism, and had claimed that he could duplicate the feats of various mediums. When he announced that he could duplicate the pellet reading of Charles Foster, Foster stood up and challenged him to do so. Bishop agreed, and the battle commenced, with Foster going first.

The chairman selected an individual whom Foster did not know, who wrote down the name of a deceased relative on a piece of paper. This was rolled up into a pellet, mixed in among several other pellets and, though Foster neither saw nor touched the paper (or so it would have seemed), he announced the name that had been written on it. He then challenged Bishop to do the same. Bishop returned to the stage, and began to ramble. Despite being reminded by the chairman that he was there to demonstrate rather than talk, Bishop continued to make claims and challenge others, but did nothing. When the chairman finally called time, Bishop ran from the stage.[17]

This may not have been his finest hour, but Washington Irving Bishop certainly had his moments. After all, far from being a mere debunker, his career was largely concerned with demonstrating extraordinary phenomena. Only the previous year, the son of a spiritualist medium had been working with Anna Eva Fay, and had framed her demonstrations as genuine by appealing to particular scientific expertise. 'Mr Bishop begs respectfully to state that Miss Fay, the celebrated spiritual-physical medium', he had announced in an advert in the *New York Herald*, 'as to the genuineness of her manifestations, is indorsed [sic] by William Crookes, F.R.S. and other members of the Royal Society'.[18]

After three months, however, Bishop had fallen out with Fay and published an exposure of her entire act in the *Daily Graphic* entitled: 'The greatest humbug yet: how Professor Crook's [sic] 'gifted and wonderful' medium, Anna Eva Fay, performs her tricks'.[19] The article had been accompanied by a facsimile of a letter from Crookes, in which the latter declared his belief in the genuineness of Fay's powers. Bishop had also begun to perform the Fay act, followed by an explanation of how she did it, and (at least according to the advertising) included the feats of other mediums such as the Davenports, Daniel Home and Charles Foster. Despite his encounter with the latter, he continued to perform spiritualist exposures, even if these were not accurate duplications of what happened at a séance.

Following his encounter with Foster in New York, Bishop saw the thought-reading act of John Randall Brown. Brown would ask for an object to be hidden in a location that he did not know, and then by having some physical contact with the person (typically, by holding the wrist), he would ask the person to think of its location.

Brown would then find it without any apparent clues being given. His ability had been tested by George Beard, the physiologist, who gave it the name 'muscle-reading', because it depended upon reading subtle muscle movements of the person with whom the reader was in contact, and it has been performed by countless people since.[20]

Bishop quickly recognized the potential of the act, learned the secrets, then came to Britain, where it was then unknown, billing himself as the 'world's first mind reader'.[21] When he arrived in London in 1881, he met with William Benjamin Carpenter, performed some mind-reading feats for him, and obtained a letter of introduction in which Carpenter recommended Bishop's skills as 'of great value to the Physiologist and the Psychologist'.[22] This led to investigations by many of the most eminent scientists of the time, which were reported in the *Lancet*, the *British Medical Journal* and *Nature*.[23] This, in turn, provoked further disputes about what Bishop could do, and how it might be explained, and the controversy, though it has been discussed by others, deserves a closer look.

As Roger Luckhurst has shown, Bishop played a significant role in the emergence of the notion of telepathy, but he is also an ideal figure to examine the murky framing of mind-reading. Indeed, there remains some confusion about how Bishop framed what he did: it has been said that he 'never claimed more than physiological skill'; that he claimed 'genuine psychic powers'; and even that he did not claim to possess 'exceptional powers of will or receptivity' but rather an 'ability to receive thoughts and sensations via undiscovered psychological capacities... which would be named "telepathy"'.[24] If this seems confusing now, imagine how the Victorians felt, as they tried to figure out what was going on. Nevertheless, the ways in which Bishop framed what he did were fundamental to what people believed.

The confusion has come from the fact that Bishop was, like similar performers before and since, ambiguous and inconsistent. This should not really be surprising since, despite having been raised by spiritualist parents, he assisted in demonstrations of fake mediumship, then publicly debunked the feats of mediums, despite not being able to do what he claimed. Furthermore, when in London, and between anti-spiritualism performances, he applied to join the British National Association of Spiritualists (presumably for publicity reasons), and in several towns arranged charity benefits, and then took the majority of the profits (presumably for financial reasons).[25] In short, he was in the business of making a living by whatever means necessary and, unlike scientists then and academic historians since, was concerned with neither truth nor coherency. Inconsistency continued in his demonstrations of mind-reading, which were deliberately ambiguous in meaning at a time when recognizable categories were scarce.

Indeed, the framing of such performances was a complicated matter even before Bishop. Brown, the man from whom Bishop had learned the skill, and who was regularly clear that his skills were entirely physiological, nevertheless occasionally gave demonstrations that excluded this explanation: for example, in one demonstration, a man several blocks from the theatre held a long wire to his head, and simply thought of a number; Brown, holding the other end of the wire, told him the number of which he was thinking. This was not muscle-reading, but something else, possibly involving the use of a confederate.[26] However, by excluding muscle-reading as an explanation, Brown framed his performance as something more extraordinary (i.e. what would now be termed paranormal).

However, Bishop was even less consistent than Brown, claiming that he read minds, or thoughts, or bodies, or claiming not to know what he was doing. Billing himself as a 'mind-reader' and 'thought-reader', he was deliberately ambiguous about what this meant. When Carpenter wrote a letter to the *Daily Telegraph*, in which he explained Bishop's standard feats in terms of reading unconscious cues, Bishop included the letter in his advertising material, but with that explanation deleted.[27] Indeed, at times, he explicitly claimed that he could read minds without physical contact. When challenged by the MP, Henry Labouchère, to read what was in someone's mind (in this case, the serial number of a banknote sealed inside an envelope), Bishop accepted, and subsequently claimed that he had succeeded when he had not.[28]

When he demonstrated his skills in front of a group of eminent psychological scientists, including George Romanes, Francis Galton and George Croom Robertson, Bishop claimed that he did not know how he did what he did, yet maintained that he could sometimes read the thoughts of people without physical contact. This was tried, and succeeded once, but failed thereafter, and was dismissed by Romanes as an 'accident'.[29] Later, as mesmerists and spiritualists had done, Bishop claimed that such failures did not account for his successes.[30] Meanwhile, it is worth noting, because it is so easy to miss, that this was a test of non-contact mind-reading (i.e. telepathy, as it was about to be defined), conducted by some extremely eminent scientists, and published in Nature; it was, by definition, an example of psychical research.

Hardly any wonder, then, that people did not know what to believe. Clearly, Bishop was doing something that was regarded by many as extraordinary, and scientists had investigated this and provided an explanation of sorts, though how much of this was understood is difficult to say. This was not simply a matter of Bishop's inconsistency, since scientists who observed him were less than clear. In letters to the London Standard, Carpenter expressed the need to clarify what he had meant, and a fellow witness (on the same page) claimed that his explanation was inadequate.[31] However, the dispute in Nature is particularly interesting for what it reveals about the nature of belief.

In his report, Romanes criticized Carpenter ('the great opponent of all humbug') for recommending Bishop to the attention of scientists because 'the result is to endow the powers which were afterwards exhibited with a fictitious degree of importance in the eyes of the public'. To Romanes, the method was obvious enough, that Bishop was 'guided by the indications unconsciously given through the muscles of his subjects – differential pressure playing the part of the words "hot" and "cold" in the childish game which these words signify'. There was, for Romanes, nothing extraordinary to see in experiments he framed as 'an ordinary drawing-room amusement', nor was Bishop endowed with 'any unusual degree of tactile sensibility or power of distinguishing between small variations of resistance and pressure'.[32]

Accused of having made a mountain out of a molehill, Carpenter responded by framing Bishop as more extraordinary than Romanes appreciated, by citing other feats that deserved careful testing. One of these was his 'power of naming words and numbers previously written and sealed up in private'. This, Carpenter noted, Bishop had 'repeatedly performed in the presence of distinguished medical and scientific men in the United States... and, also before a like assemblage in Edinburgh'.[33] But this feat, which was framed as genuine by Carpenter by attributing it to the reading of unconscious cues, and by citing the authority of scientific experts who had observed it, was not muscle-reading.

What Bishop had performed in Edinburgh was something rather different. He had given a private demonstration to some local dignitaries, and then a public performance the following day at the music hall. The public performance had been billed as an exposure of spiritualism, and during the show he had performed a supposed duplication of the Foster pellet feat (though he had described it as a 'thought-reading trick'). He had asked someone to write the name of a deceased person on a slip of paper, this had been placed inside an envelope, and Bishop had then revealed the name. This being an exposure, he had then explained to the audience how it was done: he had switched the original slip of paper for another one hidden in his palm, the latter had been placed inside the envelope, then he had secretly read what was on the original slip, and subsequently announced the name. This technique, generally known as the 'billet switch', was actually used by Charles Foster, and has been used by performers to the present day. At this point, however, one of those present in the audience, who had also attended the private demonstration the previous evening, claimed that this did not explain what Bishop had done at the private gathering. Bishop explained that this was indeed the method, 'that he had not let the audience see him do so, but he could never have told the name if he had not examined the paper beforehand'.[34] In short, in this particular demonstration of mind-reading, Bishop was not muscle-reading; he was simply reading.

So much for the method, but the effect was mind-reading without any physical contact. Though it relied upon sleight of hand, Carpenter attributed the demonstration to Bishop's 'acute recognition of indications unconsciously given' by the person who knew what was written on the paper, and these 'indications' had to be recognized from a distance. Carpenter was referring to an effect that is very familiar today, the ability to know what people are thinking simply by looking at them. Like many today, Carpenter attributed the feat to genuine psychological abilities (which Bishop, like others since, did not actually possess). Indeed, in a rare moment of honesty, Bishop had admitted as much in Edinburgh. However, he did not admit it to Carpenter, and the expert on unconscious processes framed the feat as genuine.

Carpenter also cited another extraordinary feat he had been shown by Bishop. A subject had selected a playing card from the pack, which had been shuffled by Bishop, who then dealt sixteen cards face down onto the table, in four rows of four cards each. Bishop had held the subject's right hand, and asked him to drop his other hand onto any of the rows (vertical or horizontal) in order to eliminate it. This had been repeated until one row remained, then the subject had been given a choice of the upper two cards or the lower two of the remaining four, and then of the upper or lower of the last two. Thus, cards had been gradually eliminated, until the last card had been turned face up, and it had been the selected card. This had been done twice with members of Carpenter's family, and then with Carpenter himself, who said he could not explain how it was done, but ruled out luck (implicitly) and trickery (explicitly), and concluded that it was the result of unconscious influence.[35] Somehow, Carpenter was suggesting, he and members of his family had been guided in their choices without being aware of this.

This was indeed an extraordinary feat, assuming that it was not a trick, since as a letter in the next number of *Nature* pointed out, 'Dr Carpenter endows [Bishop] with the power of controlling the wills of his subjects'. The correspondent, Thomson Whyte, had attended Bishop's performance in Edinburgh, which he attributed to sleight of hand. He also provided a detailed explanation of how this latter feat could have been done by trickery (employing a very old technique, known to magicians as the 'equivoque'), and concluded that it was 'legerdemain by which he had duped the subjects of, I believe, the before-mentioned experiments'. However, Whyte noted, if he was wrong, and it was not 'a trick well known to schoolboys', then it was a case of 'will-compelling' and 'Dr Carpenter must invent a name for Mr Bishop's new power'.[36] Thus, the extraordinariness of Carpenter's view was appreciated at the time.

Such was Bishop's framing of his abilities that Carpenter excluded obvious ordinary explanations (such as chance and fraud) in favour of some kind of unconscious process that was as yet unexplained (hence the need for careful scientific investigation) and not simply physiological (since the first kind of feat was non-contact). Indeed, according to current scientific knowledge, this would count as paranormal, yet Carpenter felt it was compatible with 'scientific principles', while more sceptical folk begged to differ. This, of course, was not so different from what had been argued by mesmerists and spiritualists, who had long claimed that their as yet unexplained phenomena were compatible with science. It was also the position of Crookes and Cox, who had provided the new frame of 'psychic', and was soon to be the position of psychical researchers. But here it was being expressed by the most prominent sceptic of the age.

Following Thomson Whyte's letter in *Nature* was one from William Barrett, who had already proposed the formation of the society that would become the Society for Psychical Research. His letter made a distinction between the contact mind-reading associated with Bishop and non-contact mind-reading that he had observed elsewhere.[37] He would make the same distinction again, in the first paper of the *Proceedings of the SPR*, and the primary focus of the early SPR would be on this phenomenon that would soon be named 'telepathy'.[38] The meaning of the term has been discussed by Luckhurst, and the wealth of cultural associations he has identified no doubt made the notion more plausible for many.[39] As he has shown, fundamental to this was the notion of communication across space, hence the interest of SPR investigators in demonstrations that involved no physical contact between 'sender' and 'receiver'. Their early investigations of the Creery family, and of Blackburn and Smith, followed naturally from this line of enquiry (though this then raised the problem of excluding ordinary kinds of non-contact communication). Ironically, what Carpenter had described in *Nature* would have also qualified as psychic, had it been real, but Bishop (framed by Barrett as a contact mind-reader) was no longer of interest to the SPR.

Like countless similar performers since, Bishop was ambiguous about his methods, but gave the impression that there was something extraordinary going on, because extraordinary filled the theatre more successfully than ordinary. But what that meant was never clear, neither in the ways that he framed what he did, nor in how it was framed by scientists and the public. If one were to ask anyone who had seen, heard or read of Bishop, which would have been most of the reading public, whether they believed in mind-reading, a simple 'yes' or 'no' would have revealed very little about their beliefs. If Carpenter, the most prominent of scientific sceptics, could exclude chance and fraud in favour of a mysterious unexplained process (that has not been explained by science since), the less informed could hardly be blamed for believing that he could read minds and that this was in line with scientific thinking.

As it happens, Carpenter had already written about the 'psychology of belief', and had argued that extraordinary beliefs could be understood in terms of the plausibility of a given fact and the evidence for it having happened. In doing so, he had pointed out that what was plausible depended upon what one regarded as extraordinary, and what counted as adequate evidence depended upon whether observers were competent enough to exclude alternative explanations.[40] However, a science of psychology was not to appear in Britain for some time yet, while in Germany and the United States, a discipline of Psychology was already emerging. The birth of the new discipline was accompanied by a more energetic attempt to explain such beliefs, no more so than in the United States, where the boundaries between psychology and psychical research were the subject of some concern.

Scientific psychology and the psychology of error

> Weird notions and strange theories find a ready home in the disordered brains of such semi-morbid fanatics; and, when once they gain hold on the popular imagination and belief, such inhuman pages of history as those that record the horrors of witchcraft... the wide-spread misery of mental epidemics or the bestial self-tortures of crazed ascetics, must be written.[41]

Not stereotypical scientific language, but nevertheless how Joseph Jastrow introduced 'The psychology of spiritualism' to readers of *Science*, the organ of the American Association of the Advancement of Science, in 1886. For Jastrow, such beliefs were not only harmful but also proper objects of psychological enquiry, the product of 'dimly lit chambers, the brains flushed with excitement, and the judgment unsettled by intense expectancy'. Jastrow was the first American to obtain a PhD in Psychology and, less than two years later, founded one of the earliest Psychology departments in the United States. The first department had been founded in 1883, at Johns Hopkins University by G. S. Hall, a student of Wilhelm Wundt, who was about to found the *American Journal of Psychology* (*AJP*) and, a few years later, the American Psychological Association. In the first number of the *AJP*, Hall gave 18 pages to a review of the work of the SPR, in which he dismissed the evidence as inadequate, having been provided by 'amateurs and speculative psychologists', and such beliefs as harmful, the product of incompetent observation driven by wishful thinking.[42]

The birth of scientific psychology in America, then, was accompanied by active debunking of psychic phenomena. It was, after all, an opportunity to define the boundaries, and espouse the worth, of the new science. By expressing views about psychic phenomena, and those who believed in them, the new psychologists could both police the limits of the nascent discipline and demonstrate the value of psychological expertise. The attempts to draw boundaries between early American psychology and psychical research have been noted by historians for some time and, naturally enough, the dispute has been seen as an example of scientific boundary-work.[43] According to Deborah Coon, psychologists engaged in two 'modes of combat': by using the issue to pioneer a new field – the psychology of deception and belief; and by testing psychic claimants, in order to show that the phenomena were not real. Evidence of this can be seen in the activities and publications of several of the most eminent American psychologists of the time, who went about debunking spiritualism and psychical research in word and deed.[44]

However, if we consider this dispute in terms of belief, we can see that what these psychologists were doing was not so different from what had been done by earlier critics of extraordinary phenomena. After all, the 'psychology of deception and belief' was hardly a new field, amounting to little more than some articles published by a few individuals, primarily in popular journals. There was no specialist journal, no conference, not even a symposium that emerged from this endeavour. Indeed, there was precious little attempt even to synthesize the disparate writings of individual psychologists. Thus, when Norman Triplett published a doctoral dissertation on the psychology of deception in 1900, he was not even aware that Joseph Jastrow had published on the topic just a few years earlier.[45]

What Jastrow and Hall, and others too, were doing was deploying a psychology of error (at this stage, still little more than a line of argument), based upon a construction of psychological expertise, in order to debunk extraordinary phenomena. As others had done before them, they attributed belief in extraordinary phenomena to errors that they themselves, as experts, would not make. In doing so, they were warranting their own beliefs by constructing their own expertise as superior to that of believers, and the value of their expertise by presenting such beliefs as harmful. And they were doing so primarily in non-academic, rather than scientific, journals.

Thus, in another article by Jastrow, also entitled 'The psychology of spiritualism', but this time published in *Popular Science Monthly*: 'it is likely that the marvels of spiritualism will be, by believers in them, incorrectly and insufficiently reported. The first reason is to be found in the mental condition of the observer; if he be excited or deeply moved, his account can not but be affected, and essential details distorted'.[46] Once again, the psychology of error was being deployed in order to express the view that the phenomena were not real, and that belief was the result of incompetent observation, based in turn upon the 'mental condition' of the believer. Once again, the inherent incompetence of believers made scientific observation essential, and 'the fact that scientific examination everywhere reveals deception makes it extremely probable that, when exposure has not taken place, it is because there was no scientific examination'.[47] Thus, Jastrow equated belief with incompetence, a lack of detected fraud with an inability to find it, and an exposure of fraud with proper scientific examination. And, once again, there was a moral aspect to all of this: 'Let him understand that under the shelter of spiritualism men and women in all our large cities are daily and hourly preying upon the credulity of simple-minded folk, and obtaining money by means for which the law provides the jail'.[48] As Forbes and Carpenter had done, Jastrow presented such beliefs as not only wrong but also harmful, and scientific expertise as not only necessary but also desirable.

The arguments may not have been new, and may not have reflected a new field, but they were certainly worth making as the new discipline emerged; after all, it was not there yet. As Coon has pointed out, the boundary between the 'psychological' and the 'psychic' was fuzzy at best, and the position of William James only made things worse.[49] James was already generally recognized as the father figure of American psychology, having taught the subject at Harvard since 1875, and his *Principles of Psychology*, published in 1890, but based upon his thinking and teaching for many years, became a standard textbook of the discipline. However, James was also the most eminent advocate of psychical research in the United States, having helped form the American Society for Psychical Research (ASPR).

As far as James was concerned, the strongest case for psychic phenomena was supplied by Mrs Piper. Leonora Piper was a medium from Boston, who did not go in for 'physical' phenomena, but rather specialized in providing messages while in trance. She had impressed several psychical researchers, who had excluded ordinary explanations: the information contained in the messages seemed too accurate to be guesswork, and there seemed to be no other way that she could have discovered the information. This was the conclusion of Richard Hodgson, an investigator who had undoubted expertise, who had already debunked several mediums.[50] Having excluded chance and fraud, however, psychical researchers were divided upon whether this was psychic or supernatural. Hodgson came to believe that the messages were genuine spirit communications, while James attributed them to unconscious telepathy. Nevertheless, according to James, Mrs Piper was his 'white crow', since everyone agreed that there were fraudulent mediums, but it only took one genuine medium to demonstrate that psychic phenomena were real.[51]

James' psychological expertise may have been unquestionable, but his scientific expertise was not. The 'new psychology' was avowedly experimental, while James' had a preference for philosophical enquiry. Indeed, when he stressed the need for scientific evidence of psychic phenomena, it was not because he felt that such expertise was superior, but rather that it would be deemed more authoritative by the public.[52] Hence, no doubt, his ongoing frustration at the reluctance of scientific psychologists to engage with the topic.[53] The latter, of course, denied such prejudice.

Thus, the psychologist and editor of *Science*, James McKean Cattell, when accused of ignoring the investigations of Mrs Piper, denied ignorance of the matter, and claimed that he was simply unimpressed with the evidence. In doing so, he framed Mrs Piper's phenomena as the result of chance and fraud, and warranted his position with extracts from the 'five and only five well-known men of science' who had observed her séances, and who had been equally unimpressed.[54] James responded, but did not claim that he was also a man of science. Instead, he argued that this was an inadequate explanation, and accused Cattell of cherry-picking extracts; he then appealed to more impressive examples than those Cattell had cited, complained again of scientific prejudice, and challenged Cattell's philosophical expertise (accusing him of having made fundamental errors in logic).[55] As in prior disputes over extraordinary phenomena, each side appealed to different versions of expertise, and people tended to play to their strengths.

This particular dispute, of course, was also about the boundaries of scientific psychology. However, the dispute about boundaries was a disagreement about the reality of the phenomena, and it was not merely an argument between believers and disbelievers about what scientific psychology should be. The construction of a boundary between scientific psychology and psychical research was itself an expression of belief about the phenomena in question. After all, it was not the topic that was out of bounds, nor its experimental investigation, but rather how the phenomena were framed by the investigators. This, in effect, was what divided scientific psychology from unscientific psychical research.

We can see this in the dispute, just a few months later, between James and E. B. Titchener. Titchener wrote to *Science* on the subject of the 'feeling of being stared at'. This, he explained, was an erroneous belief based upon 'misinterpretation of fact', and he had carried out experiments to show this. He justified this investment of his time by appealing to the need to dispel 'a superstition which has deep and widespread roots in the popular consciousness'. He also praised the work of Lehmann and Hansen (1895), whose recent work in Germany had suggested that results in telepathy experiments could be explained by involuntary whispering of the subjects. According to Titchener, '[n]o scientifically-minded psychologist believes in telepathy. At the same time, the disproof of it . . . has probably done more for scientific psychology than could have been accomplished by any aloofness'.[56]

William James, no doubt aware that he had just been accused of not being 'scientifically minded', reproached Titchener for not having read criticisms of this paper, which showed how Lehmann and Hansen 'entirely failed to prove their point'. 'I think that an exploded document', he wrote, 'ought not to be left with the last word, even for the sake of "scientific psychology"'.[57] Titchener responded as Cattell had done: he had indeed read the criticisms, but he did not agree that the paper was 'exploded' (he had seen the fuse being handled, 'but I have not yet heard the detonation').[58] This, in turn, prompted James ('astounded at this hardness of hearing in my colleague') to write to Lehmann himself, and the latter's reply conceded that his theory was not yet established. This, concluded James, was precisely his own view, and Lehmann's work showed the latter to be an excellent psychical researcher.[59] Meanwhile, for Titchener, the paper remained 'a model of scientific method; [Lehmann] has shown us how borderland questions are to be attacked, and proved that the 'ordinary channels of sense' have unexplored resources'.[60]

Thus, what had begun (according to Titchener) as evidence against telepathy (the disproof of which he saw as part of scientific psychology) was reframed by James as possible evidence of telepathy (obtained, in James' view, via psychical research). The dispute over how to interpret the results may have ended by appealing to the author himself, but what the experiments represented was still up for grabs. For James, they had been investigating the possibility of telepathy, and this counted as psychical research. For Titchener, it was a scientific study of 'unexplored resources' on the borders of psychology. In principle, there was nothing to choose between them, since how one explained telepathy and where one drew the borders of psychology were ostensibly the topics of investigation. But each represented (and presented) different beliefs about the phenomena. What separated them was neither the worth of the investigation, nor its proper place within science, but whether the phenomena were framed as ordinary or extraordinary. This was not simply a dispute about what counted as proper objects of investigation, suitable methods or appropriate expertise – it was an expression of their different beliefs about psychic phenomena.

We can see this again in the study of Mrs Piper, supervised by Hall, and carried out in 1909 primarily by his assistant, Amy Tanner. Their aim, according to an early review of the published report, had been 'to analyze thoroughly the evidence for spirit communication and telepathy'.[61] In that sense, it was entirely in line with the aims of psychical research. However, Tanner positioned their attitude as distinct, as somewhere between the wishful thinking of believers and the intolerance of scientists, as 'an evaluation of the subject which will disclose the flaws in the evidence and yet which will do justice to the pioneer work of the Psychical Researchers and to the unsatisfied needs which have led to this outburst of belief in Spiritism'.[62] The study then went on to provide ordinary explanations for spirit communication and telepathy, and psychological evidence of a divided personality.

When the study was reviewed in the *AJP* by Jastrow, he described it as a scientific investigation of the psychology of Mrs. Piper, because her sittings 'represent distinct if evasive phases of a secondary personality. Therein lies their interest, and not in their supposed evidential revelations'.[63] Thus, on the one hand, tests of a spiritualist medium were scientific psychology so long as they were not concerned with the reality of the phenomena. However, on the other hand, such tests also represented an attempt to show that the phenomena were not real. 'Taking seriously the proposition [of telepathy]', Jastrow continued, 'psychology accepts the challenge and undertakes to show that a pervasive bias and a defective insight have shaped the data to distorted or imaginary significance'. So far as this was an investigation of Mrs Piper's psychic abilities, this could just as easily have been described as psychical research. But for Jastrow, as for Tanner, Hall and Titchener, psychic phenomena were not real, and scientific psychology studied such matters in order to provide ordinary explanations. This was what made such investigations scientific, what separated scientific psychology from psychical research, not the testing of medium's abilities, but rather the view that ordinary explanations were sufficient.

Of course, one had to appeal to the facts, and everyone was sceptical but open-minded. Hall had investigated the matter for years, he explained, and had once himself been a believer, and Tanner had begun with the view that 'probably telepathy was true, and perhaps spirit communication'.[64] Jastrow's review had noted their open-mindedness, that they had begun by 'taking seriously' the claims of psychical research. Such avowals of prior belief or, at the very least, open-mindedness had been deployed regularly by critics of mesmerism and spiritualism, just as avowals of prior scepticism had been regularly deployed by proponents. Thus, when Tanner stressed that she did not 'enter upon my work with any spirit of antagonism, but rather in a spirit of doubt that inclined toward belief', we might simply view this as one more example of a sceptical conclusion being prefaced by a denial of prejudice.[65] The rhetoric of neutrality was hardly new, though the framing of investigations of psychic phenomena as scientific psychology was, of course, a product of the emergence of scientific psychology. For most psychologists, however, despite their claims to prior open-mindedness, such investigations were only scientific when they were in the business of providing ordinary explanations. They were, in short, expressions and justifications of the belief that such phenomena were not real.

This was a simpler job in the case of other mediums, such as Eusapia Palladino, whose admitted fraudulent antics made her an easier target. Nevertheless, Palladino was no simple case: on the one hand, she was regularly caught cheating, even by those who continued to express belief; on the other hand, she was reported to have produced genuine phenomena at times, in front of experienced and (previously) sceptical observers.[66] For proponents, she was another example of the genuine but fraudulent demonstrator of extraordinary phenomena. Like George Goble, Charles Foster, and several other earlier mediums, everyone accepted that Palladino cheated, but not necessarily all of the time. Thus, when she was not caught, one had a choice to make: one could believe that the phenomena were real, or else that she had simply not been caught on this occasion. As usual, it came down to the adequacy of the conditions and the expertise of the observers. Critics pointed to the evidence of fraud, proponents pointed to the best evidence (where, they argued, fraud had been impossible), and critics argued that the investigators had simply missed it. The argument about expertise included the usual appeals to particular kinds of expertise, including experience in psychical research and knowledge of conjuring, as well as the inevitable appeals to scepticism but open-mindedness.[67]

However, in terms of the boundaries of scientific psychology, it remained the case that investigations of mediums were legitimate, so long as they provided ordinary explanations. Thus, *Science* included a report of an investigation into Palladino that framed the phenomena as trickery, and some of the most eminent psychologists, such as Jastrow and Hugo Munsterberg of Harvard, attended séances and subsequently reported to the public how they had caught the medium cheating.[68] However, when Cesar Lombroso, the Italian psychologist, investigated Palladino and announced that the phenomena were real, Jastrow dismissed this as 'a travesty of scientific procedure', despite Lombroso's 'scientific training', driven by wishful thinking, and only interesting in terms of 'the psychology of the reputable believers in disreputable tales'.[69]

Indeed, this was part of a wider and longstanding theme in disputes about extraordinary phenomena, in which scientists who excluded ordinary explanations were denounced as lacking the necessary competence to exclude them. What had been said of Crookes was said of Lombroso, and has been said of countless others since. According to the psychology of error, belief in the reality of the phenomena was both the cause and the result of incompetence, and therefore could be taken as an indication of it. Thus, Tanner could remark of Hereward Carrington, who had written a sceptical text on the phenomena of spiritualism, but had then been converted following his investigations of Palladino, that his recent change of mind 'must cast an unfortunate shadow backward on this book'.[70] Sceptical investigations that framed the phenomena according to ordinary explanations, on the other hand, could be part of scientific psychology, precisely because of the view they expressed.

However, the understandable focus upon more prominent demonstrators of extraordinary phenomena, such as Piper and Palladino, can give the impression that the boundary between ordinary and extraordinary was fairly clear-cut: either such phenomena were real (whether supernatural or psychic) or else they were the result of ordinary explanations (such as chance or fraud). This has been the general pattern of the discourse, but what is believed when one says something is real is by no means straightforward. As we have seen, Carpenter had explained certain feats of Bishop according to processes that were then unexplained, and would even now be considered paranormal. Even the most active debunkers could frame extraordinary phenomena in ambiguous ways, and Carpenter was by no means unique in this respect. In the aftermath of Palladino, another extraordinary case attracted the attention of American scientific psychology.

The case of Munsterberg and Beulah Miller

In 1913, Hugo Munsterberg, Professor of Psychology at Harvard, was diverted from his work when a ten-year-old girl from Rhode Island attracted the attention of the American nation. It was reported that Beulah Miller could tell what was in a person's pockets, or in a closed box, or on a page of a closed book. According to Dr John Quackenbos, a physician and member of the Academy of Medicine, who had tested the girl thoroughly, Beulah had powers of X-ray vision.[71]

So, when Munsterberg travelled from Harvard in order to test her, he went about drawing some boundaries.[72] He may not have been the first to test her, but he was quite clear that he was the best qualified. 'All those publicly reported experiments had been made without any actual exact records, and, moreover, by persons who overlooked the most evident sources of error', he explained. 'As a matter of course, I took notes of everything which happened, and treated the case with the same carefulness with which I am accustomed to carry on the experiments in the Harvard Psychological Laboratory'. He contrasted his own psychological expertise with that of the 'untrained observer' to justify his 'right to disregard the reports of all those who relied on their amateur art of experimenting'.

In his report, Munsterberg first excluded the obvious ordinary explanations of chance and fraud as 'equally out of the question' ('the probabilities are only one to many billions', the situation 'lacks every conceivable motive for fraud' and 'I can vouch for the honesty of the intentions of all concerned'). He also excluded 'mind-reading', pointing out that it was far more extraordinary than others realized. Some respectable and well-educated people had spoken of an 'unusual power of being able to read what is in the minds of . . . others' as if, in doing so, 'they disclaimed any belief in mysterious clairvoyance and telepathic powers'. People seemed to think that 'mere mind-reading' was somehow less problematic than 'prophetic gifts' or 'telepathic wonders'. But the reality of mind-reading 'would mean a complete break with everything which science has found in the mental world . . . we lack every possible means to connect such a wonder with anything which the scientist so far acknowledges'. Thus, such demonstrations were so extraordinary as to demand proper critical enquiry.

According to his experiments, Beulah was only successful when her mother or sister were present, when they knew the relevant information, and when Beulah could see at least one of them. In short, she was getting the information from them, but without their knowledge and without knowing this herself. 'I think everything can be explained through her subconscious noticing of unintended signs', he explained, and assured readers that there was 'nothing mysterious, nothing supernatural' going on. However, though his explanation was a natural one, it was not entirely lacking in mystery. Beulah had, he explained, an 'unusual, supernormal sensitiveness together with this abnormal power to receive the signs without their coming at once to consciousness . . . under conditions under which ordinary persons would neither see nor hear them'.

It was not muscle-reading (which was conveyed via touch, and normally received consciously by the muscle-reader) but a form of non-contact reading of almost imperceptible physical signs, unconsciously given by Beulah's mother and sister, and unconsciously received by Beulah herself. It was rather like Carpenter's explanation for Bishop's feat in Edinburgh, or the pseudo-explanations of more recent 'psychological illusionists', except that Beulah was unaware of what she was doing. There was, however, another boundary to be drawn, since there were limits to what could be read in this way. For example, Munsterberg pointed out, if somebody thinks of a letter, and the 'mind-reader' then goes through the alphabet, the latter might pick up on an unintentional reaction from the person when the thought-of letter is reached. This, after all, had been the basic explanation for early spirit messages, that sitters had pointed to letters of the alphabet one at a time, and spirit raps had appeared at the right time, because mediums were picking up on unintentional cues given by the sitter (who knew the relevant information, and inadvertently provided a cue when the correct letter was reached). However, while such basic information might be conveyed, it was 'impossible' to divine a whole word (unless it was by individual letters being obtained, one at a time, via this process).

Munsterberg's explanation framed the phenomena firmly within the boundaries of psychological science (neither supernatural nor mysterious), but left the details unexplained. He was, of course, a busy man, and no doubt felt he had covered the essentials, but only for those who understood exactly what he meant. After all, he had noted himself that even educated people did not know what 'mind-reading' meant, that they seemed to believe it was somehow more compatible with science than 'telepathy'. If the distinction between muscle-reading and mind-reading needed to be made, then the limits of non-contact 'mind-reading' must have been rather less clear. And then he had described Beulah as a person with 'abnormal power' and 'supernormal sensitiveness', who could do things that 'ordinary persons' could not do. No wonder, then, that the *New York Times* reported that 'Dr Munsterberg scouts the theory that she is possessed of what is known as "X-ray vision"... while admitting the girl possesses unusual psychic powers'.[73] And what did they mean by the word 'psychic', the meaning of which would have been no clearer to their readers than 'supernormal'?

Thus, the greatest psychologist in America (as the *New York Times* described him), in an attempt to debunk the most famous psychic claim of the day, framed the phenomena as real and extraordinary, and compatible with science, and his audience (the reading public) were told that he had confirmed her 'psychic' powers. If one had asked a reader of the *New York Times* what they believed about mind-reading or psychic phenomena, they might have reasonably replied that they believed them to be real, and that this had been confirmed by scientific psychology. If they had read the report closely, they might have said that 'mind-reading' and 'telepathy' were not real, but that the ability to know what others were thinking through supernormal abilities was real. And if they had been asked what they meant by this, they surely would have struggled. Unless, that is, they believed Dr Quackenbos, who continued to maintain that this was 'a true case of X-ray vision'.[74]

Like those of his sceptical colleagues, Munsterberg's investigation was intended to be scientific psychology, a study of the borders of the mind but no further, an expression of belief that such reported phenomena were amenable to ordinary explanations, based upon proper psychological expertise. It had, of course, been warranted as not only true but also useful, and had been accompanied by arguments about the extraordinariness of the claim. He had drawn boundaries not only between adequate and inadequate expertise, but also between ordinary and extraordinary explanations, yet the border was so thin that it was difficult to see, and so semantically ambiguous it was hard to understand. The line between supernormal sensitiveness to unconscious visual cues and extra-sensory perception (as it would later be known) may have been a valid one, but the difference between super-, extra- and para-, and how these work as explanations for demonstrations of 'mind-reading', have never been straightforward matters. These shades of grey have long been missed in the painting of belief and disbelief as black and white.

Discussion

The disputes over psychic phenomena were similar, in ways that should now be clear, to those concerning the phenomena of mesmerism and spiritualism. In particular, the disputes over the original psychic phenomena were expressions of different beliefs about whether ordinary explanations had been excluded, based upon what counted as adequate scientific expertise. For Carpenter, psychological expertise was essential, and his psychology of error could be deployed to express and warrant the view that the phenomena were not real, whilst presenting belief as both the cause and effect of incompetent observation. Thus, beliefs, observations and expertise were inextricably bound up together.

However, the line between ordinary and extraordinary was fuzzy, and even Carpenter could express belief in feats that were not explicable by scientific knowledge. One might note, of course, that the fact he was fooled by trickery suggests that psychological expertise was not sufficient after all. More importantly, in terms of belief, one might argue that his own beliefs about the potential of unconscious processes led him to make an error of his own: he believed that certain extraordinary phenomena were real, based upon his own views about what seemed plausible. But whatever was going on inside his head, his arguments were similar to those of psychical researchers, and earlier proponents, who framed particular events as real, and unexplained according to, but nevertheless compatible with, scientific knowledge.

The difficulty in distinguishing between ordinary and extraordinary was evident elsewhere, as American psychologists sought to keep psychical research outside psychology. And it was not just in the United States that early psychologists, in defence of their newly born science, engaged in combat with psychical research, since similar disputes were going on in Germany.[75] However, as we have seen, this was not simply a dispute between scientific psychology and psychical research, since what counted as psychology or psychical research was itself part of the argument. So far as 'psychologists' engaged in the testing of psychic claimants, far from combatting psychical research, they were, by definition, doing psychical research. Just as Forbes had tested mesmeric clairvoyance, and Romanes had tested the non-contact mind-reading abilities of Bishop, psychologists critical of the reality of the phenomena were engaged in testing the same hypothesis. What distinguished them from self-professed psychical researchers was, at the end of the day, their view about the reality of the phenomena. The investigation of phenomena that one did not believe were real only made sense as part of an ongoing discourse of debunking, one in which individuals deployed a psychology of error that both framed the phenomena in terms of ordinary explanations, and constructed the worth of their own expertise.

The point here is not merely that people on different sides held opposing beliefs, or that their words and deeds were driven by their different beliefs, but that their beliefs were an intrinsic part of the dispute. It is not that they merely expressed their beliefs whilst they were arguing about something else, but that the boundary between scientific psychology and psychical research was based neither upon the object of enquiry nor upon the methods used, but rather upon different beliefs about the phenomena. In other words, the disciplinary boundary-work of early American psychologists in relation to psychical research was itself an expression of beliefs about psychic phenomena. And, in expressing a sceptical view, rather than one of belief, the scientific status of Psychology could be more easily constructed. Hardly surprising, then, that such a view accompanied such an endeavour. This was also, of course, an exercise in debunking and, as we shall see, this has continued to be a feature of psychological interest in extraordinary beliefs since: the scientific study of beliefs about psychic phenomena has been, at the same time, an expression of beliefs about such phenomena, and an attempt to change them.

SIX

The making of paranormal phenomena

In 1974, Uri Geller sat in a room with some very respectable scientists. It was part of a laboratory at Stanford Research Institute, and Geller's paranormal abilities were being tested by physicists. During most of the formal tests, he was isolated in an electrically shielded room, while somebody outside drew something on a piece of paper. Despite being unable to see the drawing, or even know who was drawing it, Geller managed to draw an almost exact duplicate.

The experiments, which included several trials like this, were reported in *Nature*, and the authors were quite clear that this was an attempt 'to resolve... whether a certain class of paranormal phenomena exist'. Naturally, this required the exclusion of ordinary explanations, so 'we conducted our experiments with sufficient control, utilizing visual acoustic and electrical shielding, to ensure that all conventional paths of sensory input were blocked'. Whether such measures were 'sufficient', of course, depended upon their competence to assess what was sufficient, but they explained that they had investigated the ability before, carried out pilot studies, and both their knowledge of the literature and their observations led them to conclude that 'such abilities can be studied in laboratory conditions'. Such abilities were compatible with scientific investigation, amenable to 'analysis and hypothesis in the forms with which we are familiar in scientific study'.[1]

The authors' view that such abilities were real was based upon particular phenomena. It was widely reported, for example, that Geller could bend metal by paranormal means, and metal bending had indeed been observed in the laboratory, but these had not been 'adequately controlled experiments', so did not support the paranormal hypothesis. Furthermore, even in the attempt to duplicate drawings, there had been many failures. At times, Geller had said that 'he experienced difficulty in getting impressions', and therefore had not submitted a drawing. At other times, he had expressed dissatisfaction with the extent of possible targets, and his drawings had been no more accurate than what would have been expected by chance. However, the authors pointed out in their conclusion, '[a]s with all biological systems, the information channel appears to be imperfect'. Thus, as in so many previous cases, failures could be seen as evidence of the nature of the phenomena.

As the experimenters justified their position, the journal justified its decision to report it. In an editorial that was hardly ordinary, it warned its readers of the extraordinariness of the claim, but stressed the priority of the evidence over individual prejudice. It pointed out that the tests had been conducted by qualified scientists at a major research establishment and, though the phenomena were highly implausible, the study was nevertheless worthy of attention and scrutiny. However, the editorial also included comments by referees as to the weakness of the design and presentation, and to the authors' inadequate consideration of psychological methodology and prior parapsychological studies. Such weaknesses implied a lack of specialist expertise, and the possibility of unknown errors.[2] Thus, ordinary explanations had not necessarily been excluded.

Later, critics offered possible ordinary explanations, and claimed that conditions had been inadequate to prevent trickery. They questioned the expertise of the authors, who might be qualified scientists but, as they had no specialist knowledge of conjuring, were not competent to exclude fraud.[3] In the disputes that followed these experiments, one can find all the arguments that had been deployed in prior disputes, as sceptical psychologists and magicians claimed that they were not prejudiced but properly sceptical in the face of such extraordinary claims, pointed to Geller's many failures, appealed to duplications of his phenomena by magicians (via ordinary means), and claimed that he had been exposed as a fraud.[4] Meanwhile, proponents appealed to both scientific and conjuring expertise, citing scientists and magicians who had observed Geller, and who had ruled out trickery as an explanation, disputing the validity of failures, duplications and exposures, and even when it was admitted that Geller sometimes cheated, it was pointed out that this did not negate his genuine phenomena.[5]

In that sense, this particular dispute over extraordinary phenomena was nothing new, but it is an appropriate place to begin a consideration of beliefs about extraordinary phenomena in the twentieth century. First, it is an example of experimental parapsychology, the disputed science that had emerged from the worlds of spiritualism and psychical research, and which continued to be the basis of controversy over scientific status and expertise. Second, it is a demonstration by the most famous performer of extraordinary feats in the second half of the twentieth century, whose fame was such that, if one thought about the paranormal after the mid-1970s, it was very likely that one thought of Uri Geller. Third, the critical response to Geller was part of a wider manifestation of (dis)belief that was about to be expressed in the birth of the modern sceptical movement. The ongoing disputes over parapsychology, the extraordinary feats of performers such as Geller, and the relationship between beliefs about the paranormal and the emerging sceptical movement, are the major themes of this chapter.

The making of parapsychology

The boundary between psychical research and parapsychology has never been a straightforward one, both of them being, by definition, the scientific study of psychic phenomena. Nevertheless, just as psychical researchers since Crookes had distinguished between spiritualism and their own scientific enquiries, so early parapsychologists drew lines between psychical research and experimental parapsychology. Such boundaries needed to be drawn, because they were certainly not self-evident. When William McDougall left Harvard in 1927 to take up his position at Duke University, where he laid the foundations of the new experimental parapsychology, neither experiments nor the term 'parapsychology' were new to psychical research.[6] Indeed, in the process of arguing the worth of a new scientific psychical research, McDougall made similar arguments to those that Crookes and, later, the SPR had made.[7]

There were differences, of course. For one thing, this was part of a wider critique of the current dominance of materialism and behaviourism in American Psychology. But more importantly, in terms of belief, after McDougall recruited J. B. Rhine, what became known as the 'Rhine revolution' was an explicit attempt to reframe the scientific study of psychic phenomena in word and deed.[8] In addition to his use of particular terminology, including new terms such as 'extra-sensory perception' and 'psychokinesis', Rhine defined parapsychology as strictly experimental, laboratory- and university-based, in contrast with extra-academic psychical research.[9] He pioneered a progressive programme of experimental quantitative research, in an attempt to achieve academic and scientific status, and to show that psychic ability was common, not rare.[10] His approach was not entirely new, of course, as psychical researchers had been conducting quantitative studies for some time, much of it carried out by academic psychologists. However, this had been a minority approach within psychical research, whereas it was the basis of the new experimental parapsychology, which also had a dedicated academic base. As Rhine distanced himself from psychical research, he sought closer ties with experimental psychology, framing parapsychology as part of psychology, and looking for psychological correlates of paranormal ability.[11]

The experimental and quantitative nature of the enquiry was realized in experiments that were designed to draw operational boundaries between particular kinds of paranormal phenomena. Thus, for example, experiments in clairvoyance tested the ability to know which of five symbols was on a card, while tests for 'pure telepathy' removed the cards from the process so that the information could only be gained from the mind of the sender. However, what these different kinds of ESP had in common was that all of them, in terms of experimental evidence, amounted to statistical anomalies. Whether clairvoyance, telepathy or precognition, the reported facts of ESP experiments were deviations from chance in the process of card-guessing.

Thus, any claim that such experiments demonstrated ESP – and these were intended to be the most convincing case so far for the existence of paranormal phenomena – depended upon the exclusion of chance, based upon a new and particular kind of expertise: competence in statistics. It was on the basis of such competence that chance could be excluded as an ordinary explanation for experimental results. One also had to exclude the possibility of fraud, of course, and both Rhine and McDougall expressed the view that whether subjects were willing to cheat did not matter; it was the job of the experimenter to design things so that deception was impossible.[12] For them, like spiritualists and psychical researchers, that a subject might fake the phenomena at other times did not negate the positive results of a properly controlled experiment. What counted as a properly controlled experiment, however, what amounted to competent experimental design and proper statistical analysis, was naturally open to dispute.

These disputes have been described in remarkable detail by Seymour Mauskopf and Michael McVaugh in *The Elusive Science*. Critics challenged the statistics and the statistical competence of parapsychologists, criticizing alleged flaws in Rhine's analysis, and disputing the improbability of his results (and, therefore, the reality of ESP). As most psychologists struggled to keep up with the technical debate, professional statisticians became involved, and in turn criticized the competence of psychologists who had rejected Rhine's analysis. When Burton Camp, the president of the recently formed Institute of Mathematical Statistics, declared that Rhine's statistics were valid, he was no doubt less concerned with defending Rhine than with defending the worth of his own discipline.[13] Nevertheless, it ended, for a while at least, one more dispute about what counted as extraordinary (in this case, in relation to normal chance), and who was competent to assess the matter.

The facts could still be framed, of course, if not as chance, then as error or fraud. Critics claimed that there were basic defects in the ESP cards, and that conditions allowed for sensory cues, or errors in recording data, and even Rhine's personal competence was questioned on the basis that he was not a member of the American Psychological Association (APA).[14] Nevertheless, as Mauskopf and McVaugh show, Rhine's early results initially received a fairly warm reception, despite Rhine's low expectations. Positive reviews were published in major newspapers, and in academic psychology journals, and several psychologists began to conduct parapsychological experiments. Following the appearance of the *Journal of Parapsychology* in 1937, *Psychological Abstracts* agreed to include work from it. There were critics, of course, but they were relatively quiet until Rhine engaged in public dissemination of his results. His popular account of parapsychology, *New Frontiers of the Mind* (1937), was explicitly aimed at the public, and accompanied by a commercial approach that saw ESP cards being sold in bookshops, and ESP tests being conducted on radio. As the popular press began to report that

ESP was a 'scientific fact', critics began to appear in greater number. Nevertheless, despite the best efforts of critics such as B. F. Skinner, American psychologists were split on the validity of parapsychological evidence, while 90 per cent in an APA poll of 1938 accepted parapsychology as a legitimate science.[15] The following year, Rhine was accepted, albeit by a slim majority, as a member of the APA (thus, if nothing else, removing his lack of membership as an indication of incompetence as a psychologist). The publication of *ESP after Sixty Years* (1940), which referred back to work since the founding of the SPR, also received a mixed reception, but few psychologists rejected the work as unscientific.[16]

Clearly, then, one could believe that parapsychology was a science, and even that its results were statistically significant, without believing in the reality of 'psi'. Beliefs about extraordinary phenomena, since the days of mesmerism, had always offered related, but distinct, positions in terms of the facts, what they meant, and their relationship to science. Nevertheless, the timing and nature of the disputes suggested a deep concern among critics about the views of the public, who might not be expected to distinguish between the different threads of the argument. After all, if parapsychology was a science, and its findings counted as scientific knowledge, then nobody could be blamed for believing that paranormal phenomena were real. It is hardly surprising, then, that disputes about the scientific status of parapsychology and the validity of its results and claims were closely linked. Indeed, those who have examined the arguments over the scientific status of parapsychology, and the validity of parapsychological findings, have identified similar kinds of themes to those that have been discussed so far.[17] They may have made different lists, but the continuities are clear enough, subject to how one cuts the cake.

For example, as others have noted, one of the key rhetorical strategies of parapsychology's critics has been the accusation of fraud.[18] This, of course, has been an appeal to an ordinary explanation, and a challenge to the expertise of those who have (allegedly) failed to exclude it. Furthermore, such accusations have been based upon appeals to the extraordinariness of the phenomena, so much so that critics have not necessarily had to rely upon evidence of fraud. Thus, Price could argue, on the basis of the implausibility of ESP, that any results not attributable to chance or error, could be explained away by fraud.[19] Similarly, the psychologist, C. E. M. Hansel argued that, given the implausibility of the phenomena, one need only demonstrate that fraud was possible.[20] Thus, by stressing the extraordinariness of the phenomena, as in Hume's famous argument against miracles, any alternative explanation could be made more plausible. And, of course, it went without saying, though it was nevertheless said, that fraud was a bad thing.

In other words, however else one might wish to itemize the main arguments for and against the paranormal, it has been the case throughout the twentieth century, and unto the present, that the claims of parapsychologists have depended upon the exclusion of normal explanations, based upon appeals to scientific expertise, and to the potential compatibility of paranormal phenomena with mainstream scientific knowledge. Meanwhile, critics have rejected the facts as inadequate, appealing to the possibility of error, chance and fraud, questioned the competence of parapsychologists and stressed the extraordinariness of the claim. As proponents have appealed to the benefits, critics have stressed the dangers, and everyone has been sceptical but open-minded, while accusing their opponents of prejudice. As we shall shortly see, not only the facts, but also failures, duplications and exposures have been disputed in ways that were similar to earlier disputes.

However, it is easy to get the impression that disputes over extraordinary phenomena are between the irresistible force of scepticism and the unmoveable object of belief, that there are believers and disbelievers and never the twain shall meet. But disputes in the early years of experimental parapsychology, as before and ever since, reveal a considerably more complex picture of belief and disbelief.

Take, for example, the impressive results obtained by George Zirkle and Sarah Ownbey. According to Rhine, 'the greatest amount of really amazing work in telepathy was done by Mr Zirkle, and it was done during the period when Miss Ownbey was both sender and experimenter'.[21] In these particular experiments, Ownbey, as sender, attempted to send ESP symbols via telepathy to Zirkle who, as receiver, attempted to guess what they were. Ownbey, who was also acting as experimenter, then recorded these guesses. During the experiments, the pair were sitting in adjacent rooms, unable to see each other, and an electric fan was switched on to prevent Zirkle from hearing any unconscious whispering by the sender. Indeed, Ownbey did not speak throughout the experiments, but rather tapped a telegraph key to let Zirkle know when she was trying to send the symbol to him. After some moments, Zirkle called out his guess to Ownbey (the door separating the two rooms being open, so his raised voice could be heard), who recorded the choice, and then began to concentrate on the next symbol. As the conditions prevented the pair from communicating via unconscious sensory cues, Rhine considered these 'quite good conditions for safety'.[22]

Others pointed to the possibility of error, as Ownbey was acting as both sender and experimenter. A prominent critic of parapsychology, Hansel, found it extraordinary that nobody appeared 'to consider the possibility that the targets generated by Miss Ownbey could be influenced by her hearing Zirkle's calls, or even that she might make mistakes in her recording'.[23] However, the same criticisms had already been made, not by sceptics but rather by psychical researchers, who were not entirely convinced of the results.[24] And other psychical researchers made more general criticisms about the details of Rhine's reports, noting that they did not adequately exclude ordinary explanations.[25] These critics, who included eminent psychical researchers such as S. G. Soal and R. H. Thouless, believed in ESP, but not necessarily in this case. And, like earlier disbelievers, by pointing out the flaws of others, they presented themselves as having superior expertise in the matter.

In addition to the possibility of error, the question of fraud was also present. The well-known mentalist, Ted Annemann, came up with an ingenious method for duplicating a demonstration of telepathy in precisely the same conditions. In an article entitled 'Was Prof. J. B. Rhine hoodwinked?', which he published in *The Jinx* (a conjuring magazine that he edited), Annemann claimed that Zirkle and Ownbey could have used an old vaudeville trick, the 'mental count'. In theory, when Zirkle called out his first guess, this triggered the count, whereby both sender and receiver began silently, at a previously practised pace, to run through the symbols in sequence. When Ownbey then tapped the telegraph key (supposedly to tell Zirkle that she was now thinking of another symbol), chances were very good that they would both be thinking of the same symbol at that moment. Thus, she could have secretly communicated the symbol of which she was thinking. Of course, the system was not perfect, but it was certainly adequate to ensure results significantly above chance. Annemann did not claim that this was actually done, only that it could have been used, but he made the point that Rhine was not a magician, and that one would not 'investigate a subject explainable by chemistry . . . [without] a competent chemist present'.[26] Thus, his explanation reflected, and no doubt reinforced for its readers, the belief that conjuring expertise was needed in the scientific testing of paranormal phenomena.

What is interesting about this particular explanation, however, is that it was practical yet unnecessary. It could have been used, and would have been effective, if it had been used by Zirkle and Ownbey, but there would have been no point. What Annemann failed to mention, though Rhine had stated it explicitly, was that there was nobody else present at these experiments. 'To have supplied another observer was beyond our means at the time', he had explained, a position he justified on the grounds that these experiments were process- rather than proof-oriented (i.e. they were exploring the nature of ESP rather than testing its reality).[27] Thus, if Zirkle and Ownbey had wished to cheat, there was no need to resort to a 'mental count', or indeed to any other kind of clever technique. Since nobody was watching them, they could have simply sat down together and agreed on whatever results they wanted.

Furthermore, Annemann must have known this, since it is clear from his description that he had read Rhine's original account, and was referring to these particular experiments. Indeed, he explained that he had chosen these because they had been described as (and here he directly quoted Rhine) 'the greatest amount of really amazing work in telepathy'.[28] This matters because it shows that this was not primarily an attempt to debunk ESP. If he had merely wished to debunk the results, he could have simply pointed out that nobody was watching Zirkle and Ownbey and so, if they were prepared to cheat, fraud would have been remarkably easy. Perhaps more importantly, he could have said this in a considerably more public forum than an exclusive conjuring magazine. For that matter, even if he had somehow forgotten the details, and thought that this might actually have happened, he could have made a more public claim. After all, others later revealed this method as a possible explanation for these same results.[29]

Rather, Annemann's pseudo-explanation suggests a more subtle aspect of the role of expertise in beliefs about extraordinary phenomena. It was framed as a way of duplicating Rhine's most impressive experimental results, but it was written for an audience of magicians, not as a practical method for them to use on stage, but as a theory about how an esoteric technique might have been used in this particular parapsychology experiment. It conveyed not merely specialist knowledge but superior knowledge to that of Rhine, whose ignorance of such methods meant that his claims were based upon inadequate expertise. But it shared this knowledge with an exclusive group, readers of *The Jinx*, who were now in the know, and who could now also see themselves as more knowledgeable than Rhine on this particular matter. And, having been framed as Rhine's most impressive results in telepathy, this was no small matter. Readers of *The Jinx* could now see themselves as part of a small minority of folk who knew about such things, who possessed specialist knowledge that might explain the strongest scientific evidence for ESP. The point is not that this was true, nor even that they would have taken the article so seriously, but rather that it represented something much broader about specialist conjuring knowledge. The sharing of esoteric knowledge is an inherent part of the conjuring community, and knowledge of secrets (that, by definition, others do not know) has always been a standard indication of status and expertise in magic. It is, in short, a desirable thing to feel that one is in the know. To be faced with a phenomenon that others cannot explain, perhaps even other magicians, and to be in possession of an explanation, is obviously attractive. Whether one actually knows what happened, whether one even knows the details, one can nevertheless present oneself as a person of superior knowledge. Whatever other reasons might underlie beliefs about the paranormal, the opportunity to present oneself as one who knows what others do not is an understandable reason for expressing one view rather than another.

Of course, knowledge of how ESP might be faked is not the same as disbelief in the paranormal. One of the reasons why magicians are seen as more sceptical than most, despite evidence to the contrary, is that many magicians have pointed out that they are aware of how paranormal phenomena can be faked.[30] However, those who have expressed this view have expressed a range of views about paranormal phenomena and, as we shall see, many conjuror-debunkers have also expressed belief in the paranormal.[31] What specialist conjuring knowledge affords is the opportunity to present oneself as more informed on particular, but relevant, matters than even the most eminent parapsychologist. An expression of disbelief towards particular extraordinary phenomena, whether or not it reflects a more general view about the paranormal, can be a means of displaying one's individual expertise.[32]

Beyond the rather exclusive world of the well-informed magician, however, this minor episode reflected still wider concerns. For one thing, despite Rhine's initial insistence that experiments should be designed so that fraud was impossible, many of his experiments were, by his own admission, less than fraud-proof. This was because, according to Rhine himself, proof had been established by earlier work, and these particular experiments were concerned with establishing not that ESP existed, but rather how it worked. Nevertheless, he had presented these experiments as part of the general evidence for ESP, describing the results as impressive, and the conditions in ways that excluded (some, if not all) ordinary explanations, such that commentators later described them as more stringent than other experiments at the time.[33] Furthermore, even for those who understood that these experiments were process- rather than proof-oriented, their value as evidence of process depended upon the results being due to ESP.[34] Thus, one way or another, these experiments were presented as evidence that ESP was real.

Indeed, the very idea of process-oriented experiments was based upon the belief that ESP was real, and that this had been demonstrated by previous experiments. However, psychical researchers such as R. H. Thouless were not convinced by Rhine's evidence that ESP was so easily found, because he felt that, in many cases, Rhine had not adequately excluded ordinary explanations.[35] Thus, regardless of what one believed about ESP in general, what one made of these particular cases could depend upon quite different interpretations, both of which were quite consistent with the facts. For Rhine, they might be evidence that ESP worked in both rigorous and less rigorous conditions, but for Thouless, they were inadequate evidence of ESP because the conditions were insufficiently rigorous. The difference in views was based upon neither the facts nor a general belief about

ESP, but rather upon different criteria for what counted as adequate evidence of ESP.

As the meaning of particular facts was disputed, even by prominent proponents of ESP, so were failures, duplications and exposures. Despite Rhine's aim to demonstrate that paranormal abilities were common rather than rare, the best results were often obtained by specific experimenters, or particular 'star' subjects, all of whom attracted the suspicion of critics. In addition to allegations of fraud that were based upon the implausibility of the phenomena, evidence emerged of fraudulent activity among not only star subjects but also successful experimenters. The question of fraud by star subjects was disputed as it had always been, in terms of possible ordinary methods, the adequacy of the conditions to prevent them, and the expertise of experimenters to detect them. For critics, fraud remained a consistent option, as any successful results could be framed as the product of successful subject fraud, since the nature of successful fraud, of course, is that it is not detected. For proponents, particular cases of alleged fraud could always be disputed, and even when accepted as actual fraud, could be framed as irrelevant to other (genuine) phenomena.[36]

As for the question of experimenter fraud, it was also always a logical possibility, and for anyone who found it more plausible than psi, was a constant option as a basis for disbelief. Accusations of experimenter fraud were made towards prominent researchers, including Rhine and S. G. Soal, and actual cases of data tampering were reported in the cases of Soal and Walter Levy, Rhine's director of research.[37] In the former cases, even when critics accepted that the allegations of fraud were unfair, this was not accompanied by any shift in their general view.[38] In the latter cases, even when parapsychologists accepted that fraud had taken place, they pointed out that this also happened in other sciences, cited the results of parapsychology experiments in which no fraud had been involved, and noted that these cases of fraud had been exposed by parapsychologists, thus demonstrating that they were competent to detect fraud when it did occur.[39] Thus, exposures of fraud could be framed as consistent with the scientific status of parapsychology, and supportive of the reality of psi.

A more regular concern of parapsychologists, however, was the inconsistency of results. Though Rhine's initial results had suggested regular success, failures (in the form of statistically insignificant results) remained a continual problem. For critics, this was seen as evidence that psi was not real, and that parapsychology was not a science, since its object of study could not be demonstrated by a replicable experiment.[40] Thus, whatever results were not the product of error or fraud could be dismissed as occasional statistical anomalies, which were not so extraordinary. Parapsychologists acknowledged the problem of inconsistency, but viewed regular failures as evidence of the nature of the phenomena, for example that psi was elusive and resisted empirical enquiry.[41] Furthermore, parapsychologists conducted experiments in an attempt to identify the various factors that might underlie such inconsistent results, the most prominent of which was the possible effect of the beliefs of those present. The so-called 'sheep-goat effect', coined by Gertrude Schmeidler in the 1940s, was based upon experiments that suggested those who believed that clairvoyance would be demonstrated in the experiment ('sheep') were more successful than those who believed that it would not ('goats').[42] The sheep-goat effect gradually became a wider claim within experimental parapsychology, that beliefs about psi could affect the results of a parapsychology experiment.

While the sheep-goat effect suggested a possible solution to the problem of the elusiveness of psi that faced parapsychologists, it also reflected a longer history of failure to produce the phenomena on demand, and of claims that this might be due to the effects of the beliefs (or disbeliefs) of those present. As we have seen, this had been a common theme in disputes over the phenomena of mesmerism, spiritualism and psychical research. However, the argument that belief was a casual factor in the production of extraordinary phenomena now became part and parcel of the empirical enquiry, to be explored as an independent variable within a parapsychology experiment. Subjects were given questionnaires, to assess their belief or disbelief, so that the results of the experiment could be understood in relation to their beliefs about the paranormal. The sheep-goat effect, as a means of understanding the nature of psi, led to a new interest in belief within experimental parapsychology, one to which we shall shortly return.

Meanwhile, just as exposures and failures continued to be disputed, so were duplications of paranormal phenomena. In particular, the performances of stage mind-readers throughout the twentieth century could, like prior duplications, be framed not only as evidence of fraud, but also as evidence of something that was real, albeit something ambiguous. This ambiguity was not just a matter of reception, but was rather an intrinsic part of the public demonstration of such phenomena. A brief look at some of these individuals, and the extraordinary feats that they performed, shows how inexplicable phenomena could be framed in a remarkable variety of mysterious ways, both in performance and in reception, not only by the public but also by experts.

The making of mind-reading, c. 1900–1970

As experimental parapsychology had emerged and grown, extraordinary phenomena had continued to be demonstrated in public, as new generations of mind-readers performed in theatres, then on radio and television. These have been largely ignored by scholars, perhaps because few academics have possessed the relevant knowledge about magic and mentalism.[43] But performers of mind-reading are essential to understanding extraordinary beliefs. After all, these demonstrations reached a significantly larger audience than reports of parapsychology experiments, and they provided the public with directly observable events rather than with disputed reports. Like Uri Geller, many of these performers became household names, and would have been relevant objects of thought for anyone who was asked what they made of mind-reading. They rose to fame by demonstrating feats that were carefully designed to exclude ordinary explanations, but were framed in ambiguous ways that made the boundary between extraordinary and ordinary fuzzier than ever. Such well-known and widely discussed mind-reading feats, seemingly inexplicable and mysterious in nature, cannot have failed to shape beliefs about extraordinary phenomena, not only in terms of whether they were real, but also in terms of what was real.

Public demonstrations of mind-reading were already, in the twentieth century, part of a long tradition, one that pre-dated Louis M'Kean and the Mysterious Lady. But the tradition had grown, and continues to grow, with greater numbers of such performers today than there has ever been before. As a result, it has increasingly shaped beliefs about extraordinary phenomena. We need only consider a few examples in order to understand the key points, and these individuals provide a useful link between the performers of the nineteenth century and those of today.

For example, take S. S. Baldwin, magician, debunker of spiritualism and Indian juggling, and a performer of mind-reading feats in the late nineteenth and early twentieth centuries. He travelled the English-speaking world with a remarkably rich and varied repertoire, not only standard conjuring tricks but also pseudo-spiritualist feats, such as the spirit cabinet (cf. the Davenport brothers) and the 'pellet test' (cf. Charles Foster), and also included demonstrations of muscle-reading (cf. Washington Irving Bishop). His main feature, however, was the 'question and answer' act, of which he was a pioneer. This began with the audience writing down questions on pieces of paper, folding them up and putting them in their pockets. The act then consisted of Baldwin's wife, who was on stage, in trance, and apparently psychic, providing answers to these questions, along with other information that she (seemingly) could not have known.

Despite the obvious framing of the show as a piece of entertainment, and the inclusion of humorous exposures of the tricks of mediums, it was far from obvious that the 'question and answer' act was merely trickery. Press accounts of the show often described this section as more serious than other parts of the show, and excluded various kinds of trickery as possible explanations, sometimes referring to the bewilderment of sceptics.[44] Expert magicians and psychical researchers might provide some details of how it was done in specialist publications, but even they failed to reveal the whole story, and as one explained, it was 'practically impossible for the average person to detect the fraud that is invariably practiced, in exhibitions such as these'.[45] In addition to being seemingly inexplicable, the act was framed ambiguously both in performance and in report. On the one hand, Baldwin claimed to possess no supernatural powers; on the other hand, he also claimed that he did not use trickery. This led to ambiguous framing in the British and American press, for example: 'We do not profess to know how the results are achieved, but we can state that the manifestation is devoid of trickery'; 'Whether his mentality may be impressed by those of his visitors, or whether it be by some latent power not yet defined, he cannot tell'; 'We are willing to admit that it may be by the exercise of some natural yet unknown power, but we certainly can't admit it was mind-reading... It is a question well worth the attention of scientific men'.[46] By a 'natural yet unknown power' that is not 'mind-reading' yet is 'worth the attention of scientific men', the reporter was presumably thinking of some kind of 'psychological' rather than 'psychic' process. Nevertheless, given that 'natural yet unknown power' might easily have passed as a definition of 'psychic', the boundary between extraordinary and ordinary was extraordinarily fuzzy. Performers such as Baldwin spread mystery and ambiguity wherever they went, attracting enormous numbers of observers, and considerable space in local and national press. And he was only one of many.

In the early part of the twentieth century, as Houdini was debunking mediums, one of the most famous of American showmen was Alexander, 'the man who knows'. A former fake spiritualist medium, who became a magician and mind-reader, Alexander performed a vaudeville show in which he also mixed traditional stage magic with pseudo-spiritualist routines and a demonstration of mind-reading. The latter feat, which became his hallmark act, was a 'question and answer' act not dissimilar to that of Baldwin, though even more successful. One of the strategies that made this so convincing was that he used a variety of different methods, all of which he cannily excluded by listing them in his programme:

> Mr Alexander desires especially to call the attention of the audience to the fact that in these demonstrations he uses no confederates, no codes, no waxed pads to write upon, no exchange of your questions, thereby permitting the same to be transferred to some dressing room to an assistant to be transmitted to him via a telephone line... These are some of the methods resorted to by alleged performers, irresponsible, aspiring charlatans, pure and simple, who have copied Alexander's billing matter verbatim, and have endeavored to imitate him in the smaller houses.[47]

This provoked Houdini to complain, with no sense of irony, that Alexander was exposing the methods of those who used trickery to simulate extraordinary feats.[48] However, there has always been a fuzzy ethical line between what one should and should not do in the simulation of particular extraordinary phenomena (about the sorts of claims that should be made, and how explicit one should be), and many of the most successful performers have been remarkably inconsistent. Thus, in 1921, the *Sphinx*, a conjuror's magazine, described Alexander as 'a hater of imitators and fakers who pose as seers and soothsayers', yet he sold astrological forecasts and Ouija boards, and claimed in the press that he could predict the future (including a theatre fire that, nevertheless, destroyed all the equipment in his show).[49] When making astrological predictions, he disclaimed any 'supernatural' abilities, yet billed his demonstrations as the result of 'psychic powers' that were 'science baffling'.[50] Shortly afterwards, he presented himself as 'the world's foremost psychologist', and sold a mail-order course on *The Inner Secrets of Psychology*, which promised to 'UNLOCK the door to unlimited POWERS', including clairvoyance and telepathy.[51] His brother, who performed a similar act, presented 'psychic lectures and dream interpretations', billed himself as 'The Master Psychologist', and included in his advertising a quote from Edison that attributed his powers to 'a supersensitive brain'. He also published a monthly periodical, the *Master Mind*, devoted to 'applied psychology', which defined 'the science of Psychology' as 'the study of the human mind', and described Senator Warren Harding (then President-elect) as 'a true Psychologist'.[52]

In the years prior to the emergence of experimental parapsychology, the American public knew of Houdini and of his debunking of mediums, but they also knew of Alexander, and of the extraordinary feats that he performed. And regardless of what they believed about the spirits, they could believe that clairvoyance and telepathy were real (and, for that matter, were a part of Psychology). The combination of inexplicable feats, ambiguous frames and inconsistent claims made such characters that much more mysterious, more newsworthy and more talked about.

Alexander faded from the public eye, of course, but he was replaced by others, such as Joseph Dunninger, who joined Houdini in the debunking of mediums, but also made ambiguous claims about his own extraordinary abilities. His fame was such that, throughout his career, he performed for Thomas Edison, Pope Pius XII and several American presidents, and he pioneered the performance of mentalism on American radio and, later, television. On the one hand, he was a debunker of psychic phenomena, who challenged psychics to demonstrate feats that he could not duplicate by ordinary means, and wrote (or had ghost-written) books that debunked psychic phenomena. On the other hand, he framed what he did as 'telepathy' in the titles of his shows, in his publicity, on stage and sometimes in private conversation.[53] In one of his popular books, *The Art of Thought Reading* (1956), he claimed to teach the public how

> to receive, interpret and analyse the projected thoughts of another... There is no illusion, or anything supernatural about thought reading. It is a study, a most exacting one... if he projects to you a clear, vivid picture of his thought, you will receive his vibrations and assemble them into a pattern which clears the beamed thought in his mind.[54]

The combination of inexplicable feats and ambiguous claims was by no means a unique American phenomenon. In Britain, as Alexander bewildered Americans, the remarkable Dr Walford Bodie was mystifying fellow Brits. Another friend of Houdini, though not well remembered today, Bodie was one of the highest-paid entertainers of his time, a Freeman of the City of London, and an international star (so much so that a young Charles Chaplin began his career by performing an impersonation of him).[55] In addition to performing thought-reading, Bodie was a pioneer of stage hypnosis, and presented many of his feats as demonstrations of esoteric natural forces, such as the humbly named 'Bodic Force'. He wrote books for the public on a host of extraordinary topics, from mental suggestion, clairvoyance and telepathy to rather more esoteric matters. Among other things, for example, he claimed that nearly one per cent of the British public were buried alive every year (while in a trance state), explained how to hypnotize a chicken (or, if one preferred, a glass of water), attributed biblical miracles to hypnosis, and cited a contemporary review that compared him to Jesus.[56]

Bodie claimed to possess a string of academic, medical and scientific qualifications, and to be able to cure people through a 'natural scientific' process that he called 'bloodless surgery', a mixture of massage, electricity and hypnosis. As a result, he was the subject of several court actions, many of which he turned to his advantage. In 1909, a judge ruled, 'Dr Bodie could not be stigmatised as a quack or impostor... [and that there was] evidence of cases where other doctors had failed and which had been cured as the result of Dr Bodie's treatment'.[57] Shortly afterwards, medical students in Glasgow violently disrupted his show in what became known as the 'Bodie riot'. Even in the midst of such extraordinary demonstrations and claims, there was plenty of room to be taken seriously.

Later, as Joseph Dunninger was reading minds on American radio and television, others were demonstrating similar feats on the BBC. Al Koran, for example, though not the first to bill himself as 'the world's greatest mind-reader', nevertheless performed at the London Palladium, for British royalty (on 25 occasions, according to his own publicity).[58] He also claimed to be the son of the notorious Scottish medium, Helen Duncan, and wrote books for the public in which he claimed to possess 'extra-sensory instincts and uncanny sixth sense', that he had studied not only magic but also 'astrology, psychology and Yoga (under a Tibetan monk)', and that when asked: 'How do I read minds?... What is the secret? I tell them it is pure psychology'.[59]

There are countless further examples that might be given, but the point is merely this: these individuals, who were household names in their respective countries (and, indeed, further afield), demonstrated feats that audiences could not explain, indeed that many contemporary magicians would not have been able to explain. They framed what they did in ambiguous ways, at times as trickery but, at other times, as something more. They disclaimed certain powers, but inferred or claimed others, which were vaguely related to 'psychological' processes, most of which would count as paranormal according to orthodox scientific knowledge. It is inconceivable that a large proportion of their audiences were not, on the one hand, convinced in the reality of such demonstrations and, on the other, unsure about precisely what was going on. After all, ambiguity is mystery, and such performers made their living from creating, provoking and exploiting mystery.

Such claims had long been an essential part of showmanship, as they continue to be today, and the fact that such claims can be taken seriously has occasionally provoked a sceptical response. Such was the case with Maurice Fogel, a British mentalist who also billed himself as 'the world's greatest mind-reader'. In 1947, Fogel arranged a transatlantic 'experiment' with J. B. Rhine, which garnered enormous publicity. Rhine himself dismissed the test as meaningless, and Fogel as a showman, but in the midst of various ambiguous claims to the press, Fogel gave the clear impression that he was telepathic.[60] The following year, when three million listeners heard Fogel read minds on BBC radio, he was asked by the journalist, Arthur Helliwell, whether he could really read minds. Fogel replied: 'I do not claim any supernatural powers. All I say is that I am able to read people's minds with my own methods'.[61] This ambiguous response provoked Helliwell to discover the methods behind Fogel's mind-reading, which relied upon obtaining information from certain members of the audience before the show started, and then expose them in a national newspaper. He also criticized the BBC for having misrepresented the matter, complaining that 'Fogel's broadcast was presented with all the trimmings as a genuine and brilliant feat of "mind reading"'.[62] Certainly it seems to have convinced some, but psychical researchers were less impressed. The *Journal of the Society for Psychical Research* (*JSPR*) described Fogel as someone who claimed to have telepathic powers, but who relied upon trickery, and when Helliwell publicly exposed his feats, the *JSPR* passed on the ordinary explanations to its readers.[63]

A few months later, however, a larger controversy erupted over the Piddingtons. Sidney and Lesley Piddington were a successful telepathy act from Australia, who were booked to perform on a BBC radio series. The producer claimed, as he had done in the case of Fogel, that this was genuine telepathy.[64] During the shows, Sidney sent thoughts to Lesley when she was in a series of seemingly secure locations, in circumstances that appeared to exclude the possibility that they were relying upon codes. The Piddingtons themselves never explicitly claimed to have paranormal powers (their well known slogan was 'You are the judge'), but it was hardly difficult to get that impression: they used Zener cards, described their feats as 'tests', and made references to telepathy and parapsychology experiments. Sidney told the press that he had studied telepathy (and that, despite being a sceptic, had achieved 'some surprising results'), and claimed that his wife 'could read an average of seventy per cent of my thoughts when I am deliberately transmitting – and a disturbingly high percentage of my thoughts when I am not trying'.[65] The *JSPR* complained that such claims 'can scarcely have given any other impression than that the performers were gifted with paranormal facilities', and cited friends of members (though, notably, not actual members) who had been convinced of the reality of the phenomena.[66]

In expressing disbelief about the Piddington's feats, the *JSPR* appealed to ordinary explanations, noting that '[t]he conditions in which the broadcasts have taken place lend themselves to the employment of codes of various kinds, confederates, and mechanical aids, and anyone with knowledge of the methods of illusionists can recognise ... the manner in which many of the effects could have been achieved'.[67] SPR members subsequently declared that 'nothing more than conjuring skill is required to produce the effects achieved', cited a letter from the Magic Circle that claimed such techniques were 'perfectly well known to magicians and expert psychical researchers, however inexplicable they may seem to untrained observers', and referred to 'those who, clearly without knowledge of conjuring or parapsychology, have attributed their effects to psychic faculties'.[68]

However, unlike the case of Fogel just a few months earlier, the details of how it was done were not provided, and the *JSPR* was not alone in failing to explain the matter. Arthur Helliwell also publicly stated that the Piddingtons performed tricks, and he made some vague claims about the use of codes, but he did not explain how they could have used codes in the conditions in which they worked.[69] Indeed, this puzzled magicians too, some of whom hinted at various methods but, whether due to ignorance or else a reluctance to divulge secrets, the methods of the Piddingtons were not revealed.[70]

Now, one can easily understand why magicians, even if they did not know how it was done, would have assumed that such feats were merely tricks, but what about psychical researchers, who believed that telepathy was possible? On what basis did they reject the unexplained telepathic feats of the Piddingtons? Their disbelief was based upon an appeal to ordinary explanations, but not upon actual knowledge of those explanations. It was warranted by an appeal to specialist expertise, by claiming that experts such as themselves possessed such knowledge. However, if any psychical researchers had known the details, they certainly failed to provide them. After all, the possible use of 'codes, confederates and mechanical aids' was hardly much of an explanation, since the same could have been said for any psychic claim in history, including every one that these psychical researchers believed to be real. Furthermore, disbelief towards these particular phenomena was not on the basis that the Piddingtons were entertainers, since the SPR had investigated several such performers, and the use of trickery on some occasions was no barrier to the belief that other phenomena were real.

The argument upon which psychical researchers based their disbelief was that conditions had allowed for such things to have taken place. Indeed, this was spelt out in reference to the unqualified public, when the *JSPR* advised that they ask themselves why, if the Piddingtons were real, they did not simply say so, and submit themselves for scientific investigation?[71] This was how unexplained tricks were to be distinguished from genuine paranormal phenomena. After all, as S. G. Soal pointed out, 'any competent experimenter could in half-an-hour satisfy himself that their results were not obtained by means of telepathy'.[72] Conversely, it was noted, this was not the first time that such demonstrations had been considered genuinely paranormal by the public.[73]

Senior members of the SPR made this clear in a letter to the *Times*, in which they distinguished between the 'thought-transference performances' of the Piddingtons and 'genuine telepathic powers', the former being similar to those that could be reproduced by 'a competent illusionist', the latter having been examined 'under laboratory conditions' and accepted by 'several leading scientists'. 'We need hardly stress the importance of a thorough and impartial exploration [of telepathy] . . . It would be most regrettable if any confusion were created in the public mind between serious researches of this kind and the performances which the BBC has been transmitting'.[74] Thus, for the benefit of *Times* readers, boundaries were drawn between pseudo- and genuine telepathy, the unexplained and the paranormal, public credulity and specialist expertise, trivial entertainment and serious experimental work. As psychologists had long done in the debunking of psychic phenomena, psychical researchers expressed disbelief as they constructed both the superiority of their expertise and the worth of their discipline. In serious matters of the paranormal, the public (despite the Piddingtons' slogan) was not qualified to be 'the judge'.

This was a position of disbelief towards very particular unexplained feats, based upon the claim that conditions allowed for fraud, and that they could be duplicated by trickery. It was made by individuals who expressed a belief that telepathy was real, but not in this case, the distinction being made on the basis that no proper investigation had been permitted. So much for how, but it nevertheless begs the question: why did people who believed in telepathy not believe in these particular unexplained demonstrations of telepathy?

It has been argued throughout that belief in the reality of extraordinary phenomena depends upon the exclusion of ordinary explanations, and this is based upon (the belief that one has, or at least somebody has) the competence to exclude them. Nobody doubted that some phenomena were fake, and the ability to distinguish between the wheat and the chaff was fundamental to psychical researchers. The ability to demonstrate competence to do so was essential if they were to be taken seriously by others, and their own belief that they could do so was essential to their beliefs in the reality of any phenomena. This competence was constructed and warranted through appeals to observations and experiments, in which adequately controlled conditions excluded ordinary explanations. But belief on the basis of adequate evidence required the rejection of inadequate evidence, and if the former meant controlled experiments by experienced investigators, then the rejection of other kinds of evidence was essential to maintaining that position. Rejecting such performances because they did not count as adequate evidence did not challenge their beliefs; on the contrary, it was fundamental to their beliefs (in other, adequately investigated phenomena).

Extraordinary beliefs are based upon particular phenomena, because they are based upon a construction of 'adequate evidence', and this requires the rejection of 'inadequate evidence'. In short, believers are also disbelievers, and those who believe in (certain) phenomena have invariably rejected the evidence for (other) phenomena. In the process, they have often disagreed about which phenomena are paranormal. In disputing the facts and what they mean, the usual arguments have been deployed, even in disputes between fellow believers in the paranormal. This, of course, had long been the case, since mesmerists and spiritualists had often disagreed about the authenticity of particular phenomena. A brief examination of a more recent case shows that there has continued to be a variety of options in what to believe about particular extraordinary phenomena, regardless of what one believes about other phenomena.

The making of Marion

The SPR's rejection of the Piddington's feats was based upon an absence of experimental evidence that adequately excluded ordinary explanations. This, of course, had long been an argument of sceptics, and had been part of a longstanding dispute about who was competent to conduct such experiments, and therefore to exclude such explanations. However, when S. G. Soal noted that 'any competent investigator' could distinguish such feats from genuine telepathy, he no doubt had himself in mind. A few years earlier, he had carried out several experiments with Fredrick Marion, another stage performer, but one who did explicitly claim to have paranormal powers. Marion's claim led to him being tested by other members of the SPR, and the result was a dispute among psychical researchers about the reality of very particular phenomena, based not only upon who was competent but also upon what was extraordinary.

One of Marion's trademark effects was a demonstration of the ability to find hidden objects, much as muscle-readers such as Bishop had done, but without physical contact with any of the audience. Through a series of experiments that were described as 'outstanding' in *Nature*, Soal compared Marion's ability to find hidden objects in a number of conditions.[75] In the process, he excluded both collusion and trickery, but he also excluded paranormal abilities. As far as he was concerned, Marion's powers were remarkable and rare ('powers which are probably possessed by not one man in a million'), but were a manifestation of supersensitive not extrasensory abilities. According to Soal, Marion was able to find hidden objects by picking up on subtle visual cues from the audience, who knew where the object was hidden, and who unconsciously conveyed its location by small movements of their head and eyes.[76]

Marion also demonstrated the ability to divine the names of playing cards, which Soal attributed to 'sometimes visual and sometimes tactual cues', such as identifying subtle marks or crimps [bends] in certain cards. This, Soal explained, had been duplicated by members of the Magic Circle who had seen Marion perform.[77] It was not, however, the only ordinary explanation available. One suggestion, by a physiologist, had been that Marion might rely upon subtle differences in sound, that 'each card had a pitch or keynote of its own, perceptible only to Marion', but Soal had considered this 'far-fetched'.[78] According to Harry Price, who had also been involved in testing him, Marion's abilities were the result of hyperaesthesia, which he defined as an exaggerated sensibility or hyperacuity of the normal senses.[79] Thus, his abilities were extraordinary, indeed they had 'to be seen to be believed', but they were not paranormal.[80]

Marion was subsequently tested by R. H. Thouless and B. P. Weisner, a fellow member of the SPR, who came to the opposite conclusion. Their views were first announced in a foreword to Marion's autobiography, *In My Mind's Eye* (1949), and readers would have been in no doubt that ordinary explanations had been excluded by competent observers. Their scientific credentials were displayed in the long title of the book ('with a foreword by R. H. Thouless, MA, PhD, University Reader in Educational Psychology, Cambridge, and B. P. Weisner, DSc, PhD') and repeated again, just two pages later, above the foreword itself. There they explained how their doubts about Soal's investigation had made them 'anxious to make a new investigation', that this had been conducted 'under strictly controlled experimental conditions', and that it had 'convinced us of the reality of Marion's paranormal capacities'.[81]

In the relevant chapter of his autobiography, Marion also rejected Soal's conclusion, maintaining that he did indeed possess paranormal powers. In support, he appealed to the views of Edmond P. Gibson, whom he described as 'well qualified', being 'an American investigator of wide knowledge and repute in these matters'. He then listed Gibson's many, and sometimes sarcastic, criticisms of Soal's experimental procedures, and his view that Soal was prejudiced against admitting the telepathy hypothesis.[82] These criticisms of his competence and accusations of prejudice were, in turn, disputed by Soal when he reviewed the book for the *JSPR*, in which he questioned Gibson's repute, and claimed that '[o]nly the credulous believe that vaudeville mystery showmen perform their feats by telepathy'.[83]

However, in that remarkably well-populated territory that lies between prejudice and credulity, alongside the usual disputes over whether ordinary explanations had been excluded, and who was competent to assess this matter, there was also a disagreement about what counted as extraordinary. According to Thouless and Weisner, when they read Soal's report, '[w]e were more sceptical of the reality of sensory hyper-acuity than of the existence of paranormal ways of obtaining knowledge'.[84] Gibson also complained that Soal's prejudice had led him 'to scamper so nimbly from hypothesis to hypothesis to explain a simple phenomenon and has to invent a "hyperaesthesia" for which there is little or no real psychological proof'. For Marion's proponents, hyperaesthesia was a more extraordinary explanation for the facts than paranormal abilities.[85]

As they disputed the meaning of Marion's successes, so they disputed his failures. Soal had, as so many experimenters had done previously, reported initial success and subsequent failure, which he had attributed to increasingly tighter experimental controls. But for Weisner, this was an 'unwarranted interpretation', and Soal had shown instead 'that in certain complex situations positive results tend to disappear'.[86] Meanwhile, Thouless suggested that Marion's initial successes might actually count as evidence of paranormal capacities. He also rejected the claim by Soal that members of the Magic Circle had duplicated Marion's card feats: 'such success as Marion had with cards was under conditions not duplicated by the conjuror'. Attributing Marion's lack of consistency to a sceptical environment, they had 'found that Marion may fail altogether with a hostile or suspicious audience'. His much greater success on stage, on the other hand, was 'impossible to establish experimentally ... [but]

even if he uses trickery on stage, he might have been led to the idea of stage telepathic performance by finding that he had paranormal powers which, however, were not reliable enough to depend on by themselves for his effects'.[87]

Thus, all the facts were reframed accordingly, as failures did not discount the successes, and were merely further evidence of the nature of the phenomena, which often failed in a sceptical environment. Duplications were not proper duplications, and faking the phenomena was understandable when a psychic was under pressure to succeed. These now familiar arguments were being deployed in a very particular context, between two senior figures in psychical research who agreed on all the basics: that telepathy was real; that testing a stage performer for telepathic abilities was worthwhile; that some of his feats were not telepathy; that whether he had any telepathic abilities was a matter to be determined by proper experimental enquiry; and even that the experiments had excluded chance and fraud. Nevertheless, they framed the facts differently, not only Marion's successes but also his failures, and in ways that closely resembled longstanding disputes between believers and disbelievers.[88] In this case, however, beliefs and disbeliefs were not about the existence of telepathy, or about the reality of Marion's abilities, but about whether these particular abilities counted as telepathy.

Such differences in belief about particular phenomena are a reminder that believers do not believe in just anything, not merely in relation to paranormal categories but in relation to any given example. As spiritualists had disagreed about individual mediums, or particular demonstrations by them, so psychical researchers and parapsychologists rejected certain unexplained feats, and disputed specific experimental evidence. What they believed in, and what they believed about these things (whether they were real, whether paranormal, and what that meant in relation to science) cannot be captured by a simplistic dichotomy between belief and disbelief, because the objects and forms of extraordinary belief have always been more complicated.

Nevertheless, one could still construct a boundary between belief and disbelief, and around a kind of person who believed certain things about certain things. It seemed obvious enough, at least to some, that there were those who believed in the paranormal, that there were those who did not believe, and that the former kind of belief was not only wrong but also harmful. A new psychology of error emerged, which reflected all the old arguments but, unlike the earlier psychology of belief, was clearly a new area of academic Psychology. It began in the 1970s, as the phenomena associated with Uri Geller were being disputed around the world, and a new group of critics (which included several psychologists and magicians) were expressing their disbelief about Geller's phenomena, based upon possible ordinary explanations, the inadequacy of the conditions to exclude such explanations, a lack of specialist expertise in assessing this, and so on.[89]

However, the targets of the new sceptical movement were considerably broader than Geller, and included all claims to paranormal powers. Indeed, its roots are more directly located in an attempt to debunk astrology as erroneous, incompatible with science and reason (and, therefore, a bad thing), based upon an explicit appeal to scientific authority.[90] This particular debunking effort led to a conference at SUNY-Buffalo, New York, in 1976 on 'The New Irrationalisms: Antiscience and Pseudoscience', which in turn led to the founding of the Committee for the Scientific Inquiry of Claims of the Paranormal (CSICOP).[91] CSICOP became the heart of the new sceptical movement, first in the United States, then internationally, and as a result has played a significant role in the shaping of extraordinary beliefs.

The new sceptical movement that CSICOP represented was a manifestation of one side of the ongoing argument about extraordinary phenomena, and as it sought to debunk the paranormal, so it constructed and deployed psychological knowledge about belief. At the same time, parapsychologists were also interested in beliefs about the paranormal, albeit for quite different reasons. In the process, two identifiably different psychologies of paranormal belief emerged, each of which expressed one side of the ongoing dispute about paranormal phenomena, because each emerged from two quite different social and discursive contexts. The result was two quite different kinds of psychological knowledge, and we can see not only how such knowledge was constructed, but also how it has been constructive of people.

The making of paranormal belief

As previous chapters have explained, what can be described as a 'psychology of error' predated the emergence of Psychology as a discipline, and the early American psychologists' 'psychology of belief' was hardly an area of academic Psychology. Indeed a formal psychology of belief, in the sense of a large number of publications in scientific journals that drew upon prior work and sought to develop methods and theory, did not emerge until the twentieth century. When it did, the form(s) it took directly reflected different sides of the ongoing dispute about the reality of paranormal phenomena.

At the beginning of the twentieth century, a psychology of superstition emerged within the United States, out of a concern that superstitious beliefs persisted even among college students.[92] Within this educational context, such beliefs were seen not only as irrational, but also as a problem to be eradicated.[93] According to the questionnaires used in these early studies, the objects of superstitious belief were broad, ranging from stereotypical superstitions, concerning luck and fortune-telling, to phrenology and mesmerism, spiritualism and telepathy.[94] An extensive literature appeared over the following decades until, in the 1970s, a new psychology of paranormal belief appeared.

This new psychological research was driven by concerns about growing interest in the paranormal, it cited earlier work on superstitious belief, and described paranormal belief as a new superstition.[95] It was also associated with the new sceptical movement centred on the foundation of CSICOP and its organ, initially called *The Zetetic* and, shortly afterwards, the *Skeptical Inquirer*. Early contributors to the psychology of paranormal belief were members of CSICOP, published in its journal, cited related sceptical literature in their own articles, and discussed such beliefs in very similar ways, that is as not only wrong but also dangerous.[96] Thus, for example, in the same year that Tobacyk published the Paranormal Belief Scale (1983), he wrote in *Skeptical Inquirer* that paranormal beliefs could lead to ideologies 'destructive to individuals and society'.[97]

For such sceptical psychologists, the 'paranormal' was defined as widely as superstition had been. It included not only extrasensory perception but also a wide range of other strange phenomena such as witches, superstitions, UFOs and the Loch Ness Monster. The questionnaires used to measure paranormal belief reflected this wide definition, including statements about phenomena that, while remarkably diverse, were regarded (by those who constructed the measures) as equally erroneous.[98] Tobacyk and Milford pointed out that their questionnaire, unlike others, was based upon factor analysis, rather than upon a priori assumptions about what counted as paranormal belief.[99] However, while this might have warranted the sub-scales into which they divided paranormal belief, it did not explain the scope of their definition of paranormal belief. Indeed, when the definition was subsequently criticized as too broad, the dispute rested upon non-empirical considerations.[100] Such a wide definition of the paranormal reflected a standard view of critics of parapsychology, who had long sought to discredit such phenomena by making associations with witchcraft and the occult.[101] This association now became an intrinsic feature of the scales they used to measure beliefs, based upon the assumption that they were the same kind of thing.

The sceptical view that all such phenomena were the product of error and fraud was similarly reflected in the 'cognitive deficits' hypothesis that they offered, which explained paranormal belief in terms of low intelligence, inadequate education, and so on.[102] The ostensible purpose of this latest example of the psychology of error was, like previous versions, to explain and deter beliefs that were not only erroneous but also harmful. Moreover, as we shall see, the new methods of psychology allowed studies to be conducted into ways of reducing such beliefs.

Meanwhile, at around the same time, another psychology of paranormal belief emerged, one that had its roots in experimental parapsychology. Gertrude Schmeidler's experiments in clairvoyance, which suggested that believers were more successful than non-believers (the so-called 'sheep-goat effect') led to growing parapsychological interest in the question of belief. However, when parapsychologists conducted studies into paranormal belief, they did so in ways that were fundamentally different from those of sceptics, in terms of what was being studied, how it was being measured, what hypotheses were being explored, and why the research was being conducted.

Parapsychologists defined the paranormal more narrowly than sceptics, 'psi' being defined as ESP and psychokinesis, and sometimes including survival after death.[103] The scales that these researchers used reflected this narrower definition, which did not ask about witches or superstitions, and their papers, normally published in parapsychology journals, were unconvinced by a 'cognitive deficits' hypothesis that portrayed believers as 'illogical, irrational, credulous, uncritical and foolish'.[104] Indeed, since from their perspective, paranormal beliefs were not necessarily wrong, the purpose was not to eradicate belief but in part to provide a better understanding of how psi worked, since the elusive phenomenon might be more easily found by understanding the sheep-goat effect. This was itself a direct reflection of the longstanding views among proponents that regular failure to produce the phenomena was a result of the nature of the phenomena, and that the beliefs of those present might have an effect.

For several years, these two versions of the psychology of paranormal belief continued in parallel, with very little crossover, on the basis of different definitions, measures, hypotheses and aims, all of which directly reflected different views about the reality of the paranormal. In short, these two psychologies of paranormal belief can be seen as expressions of opposing beliefs about the paranormal; they have been manifestations of the very beliefs that they have sought to understand.

This, then, is an example of the reflexive nature of psychological knowledge, in the sense that it can be constructed in ways that are inextricably linked to those who produce it. However, it is also an example of how psychological knowledge can be constructive of people, as it has not only been shaped by, but has also shaped beliefs about the paranormal. Moreover, Ian Hacking has argued that changes in psychological knowledge can lead to the 'making up' of people, that new psychological categories can bring about new kinds of people, and thus new ways to think, feel and act in the world.[105] In this sense of constructiveness, the categorization of 'abnormality' has been a particular focus, in part because of the obvious real-world consequences of being classed in this way.[106]

However, if psychological knowledge is constructive as well as constructed, then we should find evidence of 'normal' people being made up in all sorts of ways, according to various psychological categories, as extraverts or introverts, say, or as left-brained or right-brained. And, of course, we do hear people regularly interact with such categories, describing themselves as being one or the other, and explaining and justifying their behaviour in the process. Such terms provide folk with ways of understanding themselves and their relationships with others, and cannot help but affect how they think, feel and act. However, the same might be said for zodiac signs or national identity, which are commonly associated with psychological traits, but are not part of psychological knowledge in the same sense as extraversion or hemispheric dominance. And indeed, when one describes oneself as an extravert, the link to psychological knowledge beyond the use of the term may be rather tenuous.

Thus, we need to consider carefully in what ways psychological knowledge can be constructive of its particular subject matter, or of people more generally. In this case, we are concerned with how the psychology of paranormal belief has shaped its own subject matter (beliefs about the paranormal), and how it has more generally shaped how people think and act, which (arguably) has led to the making up of a new kind of person.

The making of the modern sceptic

As noted earlier, the dominant version of the psychology of paranormal belief was associated with the new sceptical movement, at the centre of which was CSICOP, which was founded at a conference on 'anti-science and pseudo-science', which had itself emerged from a well-publicized attempt to convince the public that astrology was nonsense, based upon an appeal to scientific authority. From the beginning, then, CSICOP represented a concern about paranormal beliefs, that they were not only wrong but also harmful, and that science could and should do something about them. Its journal from 1977, *Skeptical Inquirer* (*SI*), regularly stressed the importance of explaining the origins of such beliefs, as well as expressing the desire to reduce them. During the early years, articles on belief frequently appeared in *SI*, most of them written by psychologists. Many of them presented data from empirical studies that they had carried out, all of which suggested that belief in the paranormal could be explained in terms of cognitive deficits, that is as the result of lack of knowledge, uncritical thinking, cognitive biases and other forms of ineffective cognitive functioning.[107] Readers of *SI* were thus not only told, but also provided with psychological evidence, that those who believed in the paranormal were cognitively inferior to those of a sceptical disposition.

At the same time, the value of psychological expertise was reinforced. Indeed, psychologists were portrayed as the most sceptical of scientists, because (it was suggested) they were the most knowledgeable of the evidence, and of the causes of belief.[108] Many books, written by sceptical psychologists, were reviewed in *SI*, and these books (and the reviews) reinforced the psychology of error. Marks and Kamman's *The Psychology of the Psychic* (1980) was praised for its description of various cognitive biases that induce fallacious belief.[109] Hansel's *ESP: A Critical Re-evaluation* (1980) was described as a persuasive exposure of the gullibility of parapsychologists.[110] Alcock's *Parapsychology: Science or Magic?* (1981) was described as providing an excellent discussion of why people hold erroneous beliefs.[111] Zusne and Jones' *Anomalistic Psychology* (1982) was hailed as the best book yet on how psychological principles can account for seemingly paranormal phenomena (though the reviewer, another psychologist, politely noted that it had failed to discuss adequately the role of poor reasoning skills).[112]

Most of the authors of these sceptical texts, like the reviewers, had formal links to CSICOP, and their books, along with Frazier's *Paranormal Borderlands of Science* (1981), which was a collection of articles from *SI*, became standard sceptical textbooks.[113] The importance of such books was understood as part of the battle against irrational thinking; beliefs were not only wrong but also harmful, and their reduction a clear aim of CSICOP, who regularly stressed the need for greater scientific education and increased critical thinking.

Indeed, articles also began to appear in *SI* providing psychological evidence that such beliefs could be reduced through increased understanding of scientific thinking.[114] The desire to change belief was, of course, a product of concern. According to Tobacyk, who had just published elsewhere what would become the most widely used measure of paranormal belief:

> This concern is clearly warranted, since history provides many illustrations of how certain paranormal beliefs have crystallized into ideologies destructive to individuals and society, indeed sometimes to human life itself (e.g., witchcraft, Nazism, the Jonestown case, etc.).[115]

Such harmful beliefs could be reduced, however, by the practical deployment of scientific knowledge. Changes could be induced by sceptical textbooks, most of which were written by psychologists, and recently invented belief scales could measure the extent of success. One psychologist, 'distressed' by levels of belief among his students, and 'astonished' at the lack of concern among his colleagues, 'decided to pursue [his] own quiet campaign'.[116] He introduced a college course based upon sceptical textbooks and, according to Tobacyk's scale, this resulted in a highly significant decline in belief.[117] Another psychologist also reported how his own university course, which took a sceptical approach to the paranormal, and used similar sceptical textbooks, managed to reduce belief among his students from 85 to 50 per cent. 'Although the immediate changes are quite large', he concluded, 'it is disappointing that the willingness to express belief is still quite high'.[118]

That harmful beliefs might be reduced through improvements in the dissemination of scientific knowledge was always a core theme of CSICOP. What psychologists specifically offered at this time, in addition to a significant contribution to the content and form of that knowledge, was evidence that its dissemination actually worked. What it provided for sceptical readers was evidence not only that they were cognitively superior to believers, but also that they could improve society through the dissemination of sceptical (i.e. their kind of) thinking.

CSICOP had been born of a conference, and social interaction was an obvious core feature of the emerging sceptical movement. Local groups of sceptics began to appear in 1982, initially in California, and in 1983, CSICOP held its first international conference at SUNY, Buffalo. This included a symposium entitled 'Why People Believe: the Psychology of Deception', in which academic psychologists explained to conference delegates how beliefs could result from sensory error, misattribution, lack of understanding of probability, and wishful thinking.[119] The theme of its second conference, held at Stanford in 1984, and co-sponsored by the Psychology department, was 'Paranormal Beliefs: Scientific Facts and Fiction', at which 600 delegates, in addition to hearing why UFOs, astrology and various psychic phenomena were not real, were told by a well-known psychologist about the various cognitive fallacies of believers.[120] The third international conference, held at University College London, which took the theme of 'Investigation and Belief', included data that believers were more neurotic and more stubborn than sceptics, a theme echoed by other speakers who spoke of the stubbornness of beliefs in UFOs and fringe medicine.[121] *SI* noted the importance of the social aspects of such conferences, both to the individuals who attended and in the creation of a community of sceptics seeking to create a better-informed public, and stressed the importance of understanding how erroneous beliefs come about.[122]

Throughout the following decade, psychological evidence continued to appear in *SI*, dismissing all manner of extraordinary beliefs, from astrology to reincarnation, and standard psychology textbooks were reviewed as examples of critical thinking.[123] By the mid 1990s, *SI* reflected the remarkable growth in the sceptical movement. In 1995, the magazine increased its frequency from quarterly to bi-monthly, and printed 67,500 issues of the first of the new full-size magazine format editions. The new and growing readership was treated to articles by Carl Sagan, Richard Dawkins and Francis Crick, and was also told of the recent conference of which the theme had been 'The Psychology of Belief'. There, in addition to debunking alien abductions, psychologists had presented a variety of explanations for erroneous beliefs, from misperception and misremembering to deception by others, all of which were now repeated for those who were new to scepticism, or for anyone else who had been unable to attend.[124]

There were to be plenty more opportunities to take part in sceptical social activities, however, as local groups continued to emerge and conferences grew in number and size. Local groups had emerged in the 1980s, not only in the USA but also in Australia, Canada, France, Mexico and the UK, and by the time of CSICOP's twentieth anniversary, in 1996, they existed in more than 20 countries.[125] This year also saw the first World Skeptics Congress, in New York, where over 1,200 delegates from 24 countries could meet, discuss the gullibility of others, and buy T-shirts that displayed their sceptical credentials.[126] All of this was reported in *SI*, which remained the core publication of the movement, and which continued to publish articles by psychologists who explained how erroneous beliefs came about.[127] In the process of pointing out the various ways in which beliefs were the result of cognitive errors, they reinforced the view that sceptics were less prone to error than believers.

By 2001, as it celebrated its 25th anniversary, *SI* could boast of approximately 100 sceptical organizations in 38 countries – from Argentina to Kazakhstan, and Korea to Norway – and the 'Sceptics in the Pub' groups had already begun their rapid growth in the UK. Online sites and fora have followed, and other sceptical magazines have appeared, but CSICOP and *SI* have remained at the heart of the international movement.[128] The rise of the new sceptical movement has been a remarkable success, and has gradually widened its target from paranormal and 'pseudoscientific' claims to other perceived enemies of science and rationality, such as orthodox religion and postmodernism, though the paranormal has remained a core target.

Psychologists have clearly played a significant role in the movement, but psychological knowledge has had a particular impact. It has reinforced the view that paranormal beliefs are wrong not only by debunking various bodies of evidence, but also by explaining how such beliefs are due to cognitive errors. Unlike alternative articles on belief that appeared in *SI*, such as those that focused on wider social factors, it has largely explained belief in individualistic terms, by providing evidence that paranormal belief is the result of individual cognitive deficits.[129] In doing so, it has provided sceptics with evidence that they are better informed, less gullible, more critical thinkers than believers. By explaining the harmfulness of such beliefs, and by providing evidence that they can be reduced by better education in science and critical thinking skills, it has underwritten the value of sceptical thinking in society. In short, it has played a fundamental role in making being a sceptic a desirable and worthwhile kind of person to be.

Discussion

The emergence of parapsychology saw the continuation of arguments about whether ordinary explanations had been excluded, what counted as extraordinary, and who was competent to assess the matter, not only between proponents and critics of parapsychology, but also among parapsychologists who expressed both belief and disbelief about different phenomena and different explanations. Meanwhile, the public were provided with countless demonstrations of mind-reading, which were designed to be both convincingly real and ambiguous in terms of what was going on. Faced with unexplained events that resembled telepathy, some believers in telepathy declined to believe, expressing the view that fraud was involved, despite not being able to explain the details. In the process, like so many sceptics before them, they appealed to the possibility of fraud, and presented themselves as the ones who were competent to assess what was going on.

A new psychology of error emerged in the form of a psychology of paranormal belief, which reflected the beliefs of those who sought to explain beliefs with which they disagreed, and which was deployed with a view to changing the views of those they believed to be wrong. This was part and parcel of the modern sceptical movement, from which the modern 'sceptic' emerged, though whether this is a new 'kind of person' depends upon what one means by 'kind'. At one level, there are obvious ways in which thousands of individuals identify themselves as 'sceptics': by reading, and subscribing to, sceptical magazines; by attending local sceptics' groups and larger national and international conferences; and by buying and displaying sceptical merchandise (T-shirts, mugs, badges and transfers).[130] Furthermore, since modern scepticism has been from the start an attempt to persuade others, the construction and deployment of sceptical arguments has been a fundamental part of the movement. Sceptics have engaged in sceptical discourse, among themselves and with less sceptical folk, though the line between expressions of belief (I am sceptical) and identity (I am a sceptic) is a difficult one to draw.

However, according to the psychological knowledge that has dominated the sceptical literature, this is more than an expression of identity. The thrust of the 'cognitive deficits' hypothesis has been that sceptics are cognitively different from believers. This, of course, has been disputed, primarily by psychologists associated with parapsychology, but the validity of the hypothesis is not the point here. If we wish to argue that this is an example of psychological knowledge leading to the creation of a new kind of person, then we can argue that the psychology of paranormal belief, in the form of the 'cognitive deficits' argument, has played a fundamental role in the making of the modern sceptic (who, according to this same knowledge, is cognitively different from a believer).

However, whether this counts as an example of making up people is unimportant, except as a starting point to explore how psychological knowledge can shape how people think, feel and behave. What is clear is that, as an argument against the reality of paranormal phenomena, the 'sceptical' psychology of paranormal belief has been an expression of belief about the paranormal, and has provided arguments that warrant and reinforce particular beliefs about the paranormal. These arguments can, and indeed have been, deployed not only to maintain individual positions, but also with a view to changing the beliefs of others. In the process, it has helped create a social, intellectual and political movement that has led to large numbers of people thinking, feeling and acting in particular ways that, if one wishes to, one might describe as a new kind of person. After all, Hacking has noted himself that no two stories of making up people will be the same.[131] Alternatively, one can simply note that the psychology of paranormal belief has, in fundamental and significant ways, both reflected and affected the beliefs that it has purported to explain.

SEVEN

The making of extraordinary beliefs

Since the days of mesmerism, there have been countless demonstrations of extraordinary feats, most of which, if real, would now be classed as paranormal. These have been reported by observers, and framed in various ways by those who have seen, heard or read about them. The demonstrations have been designed to be convincing, by being demonstrated in ways that seem to exclude ordinary explanations such as chance and fraud. The demonstration and reporting of these events have been accompanied by regular arguments about expertise (about who was competent to assess whether ordinary explanations had been excluded), about how extraordinary they were (in particular, in relation to contemporary science) and about the desirability of the claims being made. In the process, beliefs have been formed.

In disputing these events, everyone has appealed to the facts, though they have often disagreed about what happened, and even when they have agreed about the facts, they have been able to frame what happened in support of either belief or disbelief. Any unexplained feat could be framed as chance or fraud, and any failure, duplication or exposure as evidence in support of the reality of the phenomena. For all the changes in the terms that have been used to refer to events that were part of contemporary debates about mesmerism, spiritualism, psychical research and parapsychology, there have been remarkable continuities. In short, we have been having a very similar argument for a very long time. Some of the continuities should be clear by now, but a broader discussion might be useful, based upon how beliefs about such phenomena have been expressed since the early nineteenth century.

The particularity of extraordinary beliefs

Extraordinary beliefs are based upon particular events, the ones in which people believe. No proponent of mesmerism, no spiritualist, and no believer in psychic phenomena has believed everything they have seen. Believers have always distinguished between events that they believed to be real and those that they did not. A believer in mesmeric analgesia was not necessarily a believer in lucid somnambulism, a believer in Daniel Home was not necessarily a believer in the Davenport brothers, a believer in the powers of Palladino (or Geller) could believe that, at times, she (or he) faked it. Prominent psychical researchers have disagreed about the authenticity of particular individuals, and parapsychologists have disagreed about the validity of particular experiments. In short, all believers are also disbelievers.

What they have in common is that they all believe in something. One need only believe in one paranormal phenomenon in order to be a believer in the paranormal. As William James noted, a single white crow is sufficient. From that point on, other facts may be irrelevant, since all the wigs in the world do not demonstrate the non-existence of real hair. All the subsequent failures, duplications and exposures can be accommodated, and indeed can be seen as evidence that such phenomena are real, but inconsistent and elusive. Nevertheless, believers in one thing are not necessarily believers in another, not merely in terms of abstract categories but also in terms of particular events. Two believers in ESP, for example, might believe in quite different things, for different reasons.

Furthermore, disbelievers are also believers, who believe that all extraordinary phenomena can be explained according to ordinary processes. This has also been on the basis of particular phenomena, since nobody can examine every phenomenon, and so the claim that none of them are real has had to be based upon a more general view: extraordinary claims require extraordinary evidence, and until such evidence has been provided, the default position must be disbelief. But what counts as extraordinary, and therefore as adequate evidence, has also been an ongoing matter of dispute. Thus, we cannot understand such beliefs until we consider not only the objects of belief, but also the forms of belief: what do folk believe is going on in relation to any given event?

The history of disputes about extraordinary phenomena shows that believers have regularly expressed a range of views, not only about different events, but also in terms of what was going on in relation to any given event. There have been at least three related, but distinct, positions regarding: whether it was real; the process involved; and the relationship of that process to science. Since the days of mesmerism, people have distinguished between facts and theories, and disagreed about whether such theories are compatible with science. Throughout this time, countless folk have said that what they saw was real, without providing an explanation, or else, when discussing a particular explanation, have done so in terms that framed it as compatible with science. One might believe that mind-reading is possible, that this is the result of ESP, and that this is incompatible with current scientific knowledge, but these are nevertheless three distinct positions.

Furthermore, there has been remarkable ambiguity surrounding the various terms that have been available as descriptions for extraordinary phenomena. Those who have demonstrated such phenomena have framed similar feats in radically different ways, while scientists seeking to provide an explanation have often been unclear. One could hardly blame the public if they resorted to the view that 'something' was going on. This, after all, is the refuge of the disbeliever who, unable to explain what he assumes to be a trick, maintains that it was 'definitely something'.[1] But unless we know what folk mean by this, we do not understand their beliefs. We can provide them with a questionnaire, of course, force them to choose an option and assume that they understand it as we do, but that is a tad presumptuous.

If we must draw a line between belief and disbelief – rather than discuss a variety of beliefs – it is presumably in the distinction between the belief that some events are real and the belief that none are real. This might be found in the decision to exclude (in the case of particular events) ordinary explanations such as chance and fraud. To reject these explanations, it might be said, is to believe that a given event is real, but real in what sense? As something other than chance or fraud, as something in particular, as something that is not compatible with science? Even stereotypical scientific sceptics, such as Braid, Carpenter and Munsterberg, ruled out chance and fraud in relation to certain extraordinary events, framing what they saw as compatible with scientific knowledge (though whether current scientists would agree is quite another matter; indeed they might classify these sceptics as believers). Meanwhile, in the real world, where individuals continue to exhibit extraordinary feats of hypnosis and mind-reading, subliminal perception and non-verbal communication, appealing to scientific expertise that might well seem impressive to non-experts, and where the public can read that peer-reviewed scientific journals have published evidence for ESP, what are folk supposed to believe?

The line between belief and disbelief is meaningless until we know the object of belief, and remains meaningless unless we know what is believed about it. In the interests of doing scientific work, psychologists have reduced beliefs to a form in which they can be counted: forced-choice responses to statements about general categories, the meanings of which are often vague and variable. This is not meaningless, it is merely reductive, and provides some sense of differences between individuals. In the process, however, it misses the enormous variety and complexity of how extraordinary beliefs are expressed and warranted in the real world. Only a more open-ended approach can capture the forms that such beliefs take, and can show how they are inextricably bound up with reasons for holding them.

Extraordinary beliefs and expertise

Beliefs about extraordinary phenomena depend upon the construction of adequate expertise. One cannot believe that one (or someone else) has excluded ordinary explanations unless one believes that one (or someone else) is competent to do so. In framing extraordinary events, matters of competence have always been present, if only in deciding whether or not one's senses can be trusted. Everyone believes and disbelieves: to disbelieve X is to believe 'not X', and believers in X have disbelieved in Y. In doing so, they have distinguished between the wigs and the genuine hair, based upon the assumption that they are competent to do so. But in expressing beliefs about the facts, and in disputing whether they are facts at all, there have been ongoing circular arguments involving belief, the facts and expertise.

As we have seen, those who have expressed beliefs about mesmeric, spiritualist, psychic and paranormal phenomena have consistently attributed their beliefs to observations. However, they have also regularly attributed observations to beliefs. According to proponents, disbelief inhibits the phenomena, while belief makes success more likely. Critics agree, though for different reasons, that phenomena are less likely to succeed in front of a sceptical audience than an audience of believers. And, regardless of what is observed, it can be framed as evidence in favour of belief (or disbelief). Thus, as everyone has attributed their beliefs to the facts, both sides have also appealed to belief as an explanation for the facts, while framing the facts as supportive of their own beliefs.

Critics have regularly claimed that belief is both a cause and an effect of inadequate expertise: belief leads to misinterpretation of the facts, and is the result of misinterpretation of the facts. Thus, belief has been, for critics, an indication of a lack of adequate expertise. Indeed, disbelief has required the claims of proponents to be rejected, on the assumption that they are not sufficiently competent to assess the matter (if only because they are insufficiently sceptical). The most generous position a critic can take is that we all make mistakes but, in this case, it is you, not I, who is mistaken.

There have been appeals to different kinds of relevant expertise, but scientific and, particularly, psychological expertise has been prominent. The dominant theme has been a psychology of error, in which beliefs have been attributed to various kinds of erroneous thinking. However, the psychology of error has done more than provide an explanation for extraordinary beliefs. Since the days of mesmerism, it has been a means through which psychological scientists have been able to construct their own expertise, not only as superior to that of others, but also as a useful thing. Hardly surprising, then, that it was an attractive option to the pioneers of a new science of psychology, who made the argument in popular as well as scientific periodicals.

In doing so, they expressed their own beliefs about spiritualist and psychic phenomena. This was done via the scientific boundary-work in which they engaged, which disputed the lines between scientific psychology and psychical research, and which was less a dispute about what to study, or how to study it, than about what conclusions were drawn. Testing a medium for psychic ability, and proposing an ordinary explanation, counted as scientific psychology; a more extraordinary conclusion did not. In doing so, the psychology of error was a means of displaying expertise and worth, and of drawing a boundary between science and pseudo-science, thus separating the experts from the non-experts. Beliefs about extraordinary phenomena have been inextricably bound up with matters of personal competence, reliability and authority. In expressing a particular view, and in defending that view in particular ways, people have been able to present themselves as knowledgeable and useful folk. This has been the case for anyone who has held a particular view, and it has been the case for psychologists, because psychologists are people too.

The point is not that scientific psychology does not get at what is really going on; perhaps it does, but that depends upon the details. Nevertheless, as Graham Richards would say, we are dealing with people studying people, and so psychology is necessarily reflexive. In the form of a particular kind of psychology of paranormal belief, the psychology of error has continued to provide an explanation for extraordinary beliefs, while expressing an alternative belief about the phenomena in question, and while being deployed as part of an attempt to reduce beliefs in such phenomena. It is, then, an excellent example of the reflexive nature of psychological knowledge. It has been constructed in line with particular beliefs about the paranormal, and has been constructive of the beliefs of others via application and dissemination, and by helping to define the modern sceptic. In a variety of ways, psychological knowledge about such beliefs has been inseparable from its own subject matter.

On other beliefs about extraordinary phenomena

The previous chapters have discussed the phenomena that were the basis of mesmerism and spiritualism, and the focus of the early days of psychical research and parapsychology. Such demonstrations continued to interest not only psychical researchers and parapsychologists, but also the public and, largely because of this, sceptical psychologists. Such phenomena are, in certain respects, similar to other objects of superstitious, magical and religious belief.[2] However, despite the conceptual overlaps, we need to be wary of generalizing about beliefs in such phenomena. After all, the phenomena discussed so far were designed to be demonstrably extraordinary, presented by others as evidence of something, and framed in relation to contemporary science. Furthermore, even in relation to the phenomena discussed, we have seen that beliefs have been based upon particular phenomena, and that believers have framed very similar demonstrations in significantly different ways. Nevertheless, other phenomena than those discussed have been the objects of paranormal belief, and so deserve brief consideration.

It has often been said that personal experience is the most common factor in paranormal belief, though a personal experience might be in the company of a medium or psychic. Indeed, every account that has been discussed so far has been an account of a personal experience. However, there have been countless private experiences, in the sense that folk have been alone, or at least have experienced something extraordinary that was not a demonstration by someone else. This might include such phenomena as out-of-body-experiences, apparitions and poltergeists. It would also include experiences in which, though nothing anomalous was seen or heard, something extraordinary was deemed to have happened – a dream came true, a prayer was answered, someone was thinking of an aunt when she called – in short, what many more sceptical folk would regard as a coincidence.

Accounts of private perceptual experiences, though not debated as commonly as those discussed here, have nevertheless been examined, and there are certainly similarities. In a detailed analysis, Wooffitt has shown how such experiences have been described in ways designed to make them convincing: by discounting alternative explanations; by addressing the extraordinariness of the event; and by presenting the speaker as one who is a competent observer.[3] In describing such private experiences, accounts have been designed to portray what happened as real, rather than to express a belief that what happened was extraordinary. Nevertheless, in expressing the view that an extraordinary event *really* occurred, one is expressing the view that the event was real (though what that means may remain unclear). In short, it might be seen as a belief in the reality of an ostensibly paranormal event, but not necessarily in its paranormal nature.

In terms of meaningful coincidences, on the other hand, the reality of the events is not an issue, only the interpretation of them. Nobody would doubt that someone dreamt, or prayed, or thought of an aunt, and few would doubt the reality of subsequent events, or of the timely phone call. One could frame such a coincidence as unusual, exceptional, or even 'extraordinary' (in the sense that it is not an ordinary, everyday occurrence), but it could only count as a paranormal belief if it was framed as paranormal. One might make the connection between two events, and regard this as significant in some sense (if only in making the connection), but unless one gives this a particular name, and this refers to a process that is incompatible with science, then (by current definitions) this is not a belief in the paranormal. And unless the experient regards the named process as incompatible with science, then neither is this (depending upon how one interprets the definition) belief in the paranormal. In other words, fascinating as meaningful coincidences are, their relationship to paranormal belief depends upon the definition of the latter, and that has always been an ambiguous matter. The relevance of this to other approaches to paranormal belief shall be considered shortly.

Meanwhile, there has been a huge body of experimental work devoted to the investigation of paranormal phenomena. For parapsychologists, this work represents the most convincing argument for the reality of psi, and as such might be seen as the strongest justification for belief in the paranormal. Critics might say, on the other hand, that it merely demonstrates the inadequacy of the evidence. Both sides have regularly appealed to the evidence, disputed whether ordinary explanations have been excluded, the adequacy of expertise, and the extraordinariness of the claim. However, the parapsychologists' case may have suffered from the inheritance of certain historical arguments. The longstanding arguments about failures, the inconsistency of phenomena, and the influence of belief upon them, have come to take the form of theories, such as the 'decline effect', 'pragmatic information', 'psi missing' and the 'experimenter effect'. The idea that psi eludes empirical enquiry, and that the beliefs of those present may affect the process, has created a rhetorical dilemma for parapsychology, in which their object of scientific enquiry is defined in terms that seem to defy scientific enquiry.[4] In the long run, if psi is real and amenable to experimental investigation, then parapsychologists will no doubt eventually convince the sceptics. At present, however, the attribution of non-significant results to the nature of psi, regardless of whether or not it is true, is deeply unconvincing to those who do not already believe.

On the other hand, it has never been easier to be a sceptic, which is not necessarily good for scepticism. Being sceptical is one thing, but being a sceptic is a matter of identity, manifested in attendance at meetings, magazine subscriptions and, sometimes, the wearing of merchandise. Numerous stand-up comedians now express their disbeliefs about God or the paranormal, on stage and in rant, and growing numbers of magicians declare that psychics are frauds, including some who claim to have psychological skills that they do not have. Meanwhile, it is relativists (the ones who fly at 30,000 feet) who are accused of hypocrisy by folk who have misunderstood the argument.[5] Of course there are frauds, and there is postmodern mumbo-jumbo, just as there is bad science, but a sceptic needs to distinguish between the wheat and the chaff, and one cannot be, at the same time, both sceptical and evangelical.

Some would see the mark of the sceptic as the ability to change one's mind when faced with the facts, which is precisely what believers have done, at least that is what they tell us. The rhetoric of conversion has been a standard theme in the history of extraordinary beliefs. Believers had been sceptics once, but the facts had won them over, while those who refused to accept the facts, however extraordinary they might seem, were prejudiced and unscientific. Meanwhile, disbelievers remained sceptical, but that was the appropriate scientific response to extraordinary claims, and they were unconvinced because the facts were unconvincing to any unbiased person. Nevertheless, sceptics often claimed to have believed initially, or that they had been inclined to believe, and that they would indeed believe if only presented with genuine facts. Everyone has agreed that scepticism is good, and that prejudice is bad – in much the same sense that anything is fine up to a point, but one should not do it too much – hence, everyone has been sceptical, but open-minded.

Meanwhile, as everyone appealed to the facts, and to the need for unbiased observation of them, any of the observable evidence could be framed in line with any position. Such seeming indifference to the evidence is hardly unique, and is a reminder of the extent to which scientific knowledge is constructed.[6] After all, of what a particular observation is evidence is never self-evident. But seeming indifference is not actual indifference, and the construction of scientific knowledge is not independent of its subject matter. Thus, for example, parapsychologists can indeed frame negative findings so that they are consistent with the existence of psi.[7] Nevertheless, they distinguish between positive and negative findings, a distinction presumably prompted by something out there in the world.[8] Indeed, what these disputes show is that while proponents and critics can indeed come to opposing conclusions about even the agreed upon facts, this is not without some discursive work in order to frame the facts as evidence that supports, rather than challenges, a given position.

In short, the history of disputes shows how we have interacted with things in the real world, from stuff like 'death and furniture' to representations of the dead in the form of moving furniture, with countless other demonstrations of extraordinary feats, and with the views of others.[9] In the midst of this, we come to our own conclusions, after serious consideration, or perhaps precious little, but never without some kind of interaction with what we have seen, or read or heard.

Understanding extraordinary beliefs

According to *New Scientist*, 'whether or not you believe in the paranormal may depend entirely on your brain chemistry'. This rather enthusiastic claim was made when reporting the more sober work of Peter Brugger, whose experiments had shown that people with high levels of dopamine were more likely to find significance in coincidences, and pick out meaning and patterns where there were none.[10] For Brugger, meaningful coincidences exemplify paranormal beliefs. In an editorial of a special issue of *Cortex*, which made a tentative case for a neuropsychology of paranormal belief, he noted that coincidences 'beautifully serve to separate the scientifically-minded from the believer; while the former attempts an approximate calculation of odds and probability, the latter is simply overwhelmed by the "meaningfulness" of the coincidence... The meaningfulness of a coincidence is in the brain of the beholder'.[11]

It is an ideal match of object and method, as beliefs are created entirely within the brain, regardless of external circumstances. And such coincidences cover a wide range of paranormal phenomena, since they might be categorized as telepathy, precognition or PK, and might be viewed as evidence of astrology, spirit communication or witchcraft. Nothing extraordinary has happened; it is merely the brain misinterpreting ordinary events as something more than they really are. It is, undoubtedly, a worthwhile approach and, one suspects, there is something to it. However, it is not sufficient to justify the confinement of paranormal beliefs to the brain.

For one thing, there are many objects of paranormal belief that are observably extraordinary: anything, for example, that cannot be the result of chance, from a moving séance table to a bending spoon, or any other demonstration that has been designed to be convincing.

Such objects of belief are out there in the world, provoking us into coming up with some sort of explanation. Of course, the tendency to find meaning in randomness may correlate with beliefs about such events, but that is an empirical matter. And, in attempting to answer this question, belief scales are needed in order to distinguish between believers and disbelievers. The responses they give to general statements about kinds of paranormal phenomena are assumed to reflect the beliefs they have inside their brains. Without such expressions of belief, we can neither access nor recognize beliefs inside the brain. Linguistic expressions, of one kind or another, are essential to our understanding of paranormal beliefs, and these are necessarily out there in a place where we can see or hear them.

In the case of belief scales, people are forced to take a position towards a statement about some general category, and it is assumed that everyone is agreed upon what the terms mean. In the real world, however, beliefs are expressed in considerably more sophisticated ways, and it is often unclear what terms mean, or of what a particular event might count as an example. We cannot properly understand such beliefs without examining more detailed expressions, and by considering how they relate to beliefs themselves. There may be a culture-independent tendency to find patterns in the world, and differences in these may relate to different beliefs about the paranormal, but such tendencies themselves cannot be understood as paranormal beliefs. One cannot begin to consider paranormal beliefs until they are in a linguistic form, and whatever particular form this takes, it will depend upon meanings that come from language and culture. We cannot confine paranormal beliefs to the brain, since we cannot identify neural activity with such beliefs without using particular terms, making assumptions about what these terms mean, what they mean to others, that particular kinds of expressions represent internal stuff, and so on. We can, of course, choose to examine such beliefs as brain functions in order to study them from a neuropsychological perspective.[12] However, that is a choice of definition, shaped by a methodological preference, and there are other choices available.

This is easy to forget. The shift towards neuropsychological understandings is so common these days as to seem the obvious way to go. Beyond the more sophisticated research, there is a more general view increasingly expressed, one with direct links to the sceptical movement. According to some, the brain is a belief engine, which seeks patterns and sees agency in the world, leading to beliefs that are too easily verified, and stubborn in the face of disconfirming evidence. According to this view, we are rescued from our believing brains by science, which acts as a corrective to our flawed subjectivity. Paranormal beliefs, like other false beliefs, are held by those who ignore, or are ignorant of, the remedial effects of scientific thinking.[13]

Such a view may well explain why we hold certain false beliefs, but it does not explain which beliefs are false. For this, we must rely upon science, but how do we know whether something is science or, for that matter, whether science is right? After all, there have been countless disputes about whether certain knowledge counts as science, and countless cases in which science has been wrong. It may seem obvious in hindsight, but at any given time, we must choose for ourselves. Meanwhile, orthodox science will decide which of our beliefs are wrong, and those who hold such beliefs can be dismissed as victims of their believing brains. This argument is, in effect, an extended definition of paranormal belief (from the viewpoint of a disbeliever): people believe in things that are contrary to scientific knowledge (i.e. wrong); people ignore scientific knowledge (and are wrong). It is one more reincarnation of the psychology of error, which defines paranormal beliefs as erroneous, then explains them as the product of error.

It has been a constant theme, the attempt to explain beliefs that are out of line with scientific thinking, though many critics, in the process of rejecting such beliefs, have made their own mistakes.[14] Nevertheless, a psychology of error has dominated the psychological literature. It can be seen in the titles of journal articles, which refer to belief *in* the paranormal rather than beliefs *about* the paranormal, of books such as How We Know What Isn't So and Why People Believe Weird Things, and of various hypotheses that seek to explain 'belief' rather than 'disbelief' (e.g. the 'misattribution hypothesis', the 'cognitive deficit hypothesis', or the 'social marginality hypothesis').[15] It seems obvious that such beliefs are erroneous, being contrary to orthodox scientific knowledge, and it is part and parcel of the definition that paranormal beliefs involve a clash with scientific knowledge. However, what is obviously unscientific to some is not so obviously unscientific to others, and history shows that belief in the reality of paranormal (or other extraordinary) phenomena is not the same as belief that such phenomena are contrary to scientific knowledge. Indeed, so far as scientific knowledge has been part of the equation, most believers have taken the view that such phenomena are potentially compatible with scientific knowledge. This is a disagreement about whether current scientific knowledge is correct, and history also shows that this is not an obvious matter.

Once again, the point is not to argue, as so many proponents have done for so long, that such phenomena might be real because science is often wrong. The point is about what psychologists often take for granted in studying such beliefs, in this case that the meanings of the relevant terms and their relationship to science is self-evident. They are not self-evident, and neither is the decision to define beliefs as brain-bound. Even in the case of memory, confining the process to the inside of the head is an option: we store memories in diaries, notebooks and photographs; we recall using alarms and (not so long ago) strings on fingers and knots in handkerchiefs; we remember in the construction of monuments, and in the practicing of traditions.[16] How we define psychological categories depends upon wider theoretical and methodological matters, and the choices we make about what we study, the questions we ask and the methods we use, inevitably shape the answers we get. Thus, as we once did in relation to attitudes, we might choose to define beliefs in a way that includes things we can see directly. Indeed, we might define beliefs as things that can be seen in the actions of those who seek to demonstrate that extraordinary phenomena are real, or that they are not, in live performance and experimental enquiry, or in the founding, membership and activities of relevant societies. More specifically, however, rather than treating discourse about extraordinary phenomena as an indicator of inner states, we can see it as an intrinsic part of the construction and maintenance of extraordinary beliefs.

In doing so, the methods we use must suit the object of enquiry, and we can be empirical without having to reduce our subject matter to something that can be counted. Tempting as the quest for objectivity may be, nobody is getting at neutral facts about paranormal beliefs: one can choose a particular definition, decide which objects of belief should count, deploy a particular measure on particular people at a particular moment, assume that they understand the meanings of the statements in the way that is intended, so that they think of the sorts of things they are supposed to, then respond in ways that directly reflect what is inside their heads (then and there). That is one way of doing things, but since we must rely upon expressions of belief, we might wish to rely upon real-world examples.

In the real world, extraordinary beliefs may be processed by the brain, but this does not happen in isolation. Such beliefs, like other attitudes, are inherently argumentative, adopting one position rather than another.[17] As such, they are part of a social context in which particular events take place, are observed and reported, and different views are expressed and warranted as part of a wider discourse. Whatever one thinks or says about such things, this is a response to what one has seen or heard, and the ways in which this is done inevitably reflect wider understandings (e.g. about how extraordinary such things are, or who can be trusted to assess such things, or what others might think of a particular view being expressed). Any individual belief, whether silently thought or voiced out loud, is a position taken in relation to that wider discourse. Whatever individual factors might be at play, such beliefs are necessarily social and interactional, inseparable from the words and deeds of others.

If we wish to understand such beliefs, we can say that people frame particular events in terms of available categories. They choose one category rather than another, because they find it more plausible or desirable than the alternatives, based upon their understanding of the options. People disagree, of course, because people differ in how trusting they are of particular sources, and in how plausible and desirable they find particular positions. Psychologists, in trying to explain such beliefs, have focused upon differences between believers and disbelievers. In doing so, however, they have minimized differences in the objects and forms of such beliefs. Nevertheless, if we examine in detail what happens in the real world – the things in which people believe, what they believe about these things, and their given reasons for doing so – we can see patterns in the seeming randomness. And we can also see more general reasons for taking a particular position, regardless of whether or not, at the end of the day, it is the correct one.

In the process of expressing and justifying a particular position, one can show oneself to be a critical thinker, or a balanced person, and one can display knowledge and understanding of a topic of interest to almost everyone. One can share views with some, while disagreeing with others and, in the process, construct a viewpoint and an identity. And for those who go out of their way to explain why other people get it wrong, and why this is a bad thing, one can present oneself as a useful expert, one who is involved in a quest for truth. All of this has been the case since at least the early nineteenth century. It has taken the form of a dispute about the facts, though it has not been determined by the facts, since any of the facts can be mustered as evidence in support of any given position. But regardless of the facts, and regardless of whether extraordinary phenomena are real, and what that means, disputes about such phenomena have been longstanding and significant. They have provided opportunities to show that we are discriminating, that we are sceptical but open-minded, that we know more or better than others, that we have views that are worth being heard, that we care about what is right, and that we condemn what is wrong. They have been a means through which we have constructed and maintained our beliefs about the world in which we live, not only about what is possible in the material world, but also about what matters in the social world.

Notes

Chapter One

1 This is a personal memory of a performance witnessed in Edinburgh, during the international Edinburgh Festival Fringe, about eight years ago. However, it is fairly typical of a particular effect that has become rather common in the last decade or so.
2 Davies, *The Haunted*, 40; McCorristine, *Spectres of the Self*, 27–8.
3 Daston, 'Marvelous facts and miraculous evidence in early modern Europe'; Dear, 'Miracles, experiments, and the ordinary course of nature'; Serjeantson, 'Testimony and proof in early modern England'. On early eighteenth-century debates at the Royal Society about extraordinary objects, see Fontes Da Costa, 'The making of extraordinary facts'.
4 Despite the subsequent tales of early modern jugglers being accused of witchcraft, it is far from easy to find evidence of anyone having taken this seriously (Lamont, 'Spiritualism and a mid-Victorian crisis of evidence', 906). A similar point has been made more recently by Mangan, *Performing Dark Arts*, 39.
5 For example: Ferriar, *An Essay Towards a Theory of Apparitions*; Hibbert, *Sketches of the Philosophy of Apparitions*.
6 Cannon, 'The problem of miracles in the 1830's'; Burns, *The Great Debate on Miracles*.
7 Cook, *The Arts of Deception*, 163–213; During, *Modern Enchantments*; Lamont, 'Spiritualism', 903–6.

8 Weber, *The Protestant Ethic and the Spirit of Capitalism*; Bauman, *Intimations of Postmodernity*, x–xvi. For a recent review of the literature, see: Saler, 'Modernity and enchantment'.
9 For example: Cerullo, *The Secularization of the Soul*; Gauld, *The Founders of Psychical Research*; Turner, *Between Science and Religion*; Oppenheim, *The Other World*.
10 For example: Wilson, 'The thought of late Victorian physicists'; Noakes, 'Telegraphy is an occult art'; Noakes, 'The bridge which is between physical and psychical research'; Noakes, 'The world of the infinitely little'; Thurschwell, *Literature, Technology and Magical Thinking 1880–1920*.
11 This is a rich, diverse and growing literature but, in addition to those above, key texts include: Barrow, *Independent Spirits*; Cottom, *The Abyss of Reason*; Owen, *The Darkened Room*; Owen, *The Place of Enchantment*; Luckhurst, *The Invention of Telepathy*; Wallis (ed.), *On the Margins of Science*; Winter, *Mesmerized*.
12 For example: Sedgwick and Tyler, *A Short History of Science*; Hearnshaw, *A Short History of British Psychology*.
13 Dennett, 'Two contrasts'.
14 Tobacyk and Milford, 'Belief in paranormal phenomena'; Tobacyk, 'A revised Paranormal Belief Scale' (unpublished MS, Louisiana Tech University, 1988).
15 The problem has not gone unnoticed (e.g. Lawrence, 'How many factors of paranormal belief are there?'), though its significance may have been underestimated, as it could be said to relate to 10 of the 26 items on the PBS (3, 6, 7, 10, 13, 14, 21, 23, 24, 26).
16 For example: William Crookes, Alfred Russel Wallace or, more recently, Brian Josephson.
17 Bem, 'Feeling the future'.
18 Indeed, even if the questionnaire explicitly defined such events as contrary to scientific knowledge, would it then be measuring belief in the paranormal, or faith in scientific authority?
19 This has not gone unnoticed by those who use such questionnaires (e.g. Goulding and Parker, 'Finding psi in the paranormal', 74).
20 Potter and Wetherell, *Discourse and Social Psychology*, 43ff.
21 This episode is mentioned in every introductory textbook on parapsychology, for example: Beloff, *Parapsychology*, 47–8; Broughton, *Parapsychology*, 62–3; Irwin and Watt, *An Introduction to Parapsychology*, 22–3.

22 Potter and Wetherell, *Discourse and Social Psychology*.
23 This is no more than a reformulation of arguments that have been made by others, such as Kurt Danziger, Ken Gergen, Ian Hacking, Graham Richards and Roger Smith. See, for example: Danziger, *Constructing the Subject* and *Naming the Mind*; Gergen, 'Social psychology as history'; Graumann and Gergen, *Historical Dimensions of Psychological Discourse*; Hacking, 'Making up people'; Richards, *Putting Psychology in its Place*; Smith, *Being Human*.
24 See also: Richards, *On Psychological Language*; Leary, *Metaphors in the History of Psychology*.
25 Danziger, *Naming the Mind*.
26 Richards, *Putting Psychology in its Place*; Smith, *The Fontana History of the Human Sciences*.
27 Leary, *Metaphors*; Richards, *Putting Psychology in its Place*; Smith, *Being Human*.
28 Hacking, 'Making up people'.
29 See, respectively: Hacking, *Rewriting the Soul*; Young, *The Harmony of Illusions*.
30 Danziger, 'Prospects of a historical psychology'.
31 For example: Bunn *et al.*, *Psychology in Britain*; Coon, 'Testing the limits of sense and science'; Derksen, 'Are we not experimenting then?'; Gieryn, 'Boundary-work and the demarcation of science from non-science'; Lamont, 'Discourse analysis as method in the history of psychology'; Wolffram, 'Parapsychology on the couch'.
32 Magendie, *An Elementary Treatise on Human Physiology*, 150.
33 Flourens, *Phrenology Examined*. The latter point is made by Cooter, *The Cultural Meaning of Popular Science*, 310.
34 Young, *Mind, Brain and Adaptation in the Nineteenth Century*; Richards, *Mental Machinery*.
35 Kaufman, 'Phrenology – confrontation between Gordon and Spurzheim – 1816'.
36 Shapin, 'The politics of observation'.
37 Van Wyhe, *Phrenology and the Origins of Victorian Naturalism*.
38 Gieryn, 'Boundary-work', 789.
39 Social interests have been stressed by Shapin, 'Politics of observation', individual interests by Van Wyhe, *Phrenology*.
40 Young, *Mind, Brain and Adaptation*.
41 For example: Nixon, 'Popular answers to some psychological questions'; Gilliland, 'A study of the superstitions of college students'; Emme,

'Modification and origin of certain beliefs in superstition among 96 college students'; Scheidt, 'Belief in supernatural phenomena and locus of control'.
42 As John Elliotson noted at the time, 'where formerly *one* had been converted to the truth of phrenology, now, through mesmerism, *one hundred* were converted', cited in Cooter, *Cultural Meaning of Popular Science*, 150.

Chapter Two

1 *Trick of the Mind* (Channel 4 television, 2004), series 1, episode 5. In the following episode, Brown played a game of word association with a psychiatrist, predicting the words that the psychiatrist would name in response to his own. Afterwards the psychiatrist concluded that Brown was good at reading people and influencing their choices (*Trick of the Mind* (Channel 4 television, 2004), series 1, episode 6).
2 Singh, 'Spectacular psychology'.
3 Singh, 'Spectacular psychology'; Hill, *Paranormal Media*, 134–49.
4 Conjuring effects and methods have been categorized in various ways, and there is a rich and diverse literature on conjuring theory, written by and for magicians. These are not, as some scientists have tended to think, definitive descriptions of what is really going on, but rather a means of understanding in order to improve performance. My own particular way of organizing matters can be found in Lamont and Wiseman, *Magic in Theory*, which was written for non-magicians, and which includes a large bibliography on further reading. For some more detail on lists of effects, see Chapter 1.
5 Lamont and Wiseman, *Magic in Theory*, 7–27, 169–75.
6 Like any generalization in magic, this is not entirely true, since one can make a coin disappear from the hand, and reproduce it from inside the sleeve. However, this is only effective if the audience cannot imagine how it could have done so in the circumstances.
7 Lamont and Wiseman, *Magic in Theory*, 28–81.
8 Robert-Houdin, *Secrets of Conjuring and Magic*, 34.
9 Dawes, *The Great Illusionists*, 81.
10 Frost, *The Lives of the Conjurors*, 286.
11 According to Max Maven's delightful 'red nose' theory of mentalism: if a clown, complete with red nose and giant shoes, in between the mouth coils and the balloon animals, performs a simple card trick in which he

reveals the chosen card, at least one member of the audience will later ask if the clown does private readings (Maven, 'I'll build a stairway to a paradox').

12 The exemplary discussion of this can be found in Tamariz, *The Magic Way*.
13 For example: During, *Modern Enchantments*; Mangan, *Dark Arts*.
14 This is from Lamont, 'Magic and the willing suspension of disbelief'. However, the point has been made before, and the Peter Pan example has been used previously in order to make it (e.g. Ortiz, *Strong Magic*, 25–6; Swiss, *Shattering Illusions*, 21).
15 For example, Harris, *The Art of Astonishment*, I, 5–8.
16 For example, Tamariz, *Magic Way*.
17 Goffman, *Frame Analysis*.
18 Goffman, *Frame Analysis*, 83.
19 Nardi, 'Toward a social psychology of entertainment magic'.
20 For example: Randi, 'The role of conjurers in psi research'; Morris, 'What psi is not'.
21 Lamont, 'Magician as conjuror'.
22 This is explicitly stated in the introduction to episode one of *Mind Control* (Channel 4 television, 2000).
23 Potter and Wetherell, *Discourse and Social Psychology*, 45.
24 Lamont, 'Paranormal belief and the avowal of prior scepticism'.
25 Irwin, 'Belief in the paranormal'.
26 As we shall see, this has been a longstanding argument, and some have even claimed that it has been demonstrated by experiment (e.g. Hergovich, 'The effect of pseudo-psychic demonstrations as dependent on belief in paranormal phenomena and suggestibility').
27 Following Gilbert and Mulkay, *Opening Pandora's Box*, several key texts established a new focus upon discourse in psychology e.g. Potter and Wetherell, *Discourse and Social Psychology*; Billig, *Arguing and Thinking*; Edwards and Potter, *Discursive Psychology*; Potter, *Representing Reality*; Edwards, *Discourse and Cognition*.
28 Lamont, 'Paranormal belief', and cf. Potter, *Representing Reality*, 126.
29 Wooffitt, *Telling Tales of the Unexpected*.
30 Potter, *Representing Reality*.
31 Danziger, *Naming the Mind*, 134–56.
32 For example: Clark, *Supersizing the Mind*; Carruthers, *Language, Thought and Consciousness*; Harre and Gillett, *Discursive Mind*.

33 For example: Brugger *et al.*, 'Meaningful patterns'; Brugger, 'Functional hemispheric asymmetry and belief in ESP'; Persinger and Richards, 'Tobacyk's paranormal belief scale and temporal lobe signs'.
34 The similarities in the arguments have long been noted. See, for example: Prince, *Enchanted Boundary*; Ransom, 'Recent criticisms of parapsychology'; Collins and Pinch, 'The construction of the paranormal'; McLenon, *Deviant Science*, 79–103; Bauer, 'Criticism and controversy in parapsychology'; Hess, *Science in the New Age*; Zingrone, 'From text to self'.

Chapter Three

1 'Lecture on mesmerism: extraordinary uproar', *Morning Herald*, 5 January 1844.
2 The history of mesmerism and hypnosis is covered admirably in Crabtree, *From Mesmer to Freud* and Gauld, *History of Hypnotism*. On the British context at this time, see Winter, *Mesmerized*. On some of the more extraordinary phenomena of mesmerism in Britain and America, see Dingwall, *Abnormal Hypnotic Phenomena*.
3 Colquhoun, *Reports of the Experiments on Animal Magnetism*.
4 'Animal magnetism', *Lancet*, 30 (1838), 282–8; 'Animal magnetism: conclusion', *Lancet*, 30 (1838), 401–3.
5 'Animal magnetism, or mesmerism', *Lancet*, 30 (1838), 805–13; 'The Lancet. London, Saturday, September 15 1838.' *Lancet*, 30 (1838), 873–7; 'Experiments performed on Elizabeth and Jane O'Key', *Lancet*, 36 (1841), 694–9.
6 Gauld, *History of Hypnotism*, 205–57.
7 Winter, *Mesmerized*, 226.
8 Winter, *Mesmerized*, 181.
9 Parsinnen, 'Mesmeric performers'.
10 'Exeter', *Phrenological Journal*, 14 (1841), 102–3.
11 Vernon and Kiste, 'Phrenological visit to the Exeter Deaf and Dumb Asylum', 80.
12 'Intelligence', *Phrenological Journal* 14 (1841), 197–8, 287, 290.
13 'Intelligence', *Phrenological Journal* 17 (1844), 307.
14 Indeed, some months later, an article in that journal reported his involvement in a rare case of 'cross-mesmerism', in which he engaged in something of a battle of wills with his own subject. According to

a witness, a young lady of 'a highly nervous temperament' had been mesmerized by Vernon, such that 'she obeyed his commands, which were only mentally expressed, and also seemed to penetrate into all his thoughts'. She then proposed 'to magnetise Mr Vernon, and at once proceeded to do so... to the great amusement of the parties present. For about a minute, Mr V. sat passively under her manipulations.' At some point, however, he retaliated by 'throwing upon her his own influence', the result being that 'the young lady was almost instantaneously overpowered by him, and fell back in her chair in a state of coma'. For the next five days, we are told, she remained in 'a delirious state, and required constant attendance' (Holmes, 'Case of cross-mesmerism', 138–40). Such antics reflected the theatrical nature of so many displays of mesmeric phenomena.

15 Cooter, *Cultural Meaning of Popular Science*, 150.
16 'Mesmeric case at Deptford', *People's Phrenological Journal*, 2 (1844), 137.
17 'Mesmeric case at Deptford', *People's Phrenological Journal*, 2 (1844), 137–8.
18 'Lecture hall, Greenwich', broadsheet for Vernon lecture, 4 January 1844 (Purland Papers).
19 'Lecture on mesmerism'. This is an unidentified clipping from the Purland Papers, but its origin in the *Morning Herald* (5 January 1844) is confirmed elsewhere ('The People', *People's Phrenological Journal*, 2, 1844, 171).
20 The story seems to have done the rounds of the provincial press (e.g. 'Extraordinary uproar', *Northern Star and Leeds Advertiser*, 13 January 1844, 2).
21 This was also picked up by the *People's Phrenological Journal*, which noted: '[i]t would puzzle the Great Wizard of the North to receive such a blow and show his hand without a mark' ('The People', 172). The 'Great Wizard' in question was John Henry Anderson, the most famous conjuror in Britain at the time, who shortly after this became the first magician-debunker of spiritualism.
22 'Mesmeric intelligence', *People's Phrenological Journal*, 2 (1844), 183–5.
23 'Lecture on mesmerism: extraordinary uproar', *Morning Herald*, 5 January 1844.
24 Winter, *Mesmerized*, 125.
25 This was hardly unusual at the time, the combination of 'instruction and amusement' being part and parcel of rational recreations. On the fuzzy boundary between scientific dissemination and

entertainment, see Goodall, *Performance and Evolution in the Age of Darwin*.
26 'Extraction of teeth in the mesmeric state', *Zoist*, 3 (1845), 214–16; advert in *Times*, 24 March 1845 (Purland Papers).
27 Elliotson, 'Cure of uterine disease with mesmerism, by Mr Vernon'.
28 'Lecture on mesmerism', newspaper clipping, content suggests from *Kentish Mercury*, c. March 1845 (Purland Papers).
29 'Public medical challenge', broadsheet for Vernon lecture (Purland Papers).
30 'Lecture on mesmerism', newspaper clipping dated 27 December 1842 (Purland Papers).
31 Sandby, *Mesmerism and its Opponents with a Narrative of Cases*, 199.
32 'Lectures on mesmerism', newspaper clipping from *Maidstone Journal and Kentish Advertiser*, 3 January 1843 (Purland Papers).
33 'Lecture on mesmerism', 27 December 1842 (Purland Papers); 'Mesmerism', newspaper clipping dated May 1843 (Purland Papers).
34 'Lecture on mesmerism', *Kentish Mercury*, c. March 1845 (Purland Papers).
35 'Lecture on mesmerism', 27 December 1842 (Purland Papers).
36 'Mesmerism', newspaper clipping dated November 1843 (Purland Papers); 'Lectures on mesmerism', *Maidstone Journal and Kentish Advertiser*, 3 January 1843 (Purland Papers).
37 'Mesmerism', May 1843 (Purland Papers).
38 'Lectures on mesmerism', *Maidstone Journal and Kentish Advertiser*, 3 January 1843 (Purland Papers); 'Mesmerism', May 1843 (Purland Papers); 'Mesmerism', November 1843 (Purland Papers).
39 'Mesmerism', newspaper clipping dated 30 March 1843 (Purland Papers); 'Lectures on mesmerism', newspaper clipping dated March 1843 (Purland Papers); 'Mesmerism', newspaper clipping from *Kentish Independent*, 10 February 1844 (Purland Papers).
40 'Lectures on mesmerism', *Maidstone Journal and Kentish Advertiser*, 3 January 1843 (Purland Papers).
41 'Mesmerism', November 1843 (Purland Papers).
42 'Mesmerism', 30 March 1843 (Purland Papers).
43 'Lectures on mesmerism', newspaper clipping dated February 1843 (Purland Papers).
44 'Lectures on mesmerism', *Maidstone Journal and Kentish Advertiser*, 3 January 1843 (Purland Papers).
45 'Lecture on mesmerism', *Kentish Mercury*, c. March 1845 (Purland Papers).
46 'Lectures on mesmerism', March 1843 (Purland Papers).

47 'Lectures on mesmerism', *Maidstone Journal and Kentish Advertiser*, 3 January 1843 (Purland Papers); 'Mesmerism', *Kentish Independent*, 10 February 1844 (Purland Papers).
48 'Mesmerism', November 1843 (Purland Papers); 'Lectures on mesmerism', March 1843 (Purland Papers).
49 'Mesmerism', *Kentish Independent*, 10 February 1844 (Purland Papers).
50 'Mesmerism', 30 March 1843 (Purland Papers); 'Mesmerism', newspaper clipping from *Kentish Mercury*, 30 January 1844 (Purland Papers). See also, for example: 'Will any man dare to say that there is a greater amount of improbability, inconsistency or absurdity in mesmerism than appears to reside in the science of electricity?' ('Mesmerism', *Kentish Independent*, 10 February 1844, Purland Papers); 'We believe in the existence of the mesmeric power, as we believe in the existence of inductive magnetism. The peculiar phenomena of the latter we have seen demonstrated by repeated experiments' ('Lecture on mesmerism', 27 December 1842, Purland Papers).
51 Brookes, for example, was 'a practiced lecturer' ('Lectures on mesmerism', March 1843, Purland Papers), a man who 'had engaged for a considerable time in lecturing on mesmerism' ('Lectures on mesmerism', February 1843, Purland Papers). According to press reports – in the course of the same lecture – he both challenged the expertise of 'great men in the medical profession' who opposed mesmerism, and appealed to the expertise of medical men who were advocates. For example: 'We might surely be pardoned for enquiring whether they knew anything of the subject itself, and if we found that they had not examined, that they would not investigate, the subject, but ventured to pronounce opinions in utter ignorance respecting it, we were justified in estimating those opinions at what they are worth, which is nothing at all.' Later, in the same lecture, he appealed to the expertise of 'men of first-rate eminence in science', and 'thousands of medical and scientific men in this country and America, who were daily experimentally demonstrating its truth' ('Mesmerism', 30 March 1843, Purland Papers).
52 For example, when a report concluded: 'we can fearlessly state that there was nothing underhanded or deceptive in the matter', this was an implicit claim to be able to assess whether deception had been present ('Lecture on mesmerism', *Kentish Mercury*, c. March 1845, Purland Papers).
53 'Lecture on mesmerism', 27 December 1842 (Purland Papers).
54 In a frequently cited quote about the phenomena of mesmerism, Coleridge was reportedly told by Dr Trevaranis: 'I have seen what I

am certain I would not have believed on your testimony, and that which I am therefore bound to suppose you cannot believe on mine' ('Animal magnetism and homeopathy', *Monthly Review*, 2 (1838), 471).

55 For example, by disagreeing with the conclusions of a 'medical correspondent' and that of 'several other medical gentlemen', and then by listing several 'medical gentlemen who attended... many of whom took most active means of satisfying themselves as to the genuineness of the illustrations' ('Mesmerism', *Kentish Mercury*, 30 January 1844, Purland Papers).

56 'Mesmerism', *Kentish Independent*, 10 February 1844, (Purland Papers).

57 'Lectures on mesmerism', *Maidstone Journal and Kentish Advertiser*, 3 January 1843 (Purland Papers); 'Mesmerism', 30 March 1843 (Purland Papers); 'Literary institution', newspaper clipping dated March 1845 (Purland Papers); 'Mesmerism', *Kentish Independent*, 10 February 1844, (Purland Papers).

58 'Lecture on mesmerism', *Kentish Mercury*, c. March 1845 (Purland Papers).

59 'Greenwich lecture hall', newspaper clipping dated 2 February 1844 (Purland Papers); 'Mesmerism', advert in the *Glasgow Herald*, 31 May 1844.

60 'Greenwich lecture hall', 2 February 1844 (Purland Papers).

61 'Literary institution', March 1845 (Purland Papers).

62 A Surgeon, 'To the editor of the Maidstone Journal', *Maidstone Journal and Kentish Advertiser*, 3 January 1843 (Purland Papers).

63 'Greenwich lecture hall', 2 February 1844 (Purland Papers).

64 'Mr Purland's letter', clipping from *Forceps*, dated 13 July 1844 (Purland Papers).

65 T. Purland, 'Mesmerism', *Kentish Mercury*, 30 January 1844 (Purland Papers); 'Literary institution', March 1845 (Purland Papers).

66 Purland, 'Mesmerism'; Hytche, 'The impostors who are exhibited in public by the professors of mesmerism'; 'Literary institution', March 1845 (Purland Papers).

67 A Surgeon, 'To the editor'.

68 'Greenwich lecture hall', 2 February 1844 (Purland Papers).

69 'Mr Purland's letter', *Forceps*, 13 July 1844 (Purland Papers).

70 Purland, 'Mesmerism'; 'Mr Purland's letter', *Forceps*, 13 July 1844 (Purland Papers); 'Literary institution', March 1845 (Purland Papers).

71 A Surgeon, 'To the editor'.

72 This theme, of course, has continued since, as critics have often argued one should keep an open mind, but not so open that one's brain falls

out. Similarly, the 'Galileo argument' ('they laughed at Galileo too') was being countered by critics of mesmerism ('Animal magnetism', Athenaeum, 555 (1838), 419), and has been countered since: as Carl Sagan put it more recently, 'they also laughed at Bozo the clown' (Sagan, Broca's Brain, 64).

73 A Surgeon, 'To the editor'.
74 'Mr Purland's letter', Forceps, 13 July 1844 (Purland Papers).
75 'Mesmerism and its opponents', Medico-Chirurgical Review and Journal of Practical Medicine, 41 (1844), 142.
76 'Animal magnetism', Times, 26 January 1844, 5.
77 A Surgeon, 'To the editor'. Similar complaints were expressed by others (e.g. Bennet, 'The mesmeric mania of 1851 with a physiological explanation of the phenomena produced').
78 'Mr Braid at the Royal Institution', Manchester Times and Gazette, 27 April 1844, 6.
79 'Mr Braid at the Royal Institution', Manchester Times and Gazette, 27 April 1844, 6.
80 On Braid's views in relation to others', see for example: Gauld, History of Hypnotism, 273ff.
81 'S', 'Hypnotism'.
82 Smethurst, 'Mesmerism unmasked', 146.
83 Weekes, 'Reply to Dr Smethurst', 322.
84 Vernon, 'Mr Vernon's experiments', 138–9.
85 Vernon, 'Mr Vernon's experiments', 94.
86 Vernon, 'Mr Vernon's experiments', 95.
87 A Lover of Truth, 'Mesmerism', 2.
88 From a playbill in Houdini, The Unmasking of Robert-Houdin, 212.
89 'The double-sighted phenomenon', reprinted in the Caledonian Mercury.
90 'The double-sighted phenomenon', reprinted in the Derby Mercury. A similarly ambiguous position was later expressed by the Sunday Times in 'The extraordinary Scotch boy'.
91 From a playbill in Houdini, The Unmasking of Robert-Houdin, 221.
92 Related events may have also led to the double-sighted Scotch phenomenon being taken less seriously. By 1833, M'Kean senior was in the news, and gaining something of a reputation of his own. In March, he got drunk, charged into his landlord's room, and threatened to 'smash his *heed* into the consistency of a well-made haggis'. When appearing before the magistrate, he admitted to having been not entirely sober,

but assured him that the landlord's head had been 'as safe from him as a glass of cold water would be, were a glass of warm toddy standing by its side' (newspaper clipping dated 27 March 1833, Ricky Jay collection). Nevertheless, the following month, while 'in a glorious state of intoxication', he assaulted a member of his audience 'by breaking a violin across his nose'. The violin, we are told, 'appeared to have been a valuable one. It was smashed into many pieces'. Back in court, M'Kean senior was found guilty. On hearing this, 'he put his hat on in a rage, and said that he had been in the company of the King four times, and could have a character [reference] from a Duke'. Such connections, however, did not excuse his breach of protocol, and when he refused to remove his hat, 'it was pulled off for him, in doing which his wig came off with it, which put him in a greater rage than ever. He was conveyed to the lock-up' ('Curious case of assault', *Morning Chronicle*, 15 April 1833, 4). Such was the fate of M'Kean senior, the excited double-Scotch phenomenon.

93 'Hertford winter assizes', *Jackson's Oxford Journal*, 3 December 1831; 'London November 28', *Newcastle Courant*, 3 December 1831.
94 'Theatrical chit-chat', *Morning Chronicle*, 23 January 1832.
95 'The Clarence vase', *New Monthly Magazine*, 36 (1832), 210.
96 Colquhoun, *Reports of the Experiments*, 246.
97 Christopher, *Panorama of Magic*, 63. She was copied by others, including the daughter of Bernardo Eagle, who was himself a pale imitation of John Henry Anderson ('Magician of the south').
98 For example: Lee, *Animal Magnetism and Magnetic Lucid Somnabulism*, 122; Paris, *Philosophy in Sport Made Science in Earnest*, 435.
99 Christopher, *Panorama of Magic*, 63; 'Mysterious Lady', *Era*, 30 March 1845, 3.
100 'Mysterious Lady', *Morning Chronicle*, 12 March 1845.
101 An Enquirer, 'The Mysterious Lady'.
102 'Anti-mesmerism', *Bristol Mercury*, 25 January 1845; 'Anti-mesmerism', *Bristol Mercury*, 8 February 1845.
103 Forbes, *Illustrations of Modern Mesmerism from Personal Investigation*, 458.
104 Forbes, 'Notes of a few more trials with the mesmerists in a second search for clairvoyance', 486–95. There were several medical men present at the different trials, including one Dr Wigan. According to Forbes, Dr Wigan 'bandaged his eyes badly', and he immediately told him so, though Wigan considered the bandaging effectual. In a

separate version, however, Wigan claimed that 'any degree of vision was impossible', but Vernon tried to distract him from Adolphe, so he 'kept [his] eyes rigidly fixed on Adolphe'. In doing so, he noticed fraud but said nothing, and the result 'seemed to give perfect satisfaction to the company... it appeared as if I were the only sceptic'. Indeed, in what presumably was an attempt to take credit for the debunking, Wigan did not even mention that Forbes was present (Wigan, 'The hallucinating fraud', 136–8).

105 Forbes, 'Notes of a few more trials', 487.
106 Forbes, 'Notes of a few more trials', 487.
107 Forbes, 'Notes of yet another trial with mesmerists', 670.
108 Carpenter, 'Mesmerism, odylism, table-turning and spiritualism considered historically and scientifically', 393.
109 Forbes, 'Notes of yet another trial', 670–3.
110 Forbes, 'Notes of yet another trial', 673–5.
111 Carpenter, 'Mesmerism, odylism', 394–5; Podmore, *Mesmerism and Christian Science*, 171.
112 Forbes, *Illustrations*, vi–ix.
113 The term 'psychology of error' loosely reflects what David Bloor has called the 'sociology of error', in that it refers to the attempt to explain why people get things wrong.
114 'Illustrations of modern mesmerism', *British and Foreign Medical Review*, 19 (1845), 277–8.
115 James Braid, 'Letter' to *The Critic*, c. 8 June 1845 (Purland Papers); 'Books received for review', *Lancet*, 46 (1845), 577; 'Sir John Forbes', *Medical Times and Gazette*, 2 (1861), 506.
116 'Dr A. Wood on electro-biology', *Monthly Journal of Medical Science*, 3 (1851), 409.
117 This comment was cited elsewhere (e.g. 'Mesmerism – clairvoyance', *Bulletin of Medical Science*, 3 (1845), 390).
118 D.E.L.E., 'Dr Forbes the real impostor'.
119 Winter, *Mesmerized*, 4, 61–2, 140–2.
120 Richards, *Mental Machinery*, 287.
121 Braid, *Neurypnology, or the Rationale of Nervous Sleep Considered in Relation to Mesmerism*.
122 Gauld, *History of Hypnotism*, 287.
123 For example: 'S', 'Hypnotism'.
124 Braid, *Neurypnology*.
125 Gregory, *Letters to a Candid Enquirer on Animal Magnetism*.
126 Hacking, *Rewriting the Soul*; Young, *Harmony of Illusions*.

127 Richards, *Psychology*, 9.
128 Gauld, *History of Hypnotism*, 179; Schmit, 'Re-visioning antebellum American psychology', 408.
129 Winter, *Mesmerized*, 203–4; Ernst, 'Colonial psychiatry, magic and religion'.
130 A similar point has been made in relation to spiritualism (e.g. Noakes, 'Telegraphy is an occult art'; Thurschwell, *Literature, Technology and Magical Thinking*).
131 For example: Richards, *Mental Machinery*, 249–85; Schmit, 'Re-visioning antebellum American psychology'.

Chapter Four

1 'Mr C. Foster', *Spiritual Magazine*, 3 (1862), 46.
2 For example: Podmore, *Modern Spiritualism*; Doyle, *The History of Spiritualism*; Moore, *In Search of White Crows*; Braude, *Radical Spirits*; Carroll, *Spiritualism in Antebellum America*.
3 Podmore, *Modern Spiritualism*, I, 184–6.
4 For example: Anon, *Table-turning by Animal Magnetism Demonstrated*; Godfrey, *Table-moving Tested, and Proved to Be the Result of Satanic Agency*; Spicer, *Facts and Fantasies*.
5 Carpenter, 'On the influence of suggestion in modifying and directing muscular movement, independently of volition'.
6 'Table-turning', *Times*, 30 June 1853, 8; 'Experimental investigation of table-moving', *Athenaeum*, 2 July 1853, 801–3.
7 This appeared in *The Leader*, 12 January 1853 (Podmore, *Modern Spiritualism*, II, 5), and was described in Anderson, *Magic of Spirit-rapping*.
8 The *Yorkshire Spiritual Telegraph* ran from April 1855 to May 1859, changing its name to the *British Spiritual Telegraph* in June 1857.
9 For example: Owen, *Darkened Room*; Barrow, *Independent Spirits*.
10 This was most obviously the case with Daniel Dunglas Home, who was wooed by several fashionable London hostesses (Lamont, *The First Psychic*, 107–8).
11 For example: Turner, *Between Science and Religion*; Noakes, 'Telegraphy is an occult art'; Noakes, 'Bridge between physical and psychical research'; Thurschwell, *Literature, Technology and Magical Thinking*.
12 For example: Cerullo, *Secularization of the Soul*; Oppenheim, *Other World*.

13 For example: 'The Westminster Review on spirits and spirit rapping by T.S.', *British Spiritual Telegraph*, 2 (1858), 79.
14 Lamont, *First Psychic*, 51.
15 Gordon, *The Home Life of Sir David Brewster*, 257–8.
16 Zorab, 'Test sittings with D. D. Home at Amsterdam'.
17 For example: 'Mr C. Foster', *Spiritual Magazine*, 3 (1862), 45–8; 'Mr S. C. Hall and Mr Foster', *Spiritual Magazine*, 3 (1862), 89–92; 'A séance with Mr Foster', *Spiritual Magazine*, 4 (1871), 66–70.
18 For example: 'The Davenport brothers', *Spiritual Magazine*, 5 (1864), 481–524; Nichols, *Supra-mundane Facts in the Life of Rev. Jesse Babcock Ferguson*, 104.
19 For example: Wason, 'Letter' to *Spiritual Magazine*, 525; Brancker, 'Letter' to *Spiritual Magazine*', 431; Alexander, *Spiritualism*, 12.
20 On Home's link to aristocracy, see: Lamont and Murphy, 'On the origins of the first psychic'.
21 Owen, *Darkened Room*, 71.
22 Nichols, *Supra-mundane Facts*, 104–11.
23 Lamont, 'Magician as conjuror', 27.
24 Lamont, 'Magician as conjuror', 27.
25 For example: Nichols, *A Biography of the Brothers Davenport*; Home, *Incidents in my Life*.
26 Lamont and Wiseman, *Magic in Theory*, 118.
27 'Mr S. C. Hall and Mr Foster', *Spiritual Magazine*, 3 (1862), 90.
28 'Mr C. H. Foster', *Spiritual Magazine*, 3 (1862), 45.
29 'The Davenport brothers', *Spiritual Magazine*, 5 (1864), 470.
30 For example: J. J. S., 'Letter', 233; Bell, 'Stranger than fiction', 215; Crosland, *Apparitions*, 23; Webster, *Scepticism and Spiritualism*, 3.
31 For example:, 'Farther facts by Dr Blank', 342; 'The conversion of an MD to spiritualism', *Spiritual Magazine*, 2 (1867), 412; 'Letter' to *Human Nature*, 133; 'Stage imitation of spiritual phenomena', *Spiritualist*, 3 (1873), 137.
32 For example: J. J. S., 'Letter', 233; Wason, 'Letter', 525; Brancker, 'Letter', 431.
33 For example: 'Spiritualism in Norwood', *Spiritual Magazine*, 4 (1869), 336; 'Farther facts by Dr Blank', *Spiritual Magazine*, 1 (1860), 342; Alexander, *Spiritualism*, 12; Guppy, 'Letter', 222.
34 For example: 'The Davenport brothers', *Spiritual Magazine*, 5 (1864), 470; 'Dr Gully's facts', *Spiritual Magazine*, 2 (1861), 64.

35 Home, *Incidents*, 163–4; Hutchison, 'Important testimony to the facts', 89–90.
36 Howitt, 'Darkness as an element of power in the divine economy?'.
37 Coleman, 'The question of cui bono answered', 143, and 'Spiritualism in America II', 341.
38 For example, Foster's letters of introduction were cited as evidence that he would not cheat ('Mr. C. Foster', *Spiritual Magazine*, 3 (1862), 45), that Ferguson was a sincere man of faith as evidence of the innocence of the Davenports (Nichols, *Supra-mundane Facts*), and that Home did not accept money as evidence that he was 'beyond suspicion' (Coleman, 'Question of cui bono', 143).
39 Coleman, 'Question of cui bono', 143.
40 'Lyon v Home', *Spiritual Magazine*, 3 (1868), 242–5.
41 'Paid mediums versus ministers', *Medium and Daybreak*, 2 (1871), 139; 'Prof Pepper on spiritualism', *Spiritualist*, 2 (1872), 29.
42 *Report on Spiritualism of the Committee of the London Dialectical Society*, 146.
43 'Dr Gully's facts', *Spiritual Magazine*, 2 (1861), 63.
44 'Spiritualism in Norwood', *Spiritual Magazine*, 4 (1869), 336.
45 Coleman, 'Passing events', 165.
46 Bell (Verax), 'Stranger than fiction'; Honestas, 'Letter' to *Spiritual Magazine*; Home, *Incidents*, 251.
47 Home, *Incidents*, 250.
48 Home, *Incidents*, 255.
49 Shorter, 'Spiritualism and the laws of nature', 104.
50 'Ring out the old, ring in the new', *Spiritual Magazine*, 3 (1868), 3.
51 'Debate on modern spiritualism', *Medium and Daybreak*, 3 (1872), 517.
52 See, for example: Crosland, *Apparitions*, 23; Rymer, *Spirit Manifestations*, 39; Baker, *Fraud, Fancy, Fact*, 3; Home, *Incidents*, 173; Webster, *Scepticism and Spiritualism*, 3; 'A séance with Baron and Mlle Guldenstubbe by Wm Tebb', *Spiritual Magazine*, 2 (1867), 324; Alexander, *Spiritualism*, 42; Mme Home, *D. D. Home*, 87.
53 'Am I a spiritualist?', *Human Nature*, 7 (1873), 162.
54 J. J. S., 'Letter', 233. See also: *Report on Spiritualism of the Committee of the London Dialectical Society*, 129, 134, 136, 139, 142, 145, 157; Home, *Incidents*, 173; Mme Home, *D. D. Home*, 87; 'Spiritualism in Norwood', *Spiritual Magazine*, 4 (1869), 336; Webster, *Scepticism and Spiritualism*, 3.
55 'Testimony of non-spiritualists', *Spiritualist*, 1 (1869), 2.

56 Home, *Incidents*, 175; 'Letter from the late Prof Gregory', *Spiritual Magazine*, 6 (1865), 451; 'The Cornhill Magazine and Professor Challis, of Cambridge on spiritualism', *Spiritual Magazine*, 4 (1863), 372.

57 Coleman, 'Spiritualism in America', 294.

58 Chambers, *On Testimony*, 18.

59 For example: Rymer, *Spirit Manifestations*, 5; 'Why Galileo was persecuted', *Spiritualist*, 1 (1869), 2; Howitt, 'Correspondence', 43.

60 'Letter from the late Prof Gregory', *Spiritual Magazine*, 6 (1865), 452.

61 Cited in Oppenheim, *Other World*, 336.

62 For example: Crosland, *Apparitions*, 6; *Spirit Manifestations*, 4; 'Punch cartoon of the spirit hand', *Spiritual Magazine*, 1 (1860), 245; Brevior, 'What is religion?', 122.

63 'The Saturday Review', *Spiritual Magazine*, 4 (1863), 177. See also: Chambers, *On Testimony*, 19–23; 'Thackeray and Dickens on spiritualism', *Spiritual Magazine*, 1 (1860), 391; 'A master of arts', *Spiritual Magazine*, 4 (1863), 171; 'Sir William a Beckett the judge', *Spiritual Magazine*, 4 (1863), 356.

64 Wilbraham, 'Letter', 266. See also: 'Saturday Review', *Spiritual Magazine*, 4 (1863), 177; 'Spiritual manifestations', *Spiritual Magazine*, 5 (1870), 21.

65 Coleman, 'Letter', 13. See also: Webster, *Scepticism and Spiritualism*, 37–8; 'Letter from the late Prof Gregory', *Spiritual Magazine*, 6 (1865), 452.

66 For example: Home, *Incidents*, 244; Coleman, 'Spiritualism in America', 294; Webster, *Scepticism and Spiritualism*, 6; Alexander, *Spiritualism*, 2; Podmore, *Modern Spiritualism*, II, 16.

67 'The medium Colchester', *Spiritual Magazine*, 6 (1865), 466. See also: Rymer, *Spirit Manifestations*, 2; Webster, *Scepticism and Spiritualism*, 3; Alexander, *Spiritualism*, 2.

68 'Dr Gully's facts', *Spiritual Magazine*, 2 (1861), 63.

69 'Mr S. C. Hall and Mr Foster', *Spiritual Magazine*, 3 (1862), 90.

70 'Mr C. Foster', *Spiritual Magazine*, 3 (1862), 46.

71 Foster, *Report on Spiritualism*, 134–5.

72 'Sir William a Beckett the judge', *Spiritual Magazine*, 4 (1863), 354. It may be worth noting that such a claim was neither in line nor easily reconcilable with what conjurors publicly stated. Both proponents and critics regularly supported their own positions by appealing to what conjurors had supposedly said or done. The truth of the matter, so far as one can ever know, shall be (for the most part) confined to footnotes,

because (for the most part) we are concerned with how beliefs were expressed and justified. In terms of rhetoric, the function of such appeals is obvious and, though their effect is unknown, their accuracy would have mattered little, since very few would have known the details.

73 For example: 'Mr C. Foster', *Spiritual Magazine*, 3 (1862), 37; 'The Davenport brothers', *Spiritual Magazine*, 5 (1864), 468; 'Evenings with Miss Nicholl', *Spiritual Magazine*, 2 (1867), 255.
74 For example: 'Dr Hooker and Wallace', *Spiritual Magazine*, 3 (1868), 480; Varley, 'Letter', 465.
75 'Letter from the late Prof Gregory', *Spiritual Magazine*, 6 (1865), 452; Home, *Incidents*, 237.
76 For example: 'Dr Gully's facts', *Spiritual Magazine*, 2 (1861), 63; Coleman, 'Question of cui bono', 142–3; Jones, 'An evening with Mr Home', 70.
77 Horton, 'Were they having fun yet?'
78 Hankins and Silverman, *Instruments and the Imagination*, 66.
79 Nenadic, 'Illegitimacy, insolvency and insanity', 6–7.
80 Pritchard, *A Treatise on Insanity*, 16; Bucknill and Tuke, *A Manual of Psychological Medicine*, 123.
81 'Modern necromancy', *British Review*, 34 (1861), 123; 'Illusions and hallucinations', *British Quarterly Review*, 36 (1862), 416.
82 For example: Brewster and G. H. Lewes were experts on optics, and Charles Lockhart Robertson was Commissioner for Lunacy, and a vocal critic of spiritualism.
83 Anderson, *Magic of Spirit-rapping*, 67–8; 'The Spirit faith in America', *Chambers Journal*, 9 February 1856, 82; 'Modern necromancy', *British Review*, 34 (1861), 123.
84 Barge, 'Letter', 266.
85 'Spiritualism and the age we live in', *Athenaeum*, 11 February 1860, 202; 'Spiritualism', *Fraser's Magazine*, 65 (1862), 522; 'Modern spiritualism', 190; 'Report on spiritualism', *Quarterly Review*, 114 (1863), 557; 'Powell's spiritualism', *Athenaeum*, 23 April 1864, 576.
86 'Modern necromancy', *North British Review*, 34 (1861), 123; 'Illusions and hallucinations', *British Quarterly Review*, 36 (1862), 416.
87 'The homoeopathic principle applied to insanity', *Asylum Journal of Mental Science*, 4 (1858), 396; 'Spirits and spirit rapping', *Westminster Review*, 13 (1858), 65.
88 'Spiritualism', *Fraser's Magazine*, 65 (1862), 522.

89 The letters appeared in the London *Morning Advertiser*, from 3 October 1855. Most are reproduced in Home, *Incidents*, 237–61.
90 Anderson, 'Letter', 3.
91 'J', 'Letter', 23 October 1855.
92 'J', 'Letter', 27 October 1855.
93 For example: Lewes, 'Seeing is believing'; 'Spirit-rapping'.
94 'Spiritualism', *Fraser's Magazine*, 65 (1862), 521–2.
95 'Elegant extracts', *Spiritual Magazine*, 2 (1861), 438.
96 For example: 'Spiritualism', *Fraser's Magazine*, 65 (1862), 521; 'Spirit conjuring', *Punch*, 25 August 1860, 73.
97 For example: 'Modern spiritualism', *Quarterly Review*, 114 (1863); 'Incidents in my life', *Times*, 9 April 1863, 4–5.
98 'Sir William a Beckett the judge', *Spiritual Magazine*, 4 (1863), 354; 'The press', *Spiritual Magazine*, 1 (1860), 485.
99 Lamont, *First Psychic*, 118–19.
100 Lamont, *First Psychic*, 120–3.
101 For example: 'Though I cannot unravel the mystery, I am persuaded it is explicable. If I visit so expert a conjuror as Herr Frickell, I see him do many things that I cannot explain, and I never doubt that he could explain them' ('A memoir of Charles Mayne Young', *Spiritual Magazine*, 4 (1871), 414).
102 'Popular scientific errors', *Yorkshire Spiritual Telegraph*, 1 (1856), 169.
103 'Spirit faith in America', *Chambers Journal*, 9 February 1856, 83.
104 'Superstition and science', *Saturday Review*, 12 January 1856, 194.
105 'On force, its mental and moral correlates', *Athenaeum*, 2 February 1867, 150.
106 'Letter from the late Prof Gregory', *Spiritual Magazine*, 6 (1865), 451–3.
107 'The Davenport brothers', *Spiritual Magazine*, 5 (1864), 503.
108 Dawes, *Great Illusionsts*, 155.
109 Home, *Incidents*, 75.
110 For example: 'Sir Charles Isham on spiritualism', *Spiritual Herald*, 1 (1856), 17; 'The Davenport Brothers', *Spiritual Magazine*, 5 (1864), 522; Alexander, *Spiritualism*, 2; Hall, *Use of Spiritualism*, 49; Trollope, *What I Remember*, 390.
111 Guppy, 'Letter', 222.
112 'Juggling, wizarding, and similar phenomena', *Family Herald*, 13 (1855), 349.
113 Lamont, *Spiritualism*, 907.
114 Price and Dingwall, *Revelations of a Spirit Medium*, 17.

115 Podmore, *Modern Spiritualism*, II, 61.
116 For example: 'The Miracle Circle', *Spiritual Magazine*, 6 (1865), 559; 'Mr Sothern and the Miracle Circle', *Spiritual Magazine*, 1 (1866).
117 'Wonderful manifestations in India', *Spiritual Magazine*, 6 (1865).
118 For example, in the well publicized case of Henry Slade, it was argued that the spirit message that was supposed to count as evidence of fraud had actually been produced by a spirit (Podmore, *Modern Spiritualism*, II, p. 89).
119 *Report on Spiritualism of the Committee of the London Dialectical Society*, 204.
120 'Mr S. C. Hall and Mr Foster', *Spiritual Magazine*, 3 (1862), 91.
121 Coleman, 'Spiritualism in America', 294.
122 'The press and the mediums', *Spiritual Magazine*, 3 (1860), 153.
123 See, for example: 'Saturday review', *Spiritual Magazine*, 4 (1863), 177; 'Mr Home and the critics', *Spiritual Magazine*, 4 (1863), 219.
124 Lombroso, *After Death – What?*, 313. See also: 'Thackeray and Dickens on spiritualism', 388; Mme Home, *D. D. Home*, 218.
125 'Spiritualism at Brighton', 127.
126 For example: 'A séance with Miss Cook', *Spiritual Magazine*, 1 (1873), 555.
127 Lamont, *First Psychic*, 58.
128 'The Allen Boy medium's manifestations', *Spiritual Magazine*, 6 (1865), 259–63.
129 'A painful controversy', *Spiritual Magazine*, 9 (1874), 280–1; 'Trickery in spiritualism', *Spiritualist*, 2 (1872), 41. See also Podmore, *Modern Spiritualism*, II, 109.
130 'Cheating mediums', *Spiritual Magazine*, 3 (1862), 273.
131 Lamont, 'Making of extraordinary psychological phenomena', 6.
132 Brewster, *Letters on Natural Magic*, 6. See also: *Magic, Pretended Miracles*; 'Spiritualism, as related to Religion and Science', *Fraser's Magazine*, 71 (1865), 22–42; and, more recently Korem and Meier, *The Fakers*.
133 'Am I a spiritualist?', *Human Nature*, 7 (1873), 163.
134 On non-Christian spiritualism, see Barrow, *Independent Spirits*.
135 Pears, 'Letter' to *Spiritual Magazine*, 86.
136 'Manifestations in England', *Spiritual Herald*, 1 (1856), 45; Mme Home, *D. D. Home*, 201. See also: Home, *Incidents*, 174, Baker, *Fraud, Fancy, Fact*, 3; Mme Home, *D. D. Home*, 87.

137 'Professor Gregory on spiritualism', *British Spiritual Telegraph*, 1 (1857), 9; 'Letter from the late Prof Gregory', *Spiritual Magazine*, 6 (1865), 453.
138 Mme Home, *D. D. Home*, 137.
139 Lamont, 'Spiritualism', 917.
140 Mme Home, *D. D. Home*, 129.
141 Lamont, 'Magic and miracles', 153.
142 Lamont, 'Spiritualism'.

Chapter Five

1 Crookes, *Researches in the Phenomena of Spiritualism*, 17.
2 Crookes, *Phenomena of Spiritualism*, 3–4.
3 For example: 'At first', he wrote, 'I believed that the whole affair was a superstition, or at least an unexplained trick', but he had seen things 'which would make unbelief impossible', facts regardless of theory ('I cannot, at present, hazard even the most vague hypothesis as to the cause of the phenomena') and quite compatible with scientific thinking ('Nothing is too wonderful to be true if consistent with the laws of nature'). Scientific enquiry was based upon having 'no preconceived notions whatever', and 'will promote exact observation and greater love of truth among enquirers' (Crookes, *Phenomena of Spiritualism*, 4–8).
4 Lamont, 'Discourse analysis'.
5 Carpenter, 'Spiritualism and its recent converts'.
6 Carpenter, 'Spiritualism', 328.
7 Carpenter, 'Spiritualism', 343.
8 Noakes, 'Spiritualism, science and the supernatural'.
9 Carpenter, 'Spiritualism', 342.
10 For example: Tylor, 'Ethnology and spiritualism', 343; Crookes, *Phenomena of Spiritualism*, 22, 43.
11 For example: Lamont, 'How convincing is the evidence for D. D. Home?'
12 Carpenter, 'Spiritualism', 343.
13 Cox, 'The province of psychology'.
14 Richards, 'Edward Cox, the Psychological Society of Great Britain (1875–1879) and the meanings of an institutional failure,' 44.
15 Richards, 'Edward Cox'.
16 Sidgwick, 'President's address', 7–12.

17 Wiley, *Indescribable Phenomenon*, 218–20.
18 Wiley, *Indescribable Phenomenon*, 200.
19 Wiley, *Indescribable Phenomenon*, 206.
20 Beard, 'Physiology of mind-reading'.
21 Jay, *Learned Pigs and Fireproof Women*, 178.
22 Carpenter, 'Re- W. I. Bishop', 188–9.
23 'Thought-reading', *Lancet*, 117 (1881), 795; 'Thought-reading demonstrations', *British Medical Journal*, 1 (1881), 814–16; Romanes, 'Thought-reading'.
24 Luckhurst, *Invention of Telepathy*, 65; Randi, *The Supernatural A–Z*, 40; During, *Modern Enchantments*, 162–3.
25 Wiley, 'Thought-reader craze'.
26 Jay, *Learned Pigs*, 177.
27 Wiley, 'Thought-reader craze', 75.
28 Jay, *Learned Pigs*, 181–3.
29 Romanes, 'Thought-reading', 172.
30 Wiley, 'Thought-reader craze', 76.
31 'Thought-reading', (London) *Standard*, 16 May 1881, 3.
32 Romanes, 'Thought-reading'.
33 Carpenter, 'Re-W. I. Bishop', 188.
34 'The exposure of spiritism', *Scotsman*, 17 January 18794.
35 Carpenter, 'Re-W. I. Bishop', 189.
36 Whyte, 'Letter'.
37 Barrett, 'Mind-reading versus muscle-reading'.
38 Barrett et al. 'Report of the committee on thought-reading', 13–34.
39 Luckhurst, *Invention of Telepathy*.
40 Carpenter, 'On the psychology of belief'.
41 Jastrow, 'The psychology of spiritualism', 567.
42 'Psychological literature', *American Journal of Psychology*, 1 (1887), 146.
43 Mauskopf and McVaugh, *The Elusive Science*, 48; Coon, 'Testing the limits'; Hess, *Science in the New Age*, 27–9.
44 Coon, 'Testing the limits'.
45 Lamont, 'Debunking and the psychology of error', 42.
46 Jastrow, 'Psychology of spiritualism', 730.
47 Jastrow, 'Psychology of spiritualism', 731.
48 Jastrow, 'Psychology of spiritualism', 732.
49 Coon, 'Testing the limits.'
50 Gauld, *Founders of Psychical Research*, 246ff.
51 James, 'Address by the President', 5.

52 Coon, 'Testing the limits', 144.
53 James, 'Address by the President'.
54 Cattell, 'Mrs Piper the medium', 534–5.
55 James, 'Mrs Piper the medium', 640–1.
56 Titchener, 'Feeling of being stared at'.
57 James, 'Lehmann and Hansen on the telepathic problem'.
58 Titchener, 'Lehmann and Hansen', 36.
59 James, 'Messrs Lehmann and Hansen on telepathy', 655.
60 Titchener, 'Professor James on telepathy', 687.
61 Jastrow, 'Studies in spiritism', 122.
62 Tanner, *Studies in Spiritism*, 1–2.
63 Jastrow, 'Studies in spiritism', 122–4.
64 Tanner, *Studies in Spiritism*, xvi, vi.
65 Cf. Petit, 'The new woman as "tied-up dog"', *History of Psychology*, 11 (2008), 155. To take one further example, the Seybert Commission (1887) was probably the best known sceptical study of spiritualism in late nineteenth-century America, was cited positively by Jastrow and others, and indeed is noted by Tanner as a catalyst in her own interest in the subject. In the introduction to the report, the committee stressed how: 'each member in turn expressed his entire freedom from all prejudices against the subject to be investigated, and his readiness to accept any conclusion warranted by the facts; one of our number, the Acting Chairman, so far from being prejudiced confessed to a leaning in favor of the substantial truth of Spiritualism' (Seybert Commission, *Preliminary Report*, 5).
66 Gauld, *Founders of Psychical Research*, 221ff.
67 See, for example: Wiseman, 'The Fielding report', and the subsequent dispute in the *Journal of the Society for Psychical Research*.
68 Wood, 'Report of an investigation of the phenomena connected with Eusapia Palladino'; Jastrow, 'The case of Paladino'; Munsterberg, 'My friends the spiritualists'.
69 Jastrow, 'The case of Lombroso', 284–6.
70 Tanner, *Studies in Spiritism*, 2.
71 'Beulah no marvel', *New York Times*, 23 April 1913.
72 Munsterberg, *Psychology and Social Sanity*.
73 'Beulah no marvel', *New York Times*, 23 April 1913.
74 'Beulah no marvel', *New York Times*, 23 April 1913.
75 Marshall and Wendt, 'Wilhelm Wundt, spiritism and the assumptions of science'; Wolffram, 'Parapsychology'.

Chapter Six

1. Targ and Puthoff, 'Information transmission under conditions of sensory shielding'.
2. 'Investigating the paranormal', 559–60.
3. On page one of his debunking book, *The Magic of Uri Geller* (1975), the magician and escapologist, James Randi, quoted the other great magician, escapologist and debunker of the twentieth century, Harry Houdini, to make his point: 'The fact that they are scientists does not endow them with an especial gift for detecting the particular sort of fraud used by mediums, nor does it bar them from being deceived...'. As Houdini had done, Randi argued that it took a magician to catch a magician. The same point was made by Fuller, *Confessions of a Psychic*, 7.
4. See, for example: Marks and Kamman, *Psychology of the Psychic*; Randi, *Uri Geller*.
5. See, for example: Panati, *The Geller Papers*.
6. Beloff, *Parapsychology*, 127.
7. See, for example: McDougall, 'Psychical research as a university study'.
8. Rhine has tended to be seen as the key figure in the emergence of professional parapsychology, but the role of McDougall was no less important in the process (Asprem, 'A nice arrangement of heterodoxies').
9. 'Editorial introduction', *Journal of Parapsychology*, 1 (1937), 7.
10. Beloff, *Parapsychology*, 127.
11. See, for example: Rhine, *Extra-Sensory Perception*, 174–91.
12. Mauskopf and McVaugh, *Elusive Science*, 181–2.
13. Mauskopf and McVaugh, *Elusive Science*, 258.
14. Mauskopf and McVaugh, *Elusive Science*, 259–64.
15. Mauskopf and McVaugh, *Elusive Science*, 278.
16. Pratt *et al. Extra-Sensory Perception after Sixty Years.*
17. Earlier reviews of arguments between parapsychologists and critics are cited in Chapter 2, note 34.
18. See also: Pinch, 'Normal explanations of the paranormal'.
19. Price, 'Science and the supernatural', 360.
20. Hansel, *ESP: A Scientific Evaluation.*
21. Rhine, *New Frontiers of the Mind*, 125.
22. Rhine, *Extra-Sensory Perception*, 60.
23. Hansel, *ESP: A Scientific Evaluation*, 53.
24. Soal and Bateman, *Modern experiments in telepathy*, 35.

25 Thouless, 'Dr Rhine's recent experiments on telepathy and clairvoyance'.
26 Annemann, 'Was Prof J B Rhine hoodwinked?', 329.
27 Rhine, *New Frontiers of the Mind*, 126.
28 Annemann, 'Was Prof J B Rhine hoodwinked?', 333.
29 Rinn, *Searchlight on Psychical Research*, 386–7; Price, *Fifty Years of Psychical Research*, 188–9.
30 Truzzi, 'Reflections on the sociology and social psychology of conjurors and their relations to psychical research', 224.
31 Hansen, 'Magicians who endorsed psychic phenomena'.
32 Thus, for example, Rinn later claimed that it was he who had told Annemann that the 'mental count' would work as an explanation for the Zirkle-Ownbey experiments (Rinn, *Searchlight on Psychical Research*, 386).
33 For example: Soal and Bateman, *Modern Experiments in Telepathy*, 35; Mauskopf and McVaugh, *Elusive Science*, 191.
34 This point was made specifically in relation to these experiments (Soal and Bateman, *Modern Experiments in Telepathy*, 35).
35 Thouless, 'Dr Rhine's recent experiments', 36.
36 For example, when Ted Serios failed to produce paranormal photographs, then declined to allow his 'gismo' to be examined, this was framed by critics as an exposure, and by proponents as no more than a failure on this occasion. Proponents of Rosa Kuleshova, like those of Geller, admitted that she used trickery at times (Beloff, *Parapsychology*, 182–92).
37 Beloff, *Parapsychology*, 145–8.
38 Price, 'Apology to Rhine and Soal'; Wheeler, 'Parapsychology – a correction'.
39 Rhine, 'A new case of experimenter unreliability'; Marwick, 'The Soal-Goldney experiments with Basil Shackleton'; Rogo, 'J. B. Rhine and the Levy scandal'.
40 The shift of focus from the single critical experiment to a replicable experiment is described by Hyman, 'A critical historical overview of parapsychology', 71.
41 Thus, it has been argued, psi may be inhibited by particular experimental conditions, including the beliefs, interests and fears of those present. For a recent discussion of the problem, see: Kennedy, 'Why is psi so elusive?'

42 Schmeidler and Murphy, 'The influence of belief and disbelief in ESP'.
43 For some genuine insight into the fuzzy relationship between magic, mentalism and the paranormal, see: Truzzi, 'Reflections'.
44 Sawyer, S. S. Baldwin and the Press, 45.
45 Carrington, The Physical Phenomena of Spiritualism, 311; A basic description is also given in Hopkins, Magic, 196–7. The partial nature of these explanations is noted by Sawyer, S. S. Baldwin and the Press, 95.
46 Sawyer, S. S. Baldwin and the Press, 71, 18, 71.
47 Charvet, Alexander: the Man who Knows, 133.
48 Charvet, Alexander, 132.
49 Charvet, Alexander, 143–8.
50 Charvet, Alexander, 146.
51 Charvet, Alexander, 160.
52 Charvet, Alexander, 221–5.
53 Rauscher, The Mind Readers, 5–11.
54 Dunninger, The Art of Thought Reading, 4–6.
55 Dawes, Great Illusionists, 117–19; Jay, Learned Pigs, 127–46; Woods and Lead, Showmen or Charlatans?
56 Bodie, The Bodie Book; Bodie, Hypnotism.
57 Pratt, 'Doctor Walford Bodie', 3.
58 Rauscher, Mind Readers, 20–2.
59 Koran, Bring Out the Magic in your Mind, 9–10.
60 'Maurice Fogel', Journal of the Society for Psychical Research, 34 (1947), 86–7.
61 Woodward and Mark, Maurice Fogel, 94.
62 Woodward and Mark, Maurice Fogel, 94–101.
63 'Editor's notes', Journal of the Society for Psychical Research, 35 (1949), 18.
64 E. O., 'The Piddingtons', 116.
65 'The Piddingtons', Journal of the Society for Psychical Research, 35 (1949), 84.
66 'The Piddingtons', Journal of the Society for Psychical Research, 35 (1949), 84–5.
67 'The Piddingtons', Journal of the Society for Psychical Research, 35 (1949), 84.
68 E. O., 'The Piddingtons', 'Misdirection and the miraculous', 245.

69 Britland, 'Psychic or magic'.
70 Britland, 'Psychic or magic'. Indeed, members of the Magic Circle were encouraged to keep their opinions to themselves (Esler, 'The Piddingtons', 253–4).
71 E. O., 'Misdirection and the miraculous', 245.
72 Soal, Some aspects of extrasensory perception', 140.
73 E. O., 'The Piddingtons', 119.
74 E. O., 'The Piddingtons', 116.
75 Soal, 'In my mind's eye', 191.
76 Soal, *Preliminary Studies of a Vaudeville Telepathist*.
77 Soal, 'In my mind's eye', 193.
78 Soal, 'In my mind's eye', 192.
79 Price, *Fifty Years*, 45.
80 Price, *Fifty Years*, 187, 222. The ambiguity of this explanation has been noted before (e.g. Truzzi, 'Reflections', 253).
81 Marion, *In My Mind's Eye*, 7–8. The experiments were described many years later in Thouless, *From Anecdote to Experiment in Psychical Research*, 172–5. At the time, however, Soal argued that it was 'impossible for me to comment on this statement since, in spite of a considerable lapse of time, no report on their experiments has yet appeared' (Soal, 'In my mind's eye', 192–3).
82 Marion, *In My Mind's Eye*, 219.
83 Soal referred to him as 'a certain Mr Edmond P. Gibson who has had some associations with the Duke University workers in parapsychology' (Soal, 'In my mind's eye', 190).
84 Marion, *In My Mind's Eye*, 7.
85 Marion, *In My Mind's Eye*, 219–28.
86 Wiesner, 'Experiments on Frederick Marion', 222.
87 Thouless, 'Experiments on Frederick Marion, 220–2.
88 Soal did not deny that a sceptical environment might lead to failure, but merely rejected it as an explanation in this particular case, by claiming that he had wanted Marion to succeed (Soal, *'In My Mind's Eye'*, 193).
89 As far as critics were concerned, Geller was only the latest in a long line of individuals who used trickery to simulate psychic phenomena, and they rejected his paranormal abilities in the same ways as prior critics had done. Thus, for example, the magician and sceptic, Martin Gardner, provided a range of ordinary explanations for how to bend cutlery, duplicate drawings and other feats associated with Geller, based upon specialist expertise. According to the introduction, '[t]he only

persons qualified to examine self-claimed psychics are magicians'. A scientific approach – of 'logical thinking' and 'deductive reasoning' – was 'exactly wrong', and 'testing methods designed to detect paranormal ability are totally inadequate'. Meanwhile, the public, ignorant of the topic and keen to believe, were 'easy prey'. As with prior critical responses to extraordinary phenomena, this was sceptical but open-minded. 'ESP may or may not exist', and there was 'nothing wrong in scientists conducting experiments in ESP. But there is something gravely wrong in the actions of those who deliberately perpetrate feigned evidence of ESP'. Such phenomena were not only feigned but also harmful ('Black Magic is not harmless'), exploiting 'human frailty and weakness... this manuscript may make it more difficult for them to ply their trade in the future' (Fuller, *Confessions of a Psychic*, 7–8). In the first two numbers of the journal that represented this new movement, psychologists also dismissed Geller's paranormal powers (Hyman, 'The Geller papers'; Marks and Kamman, 'The non-psychic powers of Uri Geller').

90 Bok and Jerome, *Objections to Astrology*.
91 Hansen, 'CSICOP and skepticism'; Pinch and Collins, 'Private science an public knowledge'.
92 Dresslar, *Superstition and Education*.
93 Dresslar, 'Suggestions on the psychology of superstition', 213.
94 For example: Conklin, 'Superstitious belief and practice among college students'; Nixon, 'Popular answers'; Emme, 'Modification and origin'.
95 Jones *et al.*, 'Belief in the paranormal scale'.
96 For example: Alcock and Otis, 'Critical thinking and belief in the paranormal'; Alcock, *Parapsychology*; Otis and Alcock, 'Factors affecting extraordinary belief'; Tobacyk, 'Reduction in paranormal belief among participants in a college course'; Tobacyk and Milford, 'Belief in paranormal phenomena'.
97 Tobacyk, 'Reduction in paranormal belief', 57.
98 For example: Jones *et al.*, 'Belief in the paranormal scale'; Otis and Alcock, 'Factors affecting extraordinary belief'; Tobacyk and Milford, 'Belief in paranormal phenomena'.
99 Tobacyk and Milford, 'Belief in the paranormal'.
100 Lawrence, 'How many factors?'; Tobacyk, 'What is the correct dimensionality of paranormal beliefs?'; Lawrence, 'Moving on from the Paranormal Belief Scale'; Tobacyk, 'Final thoughts on issues in the measurement of paranormal beliefs?'

101 Collins and Pinch, 'Construction of the paranormal', 246–7.
102 Irwin, 'Belief in the paranormal', 294.
103 For example: Van de Castle and White, 'A report on a sentence completion form of sheep-goat attitude scale'; Thalbourne and Haraldsson, 'Personality characteristics of sheep and goats'.
104 Irwin, 'Belief in the paranormal', 16; Goulding and Parker, 'Finding psi in the paranormal', 77. For a rare example of a psychology of the sceptic, in which disbelief is attributed to emotional reasons, see Irwin, 'On paranormal disbelief'.
105 Hacking, 'Making up people'.
106 For example: Hacking, *Rewriting the Soul*; Young, *Harmony of Illusions*.
107 For example: Morris, 'Believing in ESP'; Padgett, 'Belief in ESP among psychologists'; Singer & Benassi, 'Fooling some of the people all of the time'; Marks, 'Remote viewing revisited'; Falk, 'On coincidences'; Tobacyk, 'Reduction in paranormal belief'.
108 Padgett *et al.*, 'Belief in ESP among psychologists'.
109 Hyman, 'The psychology of the psychic'.
110 Gardner, 'Science and parapsychology'.
111 Neher, 'Parapsychology: science or magic?'.
112 Benassi, 'Psychology of the extraordinary'.
113 Alcock, Hansel and Kamman were Fellows, Marks was then a scientific consultant, and later became a Fellow.
114 For example: Morris, 'Believing in ESP'; Tobacyk, 'Reduction in paranormal belief'; Gray, 'University course reduces belief in paranormal'; Woods, 'Evidence for the effectiveness of a reading program in changing beliefs in the paranormal'.
115 Tobacyk, 'Reduction in paranormal belief', 57.
116 Woods, 'Evidence', 67.
117 Tobacyk, 'Reduction in paranormal belief'.
118 Gray, 'University course reduces belief', 250.
119 Frazier, 'From psychics and ESP beliefs to UFOs and quacks'.
120 Frazier, 'Scientific facts and fictions'.
121 Jones, 'CSICOP's international conference in London.'
122 For example: Frazier, 'Scientific facts and fictions', 197; Frazier, 'CSICOP's London conference'.
123 For example: Venn, 'Hypnosis and reincarnation'; Reed, 'The psychology of channeling'; Spanos, 'Past-life regression; French *et al.*, 'Belief in astrology'; Loftus, 'Remembering dangerously'; Cormack, 'Skepticism in introductory psychology texts'.

124 Genoni, 'Exploring mind, memory and the psychology of belief'.
125 Kurtz, 'CSICOP at twenty'.
126 Frazier, 'Something for everyone at world skeptics conference', 5.
127 For example: Alcock, 'The belief engine'; Beyerstein, 'Why bogus therapies seem to work'; Gilovich and Savitsky, 'Like goes with like'; Lester, 'Why bad beliefs don't die'; Wiseman et al., 'Eyewitness testimony and the paranormal'; Wiseman et al., 'Psychic crime detectives'.
128 Kurtz, 'A quarter century of skeptical inquiry'.
129 See, for example, Bartholomew, 'Collective delusions' on social factors.
130 According to the CSICOP website, 'people from all over the world [from Alaska to New Zealand] are showing their support for skepticism by requesting a free "I doubt it" decal [transfer] from CSICOP & *Skeptical Inquirer* magazine and placing it in a creative and visible area for others to see . . . and ponder', http://www.csicop.org/resources/free_i_doubt_it_decal.
131 Hacking, 'Making up people', 232.

Chapter Seven

1 Lamont et al., 'Explaining the unexplained'.
2 For recent discussions of the similarities between various paranormal, magical and religious phenomena, see: Irwin, *The Psychology of Paranormal Belief*; Subbotsky, *Magic and the Mind*.
3 Wooffit, *In Telling Tales of the Unexpected*.
4 Coelho, 'Constructing parapsychology'.
5 The remark was made by Richard Dawkins about certain 'cultural relativists' (Dawkins, *River Out of Eden*, 32), and has become something of an anti-relativist sound bite (e.g. Norris, *Against Relativism*, 314; Brown, *Tricks of the Mind*, 267). For a clarification of the position in relation to this particular remark, see: Bloor, 'Relativism at 30,000 feet'.
6 Shapin, 'Politics of observation'; Collins and Pinch, *Frames of Meaning*; Gilbert and Mulkay, *Opening Pandora's Box*.
7 Collins, *Changing Order*.
8 Barnes et al., *Scientific Knowledge*, 76.
9 Edwards et al., 'Death and furniture'.
10 Philips, 'Paranormal beliefs linked to brain chemistry'.
11 Brugger and Mohr, 'The paranormal mind', 1291–2.

12 Newberg, *Why We Believe What We Believe*, 37.
13 Shermer, *The Believing Brain*. The concept of the 'belief engine' was first proposed by James Alcock in *Skeptical Inquirer* (Alcock, 'The belief engine').
14 Lamont, 'Critically thinking about paranormal belief'.
15 Gilovich, *How We Know What Isn't So*; Shermer, *Why People Believe Weird Things*; Wiseman and Watt, 'Belief in psychic ability and the misattribution hypothesis'; Irwin, 'Belief in the paranormal'.
16 For a detailed study of the assumptions that have been made in the study of memory, see: Danziger, *Marking the Mind*.
17 Billig, *Arguing and Thinking*.

Bibliography

'A case of clairvoyance.' *Hull Packet and East Riding Times*, 26 April (1844), 2.
Advert in *Times*, 24 March (1845) (Purland Papers).
A Lover of Truth. 'Mesmerism.' *Manchester Times and Gazette*, 20 April (1844), 2.
'A master of arts.' *Spiritual Magazine*, 4 (1863), 171.
'A memoir of Charles Mayne Young.' *Spiritual Magazine*, 4 (1871), 414.
'A painful controversy.' *Spiritual Magazine*, 9 (1874), 280–1.
'A séance with Baron and Mlle Guldenstubbe by Wm Tebb.' *Spiritual Magazine*, 2 (1867), 324–5.
'A séance with Miss Cook.' *Spiritual Magazine*, 1 (1873), 555.
'A séance with Mr Foster.' *Spiritual Magazine*, 4 (1871), 66–70.
A Surgeon, 'To the editor of the Maidstone Journal.' *Maidstone Journal and Kentish Advertiser*, 3 January (1843) (Purland Papers).
An Enquirer, 'The Mysterious Lady.' *Medical Times*, 12 (1845), 150.
Alcock, J. *Parapsychology: Science or Magic?* Oxford: Pergamon Press, 1981.
Alcock, J. 'The belief engine.' *Skeptical Inquirer*, 19:3 (1995), 14–18.
Alcock, J. 'The psychology of transcendence.' *Skeptical Inquirer*, 6:4 (1982), 57–8.
Alcock, J. and Otis, L. 'Critical thinking and belief in the paranormal.' *Psychological Reports*, 46 (1980), 479–82.
Alexander, P. P. *Spiritualism: a Narrative with a Discussion.* Edinburgh, 1871.

Alvarado, C. 'Historical perspectives in parapsychology: some practical considerations.' *Journal of the Society for Psychical Research*, 51, 265–71.
'Am I a spiritualist?' *Human Nature*, 7 (1873), 161–74.
Anderson, J. H. 'Letter.' *Morning Advertiser*, 20 October 1855, 3.
Anderson, J. H. *The Magic of Spirit-rapping*. London, n.d.
'Animal magnetism.' *Athenaeum*, 555 (1838), 417–21.
'Animal magnetism.' *Lancet*, 30 (1838), 282–8.
'Animal magnetism.' *Times*, 26 January 1844, 5.
'Animal magnetism: conclusion of second report of facts and experiments.' *Lancet*, 30 (1838), 401–3.
'Animal magnetism and homeopathy by Edwin Lee, MRCS.' *Monthly Review*, 2 (1838), 471–90.
'Animal magnetism, or mesmerism'. *Lancet*, 30 (1838), 805–13.
Annemann, T. 'Was Prof. J. B. Rhine hoodwinked?' *Jinx*, 47 (1938), 329–33.
Anon. *Table-turning by Animal Magnetism Demonstrated*. London: author, 1853.
'Anti-mesmerism.' *Bristol Mercury*, 25 January 1845, 4.
'Anti-mesmerism.' *Bristol Mercury*, 8 February 1845, 8.
Asprem, E. 'A nice arrangement of heterodoxies: William McDougall and the professionalization of psychical research.' *Journal of the History of the Behavioral Sciences*, 46 (2010), 123–43.
Baker, Mrs E. *Fraud, Fancy, Fact: Which Is It? An Enquiry into the Mystery of Spiritualism, with a Narrative of Personal Experience*. London: author, 1862.
Barge, T. 'Letter', *Spiritual Magazine*, 4 (1863), 266.
Barnes, B., Bloor, D. and Henry, J. *Scientific Knowledge: a Sociological Analysis*. London: Athlone, 1996.
Barrett, W. 'Mind-reading versus muscle-reading.' *Nature*, 24 (1881), 212.
Barrett, W. F., Gurney, E. and Myers, F. W. H. 'Report of the committee on thought-reading.' *Proceedings of the Society for Psychical Research*, 1(1), 1882, 13–34.
Barrow, L. *Independent Spirits: Spiritualism and English Plebeians, 1850–1910*. London: Routledge & Kegan Paul, 1986.
Bartholomew, R. 'Collective delusions: a skeptic's guide.' *Skeptical Inquirer*, 21:3 (1997), 29–33.
Bauer, E. 'Criticism and controversy in parapsychology – an overview.' *European Journal of Parapsychology*, 5 (1984), 141–66.
Bauman, Z. 1992. *Intimations of Postmodernity*. London: Routledge, 1992.

Beard, George M. 'The physiology of mind-reading.' *Popular Science Monthly*, 10 (1877), 459–73.
Beattie, J. 'A critique and protest.' *Spiritual Magazine*, 5 (1877), 552–4.
Bell, R. 'Stranger than fiction', *Spiritual Magazine*, 1 (1860), 211–24.
Beloff, J. 'Lessons of history.' *Journal of the American Society for Psychical Research*, 88 (1994), 7–22.
Beloff, J. 'Once a cheat, always a cheat? Eusapia Palladino revisited.' *Proceedings of the 34th Annual Convention of the Parapsychological Association*, 1991, 35–45.
Beloff, J. *Parapsychology: a Concise History*. London: Athlone, 1993.
Bem, D. 'Feeling the future: experimental evidence for anomalous retroactive influences on cognition and affect.' *Journal of Personality and Social Psychology*, 100 (2011), 407–25.
Benassi, V. 'Psychology of the extraordinary', *Skeptical Inquirer*, 7:3 (1983), 63–5.
Bennet, J. H. *The Mesmeric Mania of 1851, with a Physiological Explanation of the Phenomena Produced*. Edinburgh: Sutherland and Knox, 1851.
'Beulah no marvel, says Munsterberg.' *New York Times*, 23 April 1913, available at http://query.nytimes.com/mem/archive-free/pdf?res= 9D05E4DA173FE633A25750C2A9629C946296D6CF (accessed 15 September 2012).
Beyerstein, B. 'Why bogus therapies seem to work.' *Skeptical Inquirer*, 21 (1997), 29–34.
Billig, M. *Arguing and Thinking*. Cambridge University Press, 1987.
Blackmore, S. 'Into the unknown.' *New Scientist*, 2263 (2000), 55.
Bloor, D. 'Relativism at 30,000 feet'. In M. Mazzotti, ed., *Knowledge as Social Order: Rethinking the Sociology of Barry Barnes*. Aldershot: Ashgate Publishing Limited, 2008, 13–34.
Bodie, W. *Hypnotism*. Macduff: Author, 1912.
Bodie, W. *The Bodie Book*. London: Coxton Press, 1906.
Bok, B. J. and Jerome, L. E. *Objections to Astrology*. Buffalo, NY: Prometheus Books, 1975.
'Books received for review.' *Lancet*, 46 (1845), 577.
Boring, E. *A History of Experimental Psychology*. New York: Century, 1929.
Boring, E. G. 'Introduction.' In Hansel, *ESP: a Scientific Evaluation*, xiii–xxi.
Braid, J. 'Letter' to *The Critic*, c. 8 June 1845 (Purland Papers).
Braid, J. *Neurypnology, or the Rationale of Nervous Sleep Considered in Relation to Mesmerism*. London: John Churchill, 1843.
Brancker, A. 'Letter.' *Spiritual Magazine*, 2 (1861), 431.

Braude, A. *Radical Spirits: Spiritualism and Women's Rights in Nineteenth Century America*. Boston: Beacon Press, 1989.

Braude, S. *The Limits of Influence: Psychokinesis and the Philosophy of Science*. Lanham, NY: University Press of America, 1997.

Brevior, T. 'What is religion?' *Spiritual Magazine*, 2 (1866), 122–7.

Brewster, D. *Letters on Natural Magic*. London: John Murray, 1832.

Britland, D. 'Psychic or magic: what's paranormal?' *Magic*, 9 (1998), 50–5.

Broughton, R. *Parapsychology: the Controversial Science*. New York: Ballantine Books, 1991.

Brown, D. *Trick of the Mind*. London: Channel 4 Books, 2006.

Brugger, P. 'Functional hemispheric asymmetry and belief in ESP: towards a "neuropsychology of belief".' *Perceptual and Motor Skills*, 77 (1993), 1299–308.

Brugger, P. and Mohr, C. 'The paranormal mind: how the study of anomalous experiences and beliefs may inform cognitive neuroscience.' *Cortex*, 44 (2008), 1291–396.

Brugger, P., Regard, M., Landis, T., Cook, N., Krebs, D. and Niederberger, J. '"Meaningful" patterns in visual noise: effects of lateral stimulation and the observer's belief in ESP.' *Psychopathology*, 26 (1993), 261–5.

Bucknill, J. C. and Tuke, D. H. *A Manual of Psychological Medicine: Containing the History, Nosology, Description, Statistics, Diagnosis, Pathology and Treatment of Insanity*. London: John Churchill, 1858.

Bunn, G., Lovie, A., and Richards, G. *Psychology in Britain: Historical Essays and Personal Reflections*. Leicester: BPS Books, 2001.

Burns, R. M. *The Great Debate on Miracles: from Joseph Glanvill to David Hume*. London: Associated University Press, 1981.

Cannon, W. 'The problem of miracles in the 1830's.' *Victorian Studies*, 4:1 (1960), 5–32.

Carpenter, W. B. 'Fallacies of testimony in relation to the supernatural.' *Contemporary Review*, 27 (1876), 279–95.

Carpenter, W. B. 'Mesmerism, odylism, table-turning and spiritualism, considered historically and scientifically.' *Fraser's Magazine*, 15 (1877), 382–405.

Carpenter, W. B. 'On the influence of suggestion in modifying and directing muscular movement, independently of volition.' *Proceedings of the Royal Institution of Great Britain*, 1 (1852), 147–53.

Carpenter, W. B. 'On the psychology of belief.' *Contemporary Review*, 23 (1873), 123–45.

Carpenter, W. B. 'Psychological curiosities of spiritualism.' *Fraser's Magazine*, 16 (1877), 541–64.

Carpenter, W. B. 'Re- W. I. Bishop.' *Nature*, 24 (1881), 188–9.
Carpenter, W. B. 'Spiritualism and its recent converts.' *Quarterly Review*, 131 (1871), 301–53.
Carrington, H. *The Physical Phenomena of Spiritualism: Fraudulent and Genuine*. Boston: Herbert T. Turner, 1907.
Carroll, B. E. *Spiritualism in Antebellum America*. Bloomington: Indiana University Press, 1997.
Carruthers, P. *Language, Thought and Consciousness: an Essay in Philosophical Psychology*. Cambridge: Cambridge University Press, 1998.
Cattell, J. 'Mrs Piper the medium.' *Science*, 7 (1898), 534–5.
Cerullo, J. J. *The Secularization of the Soul*. Philadelphia: Institute for the Study of Human Issues, Inc., 1992.
Chambers, R. *On Testimony: Its Posture in the Scientific World*. London, 1859.
Charvet, D. *Alexander: the Man Who Knows*. Pasadena, CA: Mike Caveney's Magic Words, 2004.
'Cheating mediums.' *Spiritual Magazine*, 3 (1862), 273.
Christopher, M. *Panorama of Magic*. New York: Dover Publications, 1962.
'Clairvoyance extraordinary.' *Manchester Times and Gazette*, 11 May 1844, 5.
Clark, A. *Supersizing the Mind: Embodiment, Action and Cognitive Extension*. Oxford: Oxford University Press, 2008.
Coelho, C. 'Constructing parapsychology: a discourse analysis of accounts of experimental parapsychologists.' Unpublished doctoral thesis. University of Edinburgh, 2005.
Coleman, B. 'Letter.' *The Spiritualist*, 2 (1871), 13.
Coleman, B. 'Passing events.' *Spiritual Magazine*, 5 (1864), 164–70.
Coleman, B. 'Spiritualism in America.' *Spiritual Magazine*, 2 (1861), 294.
Coleman, B. 'Spiritualism in America II.' *Spiritual Magazine*, 2 (1861), 341–3.
Coleman, B. 'The question of cui bono answered.' *Spiritual Magazine*, 2 (1861), 142–3.
Collins, H. *Changing Order: Replication and Induction in Scientific Practice*. London: Sage, 1992.
Collins, H. and Pinch, T. *Frames of Meaning: the Social Construction of Extraordinary Science*. London: Routledge and Kegan Paul, 1982.
Collins, H. and Pinch, T. (1979). 'The construction of the paranormal: nothing unscientific is happening.' In Wallis, R., ed., *On the Margins of Science*, 237–70.

Colquhoun, J. C. *Reports of the Experiments on Animal Magnetism*. Edinburgh: Robert Caddell, 1833.
Conklin, E. S. 'Superstitious belief and practice among college students.' *American Journal of Psychology*, 30 (1919), 83–102.
Cook, J. *The Arts of Deception*. Cambridge, MA: Harvard University Press, 2001.
Coon, D. 'Testing the limits of sense and science: American experimental psychologists combat spiritualism.' *American Psychologist*, 47 (1992), 143–51.
Cooter, R. *The Cultural Meaning of Popular Science: Phrenology and the Organization of Consent in Nineteenth-Century Britain*. Cambridge: Cambridge University Press, 1984.
Cormack, R. H. 'Skepticism in introductory psychology texts'. *Skeptical Inquirer*, 15 (1991), 302–7.
Cottom, D. *The Abyss of Reason: Cultural Movements, Revelations and Betrayals*. Oxford: Oxford University Press, 1991.
Couttie, B. *Forbidden Knowledge: the Paranormal Paradox*. Cambridge: Lutterworth Press, 1988.
Cox, S. 'The province of psychology.' *Proceedings of the Psychological Society of Great Britain, 1875–1879*. London: privately printed, 1880, 1–37.
Cox, W. E. 'Parapsychology and magicians.' *Parapsychology Review*, 5:3 (1974), 12–14.
Crabtree, A. *From Mesmer to Freud: Magnetic Sleep and the Roots of Psychological Healing*. New Haven: Yale University Press, 1993.
Crawford, W. J. *The Reality of Psychic Phenomena*. London: John M. Watkins, 1916.
Crookes, W. *Researches in the Phenomena of Spiritualism*. London: J. Burns, 1874.
Crosland, N. *Apparitions*. London: Effingham Willson & Bosworth & Harrison, 1856.
'Curious case of assault.' *Morning Chronicle*, 15 April 1833, 4.
D.E.L.E. 'Dr Forbes the real impostor.' *Zoist*, 3 (1846), 537–43.
Danziger, K. *Constructing the Subject: Historical Origins of Psychological Research*. Cambridge: Cambridge University Press, 1990.
Danziger, K. *Marking the Mind: A History of Memory*. New York: Cambridge University Press, 2008.
Danziger, K. *Naming the Mind: How Psychology Found Its Language*. London: Sage Publications, 1997.

Danziger, K. 'Prospects of a historical psychology.' *History and Philosophy of Psychology Bulletin*, 15 (2003), 4–10.
Darnton, R. *Mesmerism and the End of the Enlightenment in France.* Cambridge, MA: Harvard University Press, 1968.
Daston, L. 'Marvelous facts and miraculous evidence in early modern Europe.' *Critical Inquiry*, 18 (1991), 93–124.
Davies, O. *The Haunted: a Social History of Ghosts.* Basingstoke: Palgrave Macmillan, 2007.
Dawes, E. *The Great Illusionists.* Secaucus, NJ: Chartwell Books, 1979.
Dawkins, R. *River Out of Eden: a Darwinian View of Life.* New York: Basic Books, 1995.
Dear, P. 'Miracles, experiments and the ordinary course of nature.' *Isis*, 81 (1990), 663–83.
'Debate on modern spiritualism – Bradlaugh v Burns.' *Medium and Daybreak*, 3 (1872), 512–17.
Dennet, D. 'Two contrasts: folk craft versus folk science, and belief versus opinion.' In J. D. Greenwood, ed., *The Future of Folk Psychology: Intentionality and Cognitive Science*, 1991, 135–48.
Derksen, M. 'Are we not experimenting then? The rhetorical demarcation of psychology and common sense.' *Theory and Psychology*, 7 (1997), 435–56.
Dingwall, E. J., ed. *Abnormal Hypnotic Phenomena: a Survey of Nineteenth Century Cases.* New York: Barnes and Noble, 1968.
Dixon, T. *From Passions to Emotions: the Creation of a Secular Psychological Category.* Cambridge: Cambridge University Press, 2003.
Doyle, A. C. *The Edge of the Unknown.* London: John Murray, 1930.
Doyle, A. C. *The History of Spiritualism*, 2 vols. London: Catell and Co. Ltd, 1926.
'Dr A. Wood on electro-biology.' *Monthly Journal of Medical Science*, 3 (1851), 407–35.
'Dr Gully's facts.' *Spiritual Magazine*, 2 (1861), 63–4.
'Dr Hooker and Wallace.' *Spiritual Magazine* 3 (1868), 480.
Dresslar, F. B. 'Suggestions on the psychology of superstition.' *American Journal of Insanity*, 67 (1910), 213.
Dresslar, F. B. *Superstition and Education.* Berkeley: University of California Press, 1907.
Dunninger, J. *The Art of Thought Reading.* Evanston, IL: Clark Publishing Company, 1962.

During, S. *Modern Enchantments: the Cultural Power of Secular Magic.* Cambridge, MA: Harvard University Press, 2002.
E. O. 'Misdirection and the miraculous.' *Journal of the Society for Psychical Research,* 35 (1949), 244–5.
E. O. 'The Piddingtons.' *Journal of the Society for Psychical Research,* 35 (1949), 116–19.
'Editorial introduction.' *Journal of Parapsychology,* 1 (1937), 1–9.
'Editor's notes.' *Journal of the Society for Psychical Research,* 35 (1949), 18.
Edwards, D. *Discourse and Cognition.* London: Sage, 1992.
Edwards, D. and Potter, J. *Discursive Psychology.* London: Sage, 1992.
Edwards, D., Potter, J. and Ashmore, M. 'Death and furniture: the rhetoric, politics and theology of bottom line arguments against relativism.' *History of the Human Sciences,* 8 (1995), 25–49.
'Elegant extracts.' *Spiritual Magazine,* 2 (1861), 433–41.
Ellenberger, H. *The Discovery of the Unconscious: the History and Evolution of Dynamic Psychiatry.* New York: Basic Books, 1970.
Elliotson, J. 'Cure of uterine disease with mesmerism, by Mr Vernon.' *Zoist,* 3 (1845), 82–6.
Emme, E. E. 'Modification and origin of certain beliefs in superstition among 96 college students.' *Journal of Psychology,* 10 (1940), 279–91.
Ernst, W. 'Colonial psychiatry, magic and religion: the case of mesmerism in British India.' *History of Psychiatry,* 15 (2004), 57–71.
Esler, J. A. 'The Piddingtons.' *Magic Circular,* 43 (1948), 253–4.
'Evenings with Miss Nicholl.' *Spiritual Magazine,* 2 (1867), 255.
'Exeter.' *Phrenological Journal,* 14 (1841), 102–3.
'Experimental investigation of table-moving.' *Athenaeum,* 2 July 1853, 801–3.
'Experiments performed on Elizabeth and Jane O'Key at the house of Mr Wakley, Bedford Square in August 1838.' *Lancet,* 36 (1841), 694–9.
'Extraction of teeth in the mesmeric state.' *Zoist,* 3 (1845), 214–16.
'Extraordinary uproar: lecture on mesmerism.' *Northern Star and Leeds Advertiser,* 13 January 1844, 2.
Falk, R. 'On coincidences', *Skeptical Inquirer,* 6:2 (1981), 18–31.
'Farther facts by Dr Blank.' *Spiritual Magazine,* 1 (1860), 342.
Ferriar, J. *An Essay Towards a Theory of Apparitions.* London: Cadell and Davies, 1813.
Flourens, P. *Phrenology Examined.* Philadelphia: Hogan and Thompson, 1846.

Fontes da Costa, P. 'The making of extraordinary facts: authentication of singularities of nature at the Royal Society of London in the first half of the eighteenth century.' *Studies of History and Philosophy of Science*, 33 (2002), 265–88.

Forbes, J. *Illustrations of Modern Mesmerism from Personal Investigation*. London: John Churchill, 1845.

Forbes, J. 'Notes of a few more trials with the mesmerists in a second search for clairvoyance.' *Medical Gazette*, 35 (1845), 486–95.

Forbes, J. 'Notes of yet another trial with the mesmerists.' *Medical Gazette*, 35 (1845), 669–75.

Frazier, K. 'CSICOP's London conference: musings, thoughts and themes.' *Skeptical Inquirer*, 10:2 (1986), 100.

Frazier, K. 'From psychics and ESP beliefs to UFOs and quacks: highlights of CSICOP's first international conference.' *Skeptical Inquirer*, 8 (1984), 194–202.

Frazier, K. *Paranormal Borderlands of Science*. Buffalo, NY: Prometheus, 1981.

Frazier, K. 'Scientific facts and fictions: on the trail of paranormal beliefs at CSICOP "84".' *Skeptical Inquirer*, 9 (1985), 197–201.

Frazier, K. 'Something for everyone at world skeptics congress.' 20:5 (1996), 5.

French, C., Fowler, M., McCarthy, K. and Peers, D. 'Belief in astrology: a test of the Barnum effect.' *Skeptical Inquirer*, 15 (1991), 166–72.

Frost, T. *The Lives of the Conjurors*. London: Tinsley Brothers, 1876.

Fuller, U. *Confessions of a Psychic*. Teaneck, NJ: Karl Fulves, 1975.

Gardner, M. 'Science and parapsychology', *Skeptical Inquirer*, 4:3 (1980), 60–3.

Gauld, A. *A History of Hypnotism*. Cambridge: Cambridge University Press, 1995.

Gauld, A. *The Founders of Psychical Research*. London: Routledge and Kegan Paul, 1968.

Genoni, T. 'Exploring mind, memory and the psychology of belief.' *Skeptical Inquirer*, 19:1 (1995), 10–13.

Gergen, K. 'Social psychology as history.' *Journal of Personality and Social Psychology*, 26 (1973), 309–20.

Gieryn, T. 'Boundary-work and the demarcation of science from non-science: strains and interests in professional ideologies of scientists.' *American Sociological Review*, 48 (1983), 781–95.

Gilbert, N. and Mulkay, M. *Opening Pandora's Box: a Sociological Analysis of Scientists' Discourse*. Cambridge: Cambridge University Press, 1984.

Gilliland, A. R. 'A study of the superstitions of college students.' *Journal of Abnormal and Social Psychology*, 24 (1930), 472–9.
Gilovich, T. *How We Know What Isn't So: the Fallibility of Human Reason in Everyday Life*. New York: Free Press, 1991.
Gilovich, T. and Savitsky, K. 'Like goes with like: the role of representativeness in erroneous and pseudoscientific beliefs.' *Skeptical Inquirer*, 20:2 (1996), 34–40.
Godfrey, N. S. *Table-moving Tested, and Proved to Be the Result of Satanic Agency*. London: author, 1853.
Goffman, E. *Frame Analysis: an Essay on the Organization of Experience*. New York: Harper Row, 1974.
Goodall, J. *Performance and Evolution in the Age of Darwin: Out of the Natural Order*. London: Routledge, 2002.
Gordon, Mrs M. M. *The Home Life of Sir David Brewster*. Edinburgh: Edmonston and Douglas, 1870.
Goulding, A. and Parker, A. 'Finding psi in the paranormal: psychometric measures used in research on paranormal beliefs/experiences and in research on psi-ability.' *European Journal of Parapsychology*, 16 (2001), 73–101.
Graumann, C. F. and Gergen, K. *Historical Dimensions of Psychological Discourse*. Cambridge: Cambridge University Press, 1996.
Gray, T. 'University course reduces belief in paranormal.' *Skeptical Inquirer*, 8:3 (1984), 247–51.
Gregory, W. *Letters to a Candid Enquirer on Animal Magnetism*. London: Taylor, Walton and Maberly, 1851.
'Greenwich lecture hall', newspaper clipping, 2 February 1844 (Purland Papers).
Guppy, S. 'Letter.' *The Spiritualist*, 1 (1871), 222.
Hacking, I. 'Making up people.' In T. C. Heller, M. Sosna and D. E. Wellbery, eds., *Reconstructing Individualism: Autonomy, Individuality and the Self in Western Thought*. Stanford: Stanford University Press, 1986, 222–36.
Hacking, I. 'The looping effects of human kinds.' In D. Sperber, D. Premack and A. Premack, eds., *Causal Cognition: a Multidisciplinary Debate*. Oxford: Clarendon Press, 1995, 351–94.
Hacking, I. *Rewriting the Soul: Multiple Personality and the Sciences of Memory*. Princeton: Princeton University Press, 1995.
Hall, S. C. *The Use of Spiritualism*. London: E. W. Allen, 1884.
Hankins, T. and Silverman, R. *Instruments and the Imagination*. Princeton: Princeton University Press, 1995.

Hansel, C. E. M. *ESP: A Critical Re-evaluation*. Buffalo: Prometheus Books, 1980.

Hansel, C. E. M. *ESP: A Scientific Evaluation*. London: MacGibbon and Kee Ltd, 1966.

Hansen, G. P. 'CSICOP and skepticism: an emerging social movement.' *Proceedings of the Parapsychological Association*, 1987, 318–31.

Hansen, G. P. 'Magicians who endorsed psychic phenomena.' *Linking Ring*, 70:8 (1990), 65, 109.

Hansen, G. P. *The Trickster and the Paranormal*. Xlibris: New York, 2001.

Harre, R. and Gillett, G. *The Discursive Mind*. Thousand Oaks, CA: Sage Publications Inc., 1994.

Harris, P. *The Art of Astonishment: Pieces of Strange to Unleash the Moment. Book 1*. Sacramento, CA: A-1 Multimedia.

Hearnshaw, L. S. *A Short History of British Psychology, 1840–1940*. London: Methuen & Co. Ltd, 1964.

Hergovich, A. 'The effect of pseudo-psychic demonstrations as dependent on belief in paranormal phenomena and suggestibility.' *Personality and Individual Differences*, 36 (2004), 365–80.

'Hertford winter assizes.' *Jackson's Oxford Journal*, 3 December 1831.

Hess, D. J. *Science in the New Age: the Paranormal, its Defenders and Debunkers, and American Culture*. Madison: University of Wisconsin Press, 1993.

Hibbert, S. *Sketches of the Philosophy of Apparitions*. Edinburgh: Oliver & Boyd, 1825.

Hill, A. *Paranormal Media: Audiences, Spirits and Magic in Popular Culture*. Abingdon: Routledge, 2011.

Holmes, G. 'Case of cross-mesmerism.' *People's Phrenological Journal*, 2 (1844), 138–40.

Home, Mme. *D. D. Home: His Life and Mission*. London: Kegan Paul, Trench, Trubner, 1921.

Home, D. D., *Incidents in My Life*. Secaucus, NJ: University Books, 1972 (originally published 1863).

Honestas. 'Letter.' *Spiritual Magazine*, 2 (1868), 216–19.

Hopkins, A. *Magic: Stage Illusions and Scientific Diversions, Including Trick Photography*. New York: Munn & Co., 1898.

Horton, S. 'Were they having fun yet? Victorian optical gadgetry, modernist selves.' In C. Christ and J. Jordan, eds., *Victorian Literature and the Visual Imagination*. Berkeley: University of California Press, 1995.

Houdini, H. *The Unmasking of Robert-Houdin*. New York: Publishers Printing Co., 1908.
Howitt, W. 'Correspondence.' *Spiritual Magazine*, 3 (1862), 43.
Howitt, W. 'Darkness as an element of power in the divine economy?' *Spiritual Magazine*, 6 (1865), 340.
Hutchison, J. 'Important testimony to the facts.' *Spiritual Magazine*, 1 (1861), 89–90.
Hyman, R. 'A critical overview of parapsychology.' In Kurtz, A *Skeptic's Handbook of Parapsychology*, 3–96.
Hyman, R. 'The Geller papers.' *Zetetic*, 1 (1976), 73–80.
Hyman, R. 'The psychology of the psychic.' *Skeptical Inquirer*, 5:2 (1980), 60–3.
Hytche, E. 'The impostors who are exhibited in public by the professors of mesmerism.' *Lancet*, 43 (1844), 576–7.
'Illusions and hallucinations.' *British Quarterly Review*, 36 (1862), 387–418.
'Illustrations of modern mesmerism.' *British and Foreign Medical Review*, 19 (1845), 277–8.
'Illustrations of modern mesmerism from personal investigations, by John Forbes'. *British and Foreign Medical Review*, 20 (1846), 277–8.
'Incidents in my life.' *Times*, 9 April 1863, 4–5.
'Intelligence.' *Phrenological Journal* 14 (1841), 197–8, 287, 290.
'Intelligence.' *Phrenological Journal* 17 (1844), 307.
'Investigating the paranormal.' *Nature*, 251 (1974), 559–60.
Irwin, H. 'Belief in the paranormal: a review of the empirical literature.' *Journal of the American Society for Psychical Research*, 87 (1993), 1–39.
Irwin, H. 'On paranormal disbelief: the psychology of the sceptic.' In G. Zollschan, J. Schumaker and G. Walsh, eds., *Exploring the Paranormal: Perspectives on Belief and Experience*. Bridport: Prism Press, 1989, 306–12.
Irwin, H. *The Psychology of Paranormal Belief*. Hatfield: University of Hertfordshire, 2009.
Irwin, H. and Watt, C. *An Introduction to Parapsychology*. Jefferson, NC: McFarland, 2007.
J. 'Letter.' *Morning Advertiser*, 23 October 1855, 3.
J. 'Letter.' *Morning Advertiser*, 27 October 1855, 5.
J. J. S. 'Letter.' *Spiritual Magazine*, 1 (1860), 233.

James, W. 'Address by the president before the Society of Psychical Research'. *Proceedings of the Society for Psychical Research*, 12 (1896), 2–10.
James, W. 'Lehmann and Hansen on the telepathic problem.' *Science*, 8 (1898), 956.
James, W. 'Messrs Lehmann and Hansen on telepathy.' *Science*, 9 (1899), 654–5.
James. W. 'Mrs Piper the medium.' *Science*, 7 (1898), 640–1.
James, W. *Principles of Psychology*, 2 vols. New York: Henry Holt, 1890.
James, W. 'Psychical research.' *Proceedings of the Psychological Society of Great Britain, 1875–1879*. London: privately printed 1880, 650.
Jastrow, J. 'Studies in spiritism.' *American Journal of Psychology*, 22 (1911), 122–4.
Jastrow, J. 'The case of Lombroso.' *Dial*, 47 (1909), 284–6.
Jastrow, J. 'The case of Paladino.' *American Monthly Review of Reviews*, 42 (1910), 74–84.
Jastrow, J. 'The psychology of spiritualism.' *Popular Science Monthly*, 34 (1889), 721–33.
Jastrow, J. 'The psychology of spiritualism.' *Science*, 8 (1886), 567–8.
Jay, R. *Learned Pigs and Fireproof Women*. New York: Villard Books, 1987.
Jones, J. 'An evening with Mr Home.' *Spiritual Magazine*, 2 (1861), 68–70.
Jones, L. 'CSICOP's international conference in London: investigation and belief, past lives and prizes', *Skeptical Inquirer*, 10:2 (1986), 98–104.
Jones, W., Russell, D. and Nickel, T. 'Belief in the paranormal scale: an objective instrument to measure belief in magical phenomena and causes.' *Journal Supplement Abstract Service, Catalog of Selected Documents in Psychology*, 7, 100 (MS 1577), 1977.
'Juggling, wizarding, and similar phenomena.' *Family Herald*, 13 (1855), 349–50.
Kaufman, M. H. 'Phrenology – confrontation between Gordon and Spurzheim – 1816.' *Proceedings of the Royal College of Physicians of Edinburgh*, 29 (1999), 159–70.
Kennedy, J. E. 'Why is psi so elusive? A review and proposed model.' *Journal of Parapsychology*, 65 (2001), 219–46.
Koran, A. *Bring Out the Magic in Your Mind*. Preston: A. Thomas & Co., 1964.
Korem, D. and Meier, P. *The Fakers*. Old Tappan, NJ: Fleming H. Revell Co., 1980.

Kurtz, P. 'A quarter century of skeptical inquiry', *Skeptical Inquirer*, 25:4 (2001), 42–7.
Kurtz, P. ed., *A Skeptic's Handbook of Parapsychology*. Buffalo, NY: Prometheus Press, 1985.
Kurtz, P. 'CSICOP at twenty.' *Skeptical Inquirer*, 20:4 (1996), 5–8.
Kusch, M. *Psychological Knowledge: a Social History and Philosophy*. London: Routledge, 1999.
Lamont, P. 'Critically thinking about paranormal belief.' In S. Della Sala, ed., *Tall Tales about the Mind and Brain*. Oxford University Press, 2007, 23–35.
Lamont, P. 'Debunking and the psychology of error: a historical analysis of psychological matters.' *Qualitative Research in Psychology*, 7 (2010), 34–44.
Lamont, P. 'Discourse analysis as method in the history of psychology.' *History and Philosophy of Psychology*, 9:2 (2007), 34–44.
Lamont, P. 'How convincing is the evidence for D. D. Home?' *Proceedings of the Parapsychological Association International Conference*, 1999, 166–79.
Lamont, P. *Magic and Miracles in Victorian Britain*. Unpublished PhD thesis, University of Edinburgh.
Lamont, P. 'Magic and the willing suspension of disbelief.' In J. Allen and S. O'Reilly, eds., *Magic Show*. London: Southbank Centre/Hayward Publishing, 2010, 30–1.
Lamont, P. 'Magician as conjuror: a frame analysis of Victorian mediums.' *Early Popular Visual Culture*, 4 (2006), 131–42.
Lamont, P. 'Paranormal belief and the avowal of prior scepticism.' *Theory and Psychology*, 17 (2007), 681–96.
Lamont, P. 'Reflexivity, the role of history, and the case mesmerism in early Victorian Britain.' *History of Psychology*, 13 (2010), 393–408.
Lamont, P. 'Spiritualism and a mid-Victorian crisis of evidence.' *Historical Journal*, 47 (2004), 897–920.
Lamont, P. *The First Psychic: the Peculiar Mystery of a Notorious Victorian Wizard*. London: Little Brown, 2005.
Lamont, P. 'The making of extraordinary psychological phenomena.' *Journal of the History of the Behavioral Sciences*, 48:1 (2012), 1–15.
Lamont, P. and Murphy, M. 'The origins of the first psychic and other misrepresentations.' *Journal of the Society for Psychical Research*, 70 (2006), 176–80.

Lamont, P. and Wiseman, R. *Magic in Theory: an Introduction to the Theoretical and Psychological Elements of Conjuring*. Hatfield: University of Hertfordshire Press, 1999.

Lamont, P., Coelho, C., and McKinlay, A. (2009). 'Explaining the unexplained: warranting disbelief in the paranormal.' *Discourse Studies*, 11:5, 543, 559.

Lawrence, T. R. 'Gathering in the sheep and goats: a meta-analysis of forced-choice sheep-goat ESP studies, 1947–1993.' *Proceedings of the Parapsychological Association 36th Annual Convention*, 1993, 75–86.

Lawrence, T. R. 'How many factors of paranormal belief are there? A critique of the Paranormal belief scale.' *Journal of Parapsychology*, 59 (1995), 3–25.

Lawrence, T. R. 'Moving on from the Paranormal Belief Scale: a final reply to Tobacyk.' *Journal of Parapsychology*, 59 (1995), 131–40.

Leahey, T. H. and Leahey, G. E. *Psychology's Occult Doubles: Psychology and the Problem of Pseudo-science*. Chicago: Nelson Hall, 1984.

Leary, D. E., ed., *Metaphors in the History of Psychology*. Cambridge: Cambridge University Press, 1994.

'Lecture hall, Greenwich', broadsheet for Vernon lecture, 4 January 1844 (Purland Papers).

'Lecture on mesmerism', newspaper clipping, 27 December 1842 (Purland Papers).

'Lecture on mesmerism', newspaper clipping, *Kentish Mercury* (?), c. March 1845 (Purland Papers).

'Lecture on mesmerism.' *People's Phrenological Journal*, 2 (1844), 172.

'Lecture on mesmerism: extraordinary uproar and disgraceful attack on one of the patients.' *Morning Herald*, 5 January 1844.

Lectures on mesmerism', newspaper clipping from *Maidstone Journal and Kentish Advertiser*, 3 January 1843 (Purland Papers).

'Lectures on mesmerism', newspaper clipping, March 1843 (Purland Papers).

Lee, E. *Animal Magnetism and Magnetic Lucid Somnambulism*. London: Longmans, Green and Co., 1866.

Lester, G. 'Why bad beliefs don't die.' *Skeptical Inquirer*, 24:6 (2000), 40–3.

'Letter', *Human Nature*, 4 (1870), 133.

'Letter from the late Prof. Gregory.' *Spiritual Magazine*, 6 (1865), 451–3.

Lewes, G. H. 'Seeing is believing.' *Blackwood's Edinburgh Magazine*, 88 (1860), 381–95.

'Literary institution', newspaper clipping, March 1845 (Purland Papers).

Loftus, E. 'Remembering dangerously.' *Skeptical Inquirer*, 19:2 (1995), 20–9.
Lombroso, C. *After Death – What?* Boston: Small, Maynard & Company, 1909.
'London November 28.' *Newcastle Courant*, 3 December 1831.
Luckhurst, R. *The Invention of Telepathy*. Oxford: Oxford University Press, 2001.
'Lyon v Home.' *Spiritual Magazine*, 3 (1868), 241–81.
Mackay, C. *Memoirs of Extraordinary Popular Delusions*. London: Richard Bentley, 1841.
Macmillan, K. and Edwards, D. 'Who killed the princess? Description and blame in the British press.' *Discourse Studies*, 1 (1999), 151–74.
Magendie, F. *An Elementary Treatise on Human Physiology*. Trans. John Revere. New York: Harper and Brothers, 1855.
Magic, Pretended Miracles. London: Religious Tract Society, 1848.
'Magician of the south.' *Bristol Mercury*, 22 March 1845.
Mangan, M. *Performing Dark Arts: a Cultural History of Conjuring*. Bristol: Intellect Books, 2007.
'Manifestations in England.' *Spiritual Herald*, 1 (1856), 43–5.
Margolis, J. *Uri Geller: Magician or Mystic?* London: Orion, 1998.
Marion, F. *In My Mind's Eye. With a Foreword by R. H. Thouless, MA, PhD, University Reader in Educational Psychology, Cambridge, and B. P. Weisner, DSc, PhD*. London: Rider and Co., 1949.
Marks, D. 'Remote viewing revisited.' *Skeptical Inquirer*, 6:4 (1982), 18–29.
Marks, D. and Kamman, R. 'The non-psychic powers of Uri Geller.' *Zetetic*, 1 (1977), 9–17.
Marks, D. and Kamman, R. *The Psychology of the Psychic*. Buffalo, NY: Prometheus Books, 1980.
Marshall, M. and Wendt, R. 'Wilhelm Wundt, spiritism and the assumptions of science.' In W. G. Bringmann and R. D. Tweney, eds., *Wundt Studies: a Centennial Collection*. Toronto: C. J. Hogrefe Inc., 1980, 158–75.
Marwick, B. 'The Soal-Goldney experiments with Basil Shackleton: new evidence of data manipulation.' *Proceedings of the Society for Psychical Research*, 56 (1978), 250–77.
'Maurice Fogel.' *Journal of the Society for Psychical Research*, 34 (1947), 86–7.
Mauskopf, S. and McVaugh, M. *The Elusive Science: Origins of Experimental Psychical Research*. Baltimore: John Hopkins University Press, 1980.
Maven, M. 'I'll build a stairway to a paradox.' *Magic*, 5:2 (1995), 23.

McCorristine, S. *Spectres of the Self: Thinking about Ghosts and Ghost-seeing in England, 1750–1920*. Cambridge: Cambridge University Press, 2010.
McDougall, W. 'Psychical research as a university study.' In C. Murchison, ed., *The Case For and Against Psychical Belief*, 149–62. Worcester: Clark University, 1927.
McLenon, J. *Deviant Science: the Case of Parapsychology*. Philadelphia: University of Pennsylvania Press, 1984.
'Mesmeric case at Deptford.' *People's Phrenological Journal*, 2 (1844), 137–8.
'Mesmeric intelligence.' *People's Phrenological Journal*, 2 (1844), 183–5.
'Mesmerism', advert, *Glasgow Herald*, 31 May 1844.
'Mesmerism', *Kentish Independent*, 10 February 1844, (Purland Papers).
'Mesmerism', newspaper clipping, 30 March 1843 (Purland Papers).
'Mesmerism', newspaper clipping, *Kentish Mercury*, 30 January 1844 (Purland Papers).
'Mesmerism', newspaper clipping, May 1843 (Purland Papers).
'Mesmerism', newspaper clipping, November 1843 (Purland Papers).
'Mesmerism and its opponents.' *Medico-Chirurgical Review and Journal of Practical Medicine*, 41, 1844, 142–3.
'Mesmerism – clairvoyance', *Bulletin of Medical Science*, 3 (1845), 389–90.
'Modern necromancy.' *North British Review*, 34 (1861), 110–41.
'Modern Spiritualism.' *Quarterly Review*, 114 (1863), 179–210.
Moore, R. *In Search of White Crows*. New York: Oxford University Press, 1977.
Morris, R. L. 'What psi is not: the necessity for experiments.' In H. Edge, R. L. Morris, J. Palmer, and J. Rush, eds., *Foundations of Parapsychology*. London: Routledge and Kegan Paul, 1986, 70–110.
Morris, S. 'Believing in ESP: effects of dehoaxing.' *Skeptical Inquirer*, 4:3 (1980), 18–31.
Morus, I. 'Seeing and believing science.' *Isis*, 97 (2006), 101–10.
'Mr Braid at the Royal Institution.' *Manchester Times and Gazette*, 27 April 1844, 6.
'Mr C. Foster – the medium from America.' *Spiritual Magazine*, 3 (1862), 45–8.
'Mr C. H. Foster.' *Spiritual Magazine*, 3 (1862), 37–45.
'Mr Home and the critics.' *Spiritual Magazine*, 4 (1863), 215–19.
'Mr Purland's letter.' *Forceps*, 13 July 1844 (Purland Papers).
'Mr S. C. Hall and Mr Foster.' *Spiritual Magazine*, 3 (1862), 89–92.
'Mr Sothern and the Miracle Circle.' *Spiritual Magazine*, 1 (1866), 44.

'Mr Vernon's experiments and the medical Society.' *Western Lancet: a Monthly Journal of Practical Medicine and Surgery*, 3 (1844), 138–9.

Munsterberg, H. 'My friends the spiritualists: some theories and conclusions concerning Eusapio Palladino.' *Metropolitan*, 31 (1910), 559–72.

Munsterberg, H. *Psychology and Social Sanity.* New York: Doubleday, Page and Co., 1914, 146–80.

'Mysterious Lady.' *Morning Chronicle*, 12 March 1845, 1.

'Mysterious Lady.' *Era*, 30 March 1845, 3.

Nardi, P. 'Toward a social psychology of entertainment magic.' *Symbolic Interaction*, 7 (1984), 25–42.

Neher, A. 'Parapsychology: science or magic?' *Skeptical Inquirer*, 6:4 (1982), 54–6.

Nenadic, S. 'Illegitimacy, insolvency and insanity: Wilkie Collins and the Victorian nightmares.' In A. Marwick, ed., *The Arts, Literature, and Society*. London: Routledge, 1990, 133–62.

Newberg, A. and Waldman, M. R. *Why We Believe What We Believe.* New York: Free Press, 2006.

Nichols, T. L. *A Biography of the Brothers Davenport.* London: Saunders, Otley and Co., 1864.

Nichols, T. L. *Supra-mundane Facts in the Life of Rev. Jesse Babcock Ferguson.* London: F. Pitman, 1865.

Nixon, H. K. 'Popular answers to some psychological questions.' *American Journal of Psychology*, 36 (1925), 418–23.

Noakes, R. 'Spiritualism, science and the supernatural in mid-Victorian Britain.' In N. Boun, C. Burdett and P. Thurschwell, eds., *The Victorian Supernatural*. Cambridge: Cambridge University Press, 2004, 23–43.

Noakes, R. 'Telegraphy is an occult art: Cromwell Varley and the diffusion of electricity to the other world.' *British Journal for the History of Science*, 32 (1999), 421–59.

Noakes, R. 'The bridge which is between physical and psychical research: William Fletcher Barrett, sensitive flames and spiritualism.' *History of Science*, 42 (2004), 419–64.

Noakes, R. 'The world of the infinitely little: connecting physical and psychical realities in Britain c. 1900.' *Studies in the History and Philosophy of Science*, 39 (2008), 323–33.

Norris, C. *Against Relativism: Philosophy of Science, Deconstruction and Critical Theory.* Oxford: Blackwell, 1997.

'On force, its mental and moral correlates.' *Athenaeum*, 2 February 1867, 150.

Oppenheim, J. *The Other World: Spiritualism and Psychical Research in England, 1850–1914*. Cambridge: Cambridge University Press, 1988.
Ortiz, D. *Strong Magic: Creative Showmanship for the Close-up Magician*. Silver Spring, MD: Kaufman and Greenberg, 1994.
Otis, L. and Alcock, J. 'Factors affecting extraordinary belief.' *Journal of Social Psychology*, 118 (1982), 77–85.
Owen, A. *The Darkened Room: Women, Power and Spiritualism in Late Victorian England*. London: Virago Press, 1989.
Owen, A. *The Place of Enchantment: British Occultism and the Culture of the Modern*. Chicago: University of Chicago Press, 2004.
Padgett, V. Singer, B. and Benassi, V. 'Belief in ESP among psychologists.' *Skeptical Inquirer*, 5:1 (1980), 47–8.
'Paid mediums versus ministers', *Medium and Daybreak*, 2 (1871), 139.
Panati, C., ed., *The Geller Papers*. Boston: Houghton Mifflin, 1976.
Paris, J. A. *Philosophy in Sport Made Science in Earnest*. London: John Murray, 1853.
Parsinnen, T. 'Mesmeric performers.' *Victorian Studies*, 21 (1977), 87–104.
Pears, F. 'Letter', *Spiritual Magazine*, 1 (1860), 84–6.
Persinger, M. A. and Richards, P. 'Tobacyk's paranormal belief scale and temporal lobe signs: sex differences in the experience of ego-alien intrusions.' *Perceptual and Motor Skills*, 73 (1991), 1151–6.
Petit, M. 'The new woman as "tied up dog": Amy Tanner's situated knowledges.' *History of Psychology*, 11 (2008), 145–63.
Philips, H. 'Paranormal beliefs linked to brain chemistry.' *New Scientist*, 2353 (2002), 17.
Pinch, T. 'Normal explanations of the paranormal: the demarcation problem and fraud in parapsychology.' *Social Studies of Science*, 9 (1979), 329–48.
Pinch, T. and Collins, H. 'Private science and public knowledge: the Committee for the Scientific Investigation of the [sic] Claims of the Paranormal.' *Social Studies of Science*, 14 (1984), 521–46.
Plug, C. 'The psychology of superstition: a review.' *Psychologia Africana*, 16 (1976), 93–115.
Podmore, F. (1909). *Mesmerism and Christian Science: a Short History of Mental Healing*. Philadelphia: G. W. Jacobs.
Podmore, F. *Modern Spiritualism: A History and a Criticism*, 2 Vols. London: Methuen, 1902.
'Popular scientific errors', *Yorkshire Spiritual Telegraph*, 1 (1856), 169.

Potter, J. *Representing Reality: Discourse, Rhetoric and Social Construction.* London: Sage Publications, 1996.
Potter, J. and Wetherell, M. *Discourse and Social Psychology.* London: Sage Publications, 1987.
'Powell's spiritualism, its facts and phases.' *Athenaeum*, 23 April 1864, 576.
Pratt, J. 'Doctor Walford Bodie – the most remarkable man on earth.' *Call Boy*, 27 (1990), 3.
Pratt, J. G., Rhine, J. B., Smith, B. M., Stuart, C. E., and Greenwood, J. A. *Extra-Sensory Perception after Sixty Years.* New York: Henry Holt, 1940.
Price, G. R. 'Apology to Rhine and Soal.' *Science*, 175 (1972), 359.
Price, G. R. 'Science and the supernatural.' *Science*, 122 (1955), 359–67.
Price, H. *Confessions of a Ghost-Hunter.* London: Putnam, 1936.
Price, H. *Fifty Years of Psychical Research.* London: Longman, Green and Co., 1939.
Price, H. and Dingwall, E. *Revelations of a Spirit Medium.* London: Kegan Paul, Trench, Trubner & Co. Ltd, 1922.
Prince, M. F. *The Enchanted Boundary: Being a Survey of Negative Reactions to Claims of Psychic Phenomena.* Boston: Boston Society for Psychic Research, 1930.
Pritchard, J. *A Treatise on Insanity and Other Disorders Affecting the Mind.* Philadelphia: E. L. Carey & A. Hart, 1837.
Proceedings of the Psychological Society of Great Britain, 1875–1879. London: privately printed, 1880.
'Prof Pepper on spiritualism.' *Spiritualist*, 2 (1872), 29.
'Professor Gregory on Spiritualism.' *British Spiritual Telegraph*, 1 (1857), 9.
'Psychological literature.' *American Journal of Psychology*, 1 (1887), 128–46.
'Public medical challenge,' broadsheet for Vernon lecture (n.d.) (Purland Papers).
'Punch cartoon of the spirit hand.' *Spiritual Magazine*, 1 (1860), 241–5.
Purland, T. 'Mesmerism.' *Kentish Mercury*, 30 January 1844 (Purland Papers).
Quinn, S. O. 'How Southern New England became magnetic north: the acceptance of animal magnetism.' *History of Psychology*, 10 (2007), 231–48.
Randi, J. *The Magic of Uri Geller.* New York: Ballantine Books, 1975.
Randi, J. 'The role of conjurers in psi research.' In Kurtz, *A Skeptic's Handbook of Parapsychology*, 339–50.
Randi, J. *The Supernatural A–Z.* London: Headline Book Publishing, 1995.

Ransom, C. 'Recent criticisms of parapsychology.' *Journal of the American Society of Psychical Research*, 65 (1971), 289–307.
Rauscher, W. *The Mind Readers: Masters of Deception.* Woodbury, NJ: Mystic Light Press, 2002.
Reed, G. 'The psychology of channeling', *Skeptical Inquirer*, 13 (1989), 385–90.
'Report on Spiritualism.' *Athenaeum*, 28 October 1871, 556–8.
Report on Spiritualism of the Committee of the London Dialectical Society. London: J. Burns, 1873.
Rhine, J. B. 'A new case of experimenter unreliability.' *Journal of Parapsychology*, 38 (1974), 215–25.
Rhine, J. B. *Extra-Sensory Perception.* Boston: Bruce Humphries, 1934.
Rhine, J. B. *New Frontiers of the Mind.* New York: Farrar and Rhinehart, 1937.
Rhine, J. B. 'Note on Professor Thouless's review of Extra-sensory Perception.' *Proceedings of the Society for Psychical Research*, 43 (1935), 542–4.
Richards, G. 'Edward Cox, the Psychological Society of Great Britain (1875–1879) and the meanings of an institutional failure.' In Bunn, G., Lovie, A. and Richards, G., eds., *Psychology in Britain*, 33–53.
Richards, G. *Mental Machinery: the Origins and Consequences of Psychological Ideas. Part 1, 1600–1850.* London: Athlone Press, 1992.
Richards, G. *On Psychological Language and the Basis of Human Nature.* London: Routledge, 1989.
Richards, G. *Putting Psychology in its Place: a Critical Historical Overview.* London: Routledge, 2002.
'Ring out the old, ring in the new.' *Spiritual Magazine*, 3 (1868), 1–4.
Rinn, J. *Searchlight on Psychical Research.* London: Rider and Company, 1954.
Robert-Houdin, J. E. *Secrets of Conjuring and Magic.* Trans. and ed. with notes by Professor Hoffmann. London: George Routledge and Sons, 1900.
Rogo, D. S. 'J. B. Rhine and the Levy scandal'. In Kurtz, *A Skeptic's Handbook of Parapsychology*, 313–26.
Romanes, G. 'Thought-reading.' *Nature*, 24 (1881), 171–2.
Rymer, J. S. *Spirit Manifestations.* London, 1857.
S. 'Hypnotism, or Mr Braid's mesmerism.' *Medical Times*, 10 (1844), 95.
Sagan, C. *Broca's Brain: Reflections on the Romance of Science.* New York: Random House, 1979.

Saler, M. 'Modernity and enchantment: a historiographic review.' *American Historical Review*, 111 (2006), 692–716.
Sandby, G. *Mesmerism and its Opponents with a Narrative of Cases*. London: Longman, Brown, Green and Longman's, 1844.
Sawyer, T. A. *S. S. Baldwin and the Press*. Santa Ana, CA: Author, 1993.
Scheidt, R. J. 'Belief in supernatural phenomena and locus of control.' *Psychological Reports*, 32 (1973), 1159–62.
Schmeidler, G. and Murphy, G. 'The influence of belief and disbelief in ESP.' *Journal of Experimental Psychology*, 36 (1946), 271–6.
Schmeidler, G. and McConnell, R. *ESP and Personality Patterns*. New Haven: Yale University Press, 1958.
Schmit, D. 'Re-visioning antebellum American Psychology: the dissemination of mesmerism, 1836–1854.' *History of Psychology*, 8 (2005), 403–4.
Sedgwick, W. T. and Tyler, H. W. *A Short History of Science*. London: Macmillan and Co., 1917.
Serjeantson, R. W. 'Testimony and proof in early modern England.' *Studies in History and Philosophy of Science*, 30 (1999), 195–235.
Seybert Commission, *Preliminary Report of the Commission Appointed by the University of Pennsylvania to Investigate Modern Spiritualism in Accordance with the Request of the Late Henry Seybert*. Philadelphia: J. B. Lippincott Company, 1920 (originally published 1887).
Shapin, S. *A Social History of Truth: Civility and Science in Seventeenth Century England*. Chicago: Chicago University Press, 1994.
Shapin, S. 'The politics of observation: cerebral anatomy and social interests in the Edinburgh phrenology disputes.' In Wallis, ed., *On the Margins of Science*, 139–78.
Shermer, M. *The Believing Brain*. New York: Times Books, 2011.
Shermer, M. *Why People Believe Weird Things: Pseudo-Science, Superstition and Other Confusions of Our Time*. New York: W. H. Freeman, 1997.
Shorter, T. 'Spiritualism and the laws of nature.' *British Spiritual Telegraph*, 2 (1858), 104.
Sidgwick, H. 'President's address.' *Proceedings of the Society for Psychical Research*, 1 (1882), 7–12.
Singer, B. and Benassi, V. 'Fooling some of the people all of the time', *Skeptical Inquirer*, 5:2 (1980), 17–24.
Singh, S. (2003). 'Spectacular psychology or silly psycho-babble?' Retrieved 10 September 2012 from http://simonsingh.net/media/articles/maths-and-science/spectacular-psychology-or-silly-psycho-babble/.

'Sir Charles Isham on spiritualism.' *Spiritual Herald*, 1 (1856), 15–17.
'Sir John Forbes.' *Medical Times and Gazette*, 2 (1861), 506.
'Sir William a Beckett the judge.' *Spiritual Magazine*, 4 (1863), 352–6.
Smethurst, T. 'Mesmerism unmasked.' *Medical Times*, 9 (1843), 145–7.
Smith, R. *Being Human: Historical Knowledge and the Creation of Human Nature*. New York: Columbia University Press, 2007.
Smith, R. *The Fontana History of the Human Sciences*. London: Fontana, 1997.
Smith, R. 'The history of psychological categories.' *Studies in the History and Philosophy of Biological and Biomedical Sciences*, 36 (2005), 55–64.
Soal, S. G. 'Experiments on Frederick Marion.' *Journal of the Society for Psychical Research*, 35 (1950), 251–2.
Soal, S. G. 'In my mind's eye. By Frederick Marion.' *Journal of the Society for Psychical Research*, 35 (1950), 187–95.
Soal, S. G. *Preliminary Studies of a Vaudeville Telepathist*. London: University of London Council for Psychical Investigation, 1937.
Soal, S. G. 'Some aspects of extrasensory perception.' *Proceedings of the Society for Psychical Research*, 49 (1952), 131–54.
Soal, S. G. and Bateman, F. *Modern Experiments in Telepathy*. London: Faber and Faber Limited, 1954.
Spanos, N. 'Past-life regression: a critical review.' *Skeptical Inquirer*, 12 (1987), 174–80.
Spicer, H. *Facts and Fantasies: a Sequel to Sights and Sounds*. London: T. Bosworth, 1853.
'Spirit conjuring.' *Punch*, 25 August 1860, 73.
'Spirit-rapping.' *Literary Gazette*, 8 September 1860, 180–1.
'Spirits and spirit rapping.' *Westminster Review*, 13 (1858), 29–66.
'Spiritual manifestations – experiences of Hiram Powers – the sculptor.' *Spiritual Magazine*, 5 (1870), 20–2.
'Spiritualism.' *Fraser's Magazine*, 65 (1862), 520–8.
'Spiritualism, as related to Religion and Science.' *Fraser's Magazine*, 71 (1865), 22–42.
'Spiritualism and the age we live in.' *Athenaeum*, 11 February 1860, 201–2.
'Spiritualism at Brighton – the Davenports' double.' *Spiritual Magazine*, 6 (1865), 127.
'Spiritualism in Norwood.' *Spiritual Magazine*, 4 (1869), 336.
Spurzheim, J. *The Physiognomical System of Drs Gall and Spurzheim*. London: Bladwin, Cradock and Joy, 1815.
'Stage imitation of spiritual phenomena.' *Spiritualist*, 3 (1873), 137.

Subbotsky, E. *Magic and the Mind: Mechanisms, Functions and Development of Magical Thinking and Behavior.* Oxford: Oxford University Press, 2010.
'Superstition and science.' *Saturday Review*, 12 January 1856, 194.
Swiss, J. I. *Shattering Illusions.* Seattle, WA: Hermetic Press, Inc., 2002.
'Table-turning.' *Times*, 30 June 1853, 8.
Tanner, A. *Studies in Spiritism.* New York: Appleton, 1910.
Tamariz, J. *The Magic Way.* Madrid: Frakson Books, 1988.
Targ, R. and Puthoff, H. 'Information transmission under conditions of sensory shielding.' *Nature*, 251 (1974), 602–7.
'Testimony of non-spiritualists.' *Spiritualist*, 1 (1869), 1–2.
'Thackeray and Dickens on spiritualism.' *Spiritual Magazine*, 1 (1860), 386–91.
Thalbourne, M. and Haraldsson, E. 'Personality characteristics of sheep and goats.' *Personality and Individual Differences*, 1 (1980), 180–5.
'The alleged case of clairvoyance.' *Manchester Times and Gazette*, 27 April 1844, 5.
'The Allen Boy medium's manifestations – the duplication theory.' *Spiritual Magazine*, 6 (1865), 259–63.
'The Clarence vase.' *New Monthly Magazine*, 36 (1832), 210.
'The conversion of an MD to spiritualism.' *Spiritual Magazine*, 2 (1867), 412.
'The Cornhill Magazine, and Professor Challis, of Cambridge on Spiritualism.' *Spiritual Magazine*, 4 (1863), 371–2.
'The Davenport brothers.' *Spiritual Magazine*, 5 (1864), 468–70.
'The Davenport brothers.' *Spiritual Magazine*, 5 (1864), 481–524.
'The double-sighted phenomenon.' *Caledonian Mercury*, 7 November 1831, no page number.
'The double-sighted phenomenon.' *Derby Mercury*, 7 December 1831, 2.
'The exposure of spiritism.' *Scotsman*, 17 January 1879, 4.
'The extraordinary Scotch boy', newspaper clipping, *Sunday Times*, 27 March 1833 (Ricky Jay collection).
'The homoeopathic principle applied to insanity; a proposal to treat lunacy by Spiritualism.' *Asylum Journal of Mental Science*, 4 (1858), 360–96.
'The Lancet. London, Saturday, September 15 1838.' *Lancet*, 30 (1838), 873–7.
'The medium Colchester.' *Spiritual Magazine*, 6 (1865), 464–6.
'The miracle circle.' *Spiritual Magazine*, 6 (1865), 559.
'The people.' *People's Phrenological Journal*, 2 (1844), 170–2.

'The Piddingtons.' *Journal of the Society for Psychical Research*, 35 (1949), 83–5.
'The press.' *Spiritual Magazine*, 1 (1860), 485.
'The press and the mediums.' *Spiritual Magazine*, 3 (1860), 147–53.
'The Saturday Review.' *Spiritual Magazine*, 4 (1863), 177.
'The Spirit faith in America.' *Chambers Journal*, 9 February 1856, 81–3.
'The Westminster Review on spirits and spirit rapping by T.S.' *British Spiritual Telegraph*, 2 (1858), 79.
'Theatrical chit-chat.' *Morning Chronicle*, 23 January 1832.
'Thought-reading.' *Lancet*, 117 (1881), 795.
'Thought-reading.' (London) *Standard*, 16 May 1881, 3.
'Thought-reading demonstrations.' *British Medical Journal*, 1 (1881), 814–16.
Thouless, R. H. 'Dr Rhine's recent experiments on telepathy and clairvoyance and a reconsideration of J. E. Coover's conclusions on telepathy.' *Proceedings of the Society for Psychical Research*, 43 (1935), 24–37.
Thouless, R. H. 'Experiments on Frederick Marion.' *Journal of the Society for Psychical Research*, 35 (1950), 220–2.
Thouless, Robert H. *From Anecdote to Experiment in Psychical Research*. London: Routledge & Kegan Paul, 1972.
Thurschwell, P. *Literature, Technology and Magical Thinking, 1880–1920*. Cambridge: Cambridge University Press, 2001.
Titchener, E. B. 'Lehmann and Hansen on the telepathic problem.' *Science*, 9 (1899), 36.
Titchener, E. B. 'Professor James on telepathy.' *Science*, 9 (1899), 687.
Titchener, E. B. 'The feeling of being stared at.' *Science*, 8 (1898), 895–7.
Tobacyk, J. 'Reduction in paranormal belief among participants in a college course.' *Skeptical Inquirer*, 8:1 (1983), 57–61.
Tobacyk, J. and Milford, G. 'Belief in paranormal phenomena: assessment instrument development and implications for personality functioning.' *Journal of Personality and Social Psychology*, 44 (1983), 1029–37.
Tobacyk, J. J. 'Final thoughts on issues in the measurement of paranormal beliefs?' *Journal of Parapsychology*, 59 (1995), 141–6.
Tobacyk, J. J. 'What is the correct dimensionality of paranormal beliefs? A reply to Lawrence's critique of the Paranormal Belief Scale.' *Journal of Parapsychology*, 59 (1995), 27–46.
'Trickery in spiritualism.' *Spiritualist*, 2 (1872), 41.

Triplett, N. 'Communication.' *American Journal of Psychology*, 12 (1900), 144.
Trollope, T. A. *What I Remember*. London: Richard Bentley & Sons, 1887.
Truzzi, M. 1997. 'Reflections on the sociology and social psychology of conjurors and their relations to psychical research'. In S. Krippner, ed., *Advances in Parapsychological Research, VIII*. Jefferson, NC: McFarland & Company, Inc., 1997, 221–76.
Turner, F. *Between Science and Religion: the Reaction to Scientific Naturalism in Late Victorian Britain*. New Haven: Yale University Press, 1974.
Tylor, E. B. 'Ethnology and spiritualism.' *Nature*, 5 (1872), 343.
Van de Castle, R. and White, R. A. 'A report on a sentence completion form of sheep-goat attitude scale.' *Journal of Parapsychology*, 19 (1955), 171–9.
Van Wyhe, J. *Phrenology and the Origins of Victorian Naturalism*. Aldershot: Ashgate Publishing Limited, 2004.
Varley, C. 'Letter.' *Spiritual Magazine*, 5 (1871), 465.
Venn, J. 'Hypnosis and reincarnation: a critique and case study.' *Skeptical Inquirer*, 12 (1988), 386–91.
Vernon, W. J. 'Mr Vernon's experiments and the medical Society.' *Medical Times*, 10 (1844), 94–5.
Vernon, W. J. and Kiste, A., 'Phrenological visit to the Exeter Deaf and Dumb Asylum.' *Phrenological Journal*, 14 (1841), 80–1.
Vernon, W. J. 'Letter to Medical Times', reprinted in *People's Phrenological Journal*, 2 (1844), 137–8.
Wallis, R., ed. *On the Margins of Science: the Social Construction of Rejected Knowledge*. Sociology Review monograph 27. Keele: University of Keele, 1979.
Wason, J. 'Letter.' *Spiritual Magazine*, 1 (1860), 525.
Weber, M. *The Protestant Ethic and the Spirit of Capitalism*. London: George Allen and Unwin, 1930.
Webster, Mrs. *Scepticism and Spiritualism: the Experiences of a Sceptic by the Author of Aurelia*. London: F. Pitman, 1865.
Weekes, W. H. 'Reply to Dr Smethurst.' *Medical Times*, 9 (1843), 322.
Wheeler, J. A. 'Parapsychology – a correction.' *Science*, 205 (1979), 144.
'Why Galileo was persecuted.' *Spiritualist*, 1 (1869), 2.
Whyte, T. 'Re W. I. Bishop.' *Nature*, 24 (1881), 211.
Wiesner, B. P. 'Experiments on Frederick Marion.' *Journal of the Society for Psychical Research*, 35 (1950), 222.

Wigan, A. L. 'The hallucinating fraud – mesmerism.' *Lancet*, 46 (1845), 136–8.
Wilbraham, E. B. 'Letter.' *Spiritual Magazine*, 4 (1863), 266.
Wiley, B. *The Indescribable Phenomenon: the Life and Mysteries of Anna Eva Fay*. Seattle, WA: Hermetic Press, 2005.
Wiley, B. 'The thought-reader craze.' *Gibeciere*, 4 (2009), 11–134.
Wilson, D. B. 'The thought of late Victorian physicists.' *Victorian Studies*, 15 (1971), 25–45.
Winter, A. *Mesmerized: Powers of Mind in Victorian Britain*. Chicago: University of Chicago Press, 1997.
Wiseman, R. 'The Fielding report: a reconsideration.' *Journal of the Society for Psychical Research*, 58 (1992), 129–52.
Wiseman, R. and Watt, C. 'Belief in psychic ability and the misattribution hypothesis: a qualitative review.' *British Journal of Psychology*, 97 (2006), 323–38.
Wiseman, R., Smith, M. and Wiseman, J. 'Eyewitness testimony and the paranormal.' *Skeptical Inquirer*, 19:6 (1995), 29–35.
Wiseman, R., West, D. and Stemman, R. 'Psychic crime detectives: a new test for measuring their successes and failures.' *Skeptical Inquirer*, 20:1 (1996), 38–40, 58.
Wolframm, H. 'Parapsychology on the couch: the psychology of occult belief in Germany, c.1870–1939.' *Journal of the History of the Behavioral Sciences*, 42 (2006), 237–60.
'Wonderful manifestations in India.' *Spiritual Magazine*, 6 (1865), 120.
Wood, R. 'Report of an investigation of the phenomena connected with Eusapia Palladino.' *Science*, 31 (1910), 776–80.
Woods, P. 'Evidence for the effectiveness of a reading program in changing beliefs in the paranormal.' *Skeptical Inquirer*, 9:1 (1984), 67–70.
Woods, R. and Lead, B. *Showmen or Charlatans? The Stories of 'Dr' Walford Bodie and 'Sir' Alexander Cannon*. Rossendale: authors, 2005.
Woodward, C. and Mark, R. *Maurice Fogel: In Search of the Sensational*. Seattle, WA: Hermetic Press, 2007.
Wooffitt, R. *Telling Tales of the Unexpected: the Organization of Factual Discourse*. Hemel Hempstead: Harvester Wheatsheaf, 1992.
Young, A. *The Harmony of Illusions: Inventing Post-traumatic Stress Disorder*. Princeton, NJ: Princeton University Press, 1995.
Young, R. M. *Mind, Brain and Adaptation in the Nineteenth Century*. Oxford: Clarendon Press, 1970.

Zingrone, N. 'From text to self: the interplay of criticism and response in the history of parapsychology.' Unpublished thesis, University of Edinburgh, 2006.

Zorab, G. 'Test sittings with D. D. Home at Amsterdam.' *Journal of Parapsychology*, 34 (1978), 47–63.

Zusne, L. and Jones, W. H. *Anomalistic Psychology*. Hillsdale, NJ: Erlbaum, 1982.

Index

Alexander (Claude Alexander Conlin), 216–17
Anderson, John Henry, 150, 152, 157, 158
Annemann, Ted, 207–9

Baldwin, Samri S., 214–16
belief scales, problems of, 15–18, 54–5
beliefs
  as boundary-work, 185–90, 196
  as brain-bound, 253–5, 256
  as propositional attitudes, 14
  relationship to discourse, 54–60, 257–9
biblical miracles, 8, 10, 140, 144, 164
Billig, Michael, 57, 59
Bishop, Washington Irving, 172–81, 214
Bodie, Walford, 218–19
Boyle, Robert, 10, 16
Braid, James, 67, 92–3, 94–5, 113, 115–17, 124, 245
Brewster, David, 132, 142, 147, 149, 152, 163
Brown, Derren, x, 34, 52, 53

Carpenter, William Benjamin, 107, 129, 163, 168, 169, 174, 175, 176–7, 178–9, 180–1, 184, 191, 193, 195, 245
Cattell, James McKean, 185, 186
Chambers, Robert, 129, 143
Charcot, Jean-Martin, 23
Combe, George, 30
conjuring theory
  effects, 35–6, 43–4
  magic, response to, 46–9
  magic versus psychic fraud, 136–8
  methods, 36–7
  misdirection, 37–8
  pseudo-explanations, 38–43
  the relationship between performance and belief, 39–46
  willing suspension of disbelief, 44–6
Coon, Deborah, 182, 184
Crookes, William, 166–9, 170–1, 173, 179, 190, 201
CSICOP (Committee for the Scientific Investigation of Claims of the Paranormal), 231, 234–8

Danziger, Kurt, 22, 27
Davenport brothers, 131, 132, 134, 135–6, 139, 141, 146, 158, 161, 162, 214, 243
Didier, Adolphe, 105–6
Didier, Alexis, 105, 110
discourse analysis, 55–7, 110–12
Dunninger, Joseph, 217–18

Elliotson, John, 65, 66, 67, 69, 76, 116

Faraday, Michael, 129, 144, 155, 163
Fay, Anna Eva, 134, 170, 171, 173
Flourens, Pierre, 29
Fogel, Maurice, 220
Forbes, John, 105–8, 110–13, 114
Foster, Charles, 126–7, 132, 133, 135, 139, 146, 159, 160, 172–3, 177–8, 189, 214
framing
  extraordinary psychological feats, 52–3
  frame analysis (Goffman), 50–1
  magic versus psychic fraud, 51–2

Galton, Francis, 22, 176
Geller, Uri, 198–200, 214, 229
Goble, George, 105, 106–8, 113, 135, 171
Gordon, John, 29, 68
Gregory, William, 117, 144, 157, 163

Hacking, Ian, 26, 233, 241
Hall, G. Stanley, 182, 183, 187, 188
Hall, Samuel Carter, 101, 102, 139, 146
Home, Daniel Dunglas, 131–2, 134, 139, 140, 142, 146, 152–5, 157, 158, 159, 163–4, 166, 167, 170, 171, 173, 243
Howitt, William, 139, 154

James, William, 184–7
Jastrow, Joseph, 181–4, 188, 190

Koran, Al, 219

Luckhurst, Roger, 174, 180

M'Kean, Louis, 101–4, 135
Magendie, François, 29
Marion, Frederick, 228
Martineau, Harriet, 66, 76, 85, 110, 115, 116
McDougall, William, 201, 202
mesmerism
  arrival in Britain, 65
  as explanation for séance phenomena, 141, 150
  and hypnosis, 92–5, 115–17
  medical controversy, 66–7, 76–7
  origins, 64
Miller, Beulah, 191–4
Munsterberg, Hugo, 190, 191–4
Mysterious Lady, The, 103–4, 135

Newton, Isaac, 10, 16

Ownbey, Sarah, 206–8

Palladino, Eusapia, 189–90
paranormal, meaning of, 9, 14, 15–16, 18, 230–4, 250, 255–6
parapsychology
  early years, 201–4
  sheep-goat effect, 212, 232–3
  Zirkle-Ownbey experiments, 206–8
phrenology
  boundary-work, 30
  criticisms, 29–30
  scientificity, 29–30, 31
  social context, 30–1
  as superstition, 32
phreno-mesmerism, 33, 63, 69, 80–1
Piddinton, Sidney and Lesley, 220–3
Piper, Leonora, 184–5, 189
psychical research
  origins, 172
  and Psychology, 181–91
Psychology
  and commonsense, 28
  early American, 181–2
  origins, 21–3

of paranormal belief, 230–4
and parapsychology, 201–4
and psychical research, 181–91, 195–6

Rhine, Joseph Banks, 201–4, 210–12, 220
Richards, Graham, ix, 117, 248
Robert-Houdin, Jean Eugene, 39–40, 137, 146, 153–4, 158
Romanes, George, 176–7, 196
Rumball, John Quilter, 87–90, 104

scepticism, modern, 234–9, 240
Showers, Mary Rosina, 134, 170–1
Sidgwick, Henry, 172
Soal, S. G., 206, 211, 222, 225–7
spiritualism
  arrival in Britain, 129–30
  and crises of faith, 130–1, 148, 162–4
  early debunking, 128–9
  origins, 127–8

SPR (Society for Psychical Research), 171–2, 180, 182, 201, 204, 220, 221–3, 225, 226–7
Spurzheim, Johann, 29

Tanner, Amy, 187–9, 190
Thouless, R. H., 206, 210, 226–8
Titchener, Edward Bradford, 186–7

Vernon, William John, 63–7, 83, 87, 88, 89, 91, 98, 99, 100, 103, 104, 105, 106, 113

Wakley, Thomas, 65–6, 67, 93, 116
Watson, J. B., 23, 26, 117
Winter, Alison, 66, 117
Wooffitt, Rob, x, 56, 249
Wundt, Wilhelm, 22, 23, 182

Zirkle, George, 206–8